LIVING IN THE HOPE
OF FUTURE GLORY

LIVING IN THE HOPE
OF FUTURE GLORY

TOM BARNES

SERIES EDITORS
DR JOHN D. CURRID AND ROBERT STRIVENS

EVANGELICAL PRESS

Evangelical Press
Faverdale North, Darlington, DL3 0PH England
email: sales@evangelicalpress.org

Evangelical Press USA
PO Box 825, Webster NY 14580 USA
email: usa.sales@evangelicalpress.org

www.evangelicalpress.org

First published 2006

All Scripture references, unless otherwise noted, are the author's own translation.

The EMMAUS series has been created to speak directly to pastors, teachers and students of the Word of God on those issues that impact on their everyday ministry and life.

British Library Cataloguing in Publication Data available

ISBN-13 978 0 85234 608 2   ISBN 0 85234 608 5

To Karen, my wife,
with whom I delight
in living out glory.

And to my parents,
John and Laverne Barnes,
who started me on the path.

Contents

ABBREVIATIONS

BAGD *A Greek-English Lexicon of the New Testament and Other Early Christian Literature.* Walter Bauer, William Arndt, F. W. Gingrich, Fredrick Danker

BDB *Hebrew and English Lexicon of the Old Testament.* Francis Brown, S. R. Driver, C. A. Briggs

DNTT *The New International Dictionary of New Testament Theology.*

EBC *The Expositor's Bible Commentary*

JBC *Journal of Biblical Counseling*

INTRODUCTION

THE WORDS OF ROMANS 8:29-30 have often been described as the 'golden chain' of salvation.[1] In these two verses Paul gives an overview of God's work in redeeming his church from beginning to end. The main point is that what God begins he will complete. What Christian has read these words and not been thrilled by them? 'For whom He foreknew, He also predestined to be conformed to the image of His Son, that He might be the firstborn among many brothers. Moreover whom He predestined, these He also called; whom He called, these He also justified; and whom He justified, these He also glorified.'

Having been through formal theological training, having cut my pastoral teeth upon the Westminster Shorter Catechism, and having spent many years studying the Bible, I always believed that

I had a good understanding of the terms in these verses such as 'foreknew', 'predestined', 'called', and 'justified'. There was one exception – 'glorified'.

Please do not misunderstand. Whenever I came across this concept in the Scriptures I had a general idea of what was under consideration. I knew that it was 'the final stage of the process of salvation ... the point at which the doctrine of salvation and the doctrine of the last things overlap...'[2] in other words, 'the final phase of the application of redemption'.[3] I knew that the doctrine of glorification involved the transformation of the believer and the final and ultimate stage of sanctification, and that the by-product would be the cessation of our struggle with sin and the resulting pain in this world.

Yet some issues always bothered me when I read of glorification. To begin, why does the Bible speak of God glorifying us, or of that ultimate state being one of glory (Rom. 2:7; 8:18)? Why is this process not spoken of as being 'ultimately sanctified' or simply 'made perfect'? What is behind the use of the word 'glory'?

Related to this issue, if the reader of the Bible could come to understand what was behind the use of this term, would there be some understanding of God's plan of redemption and what He is doing in the lives of saints, which many Christians have been missing?

And there are the more obvious questions: What is involved in glorification? When does it take place? What will our glorified bodies be like? Does this future reality have bearing upon the life of the saint in the present? If so, what is it? What impact does it have on the church?

Armed with all these questions, I turned to systematic theology works, theological dictionaries and other tomes, and kept my eyes open as I worked my way through scholarly journals and Christian periodicals. To my surprise, I found out that very little writing has been done in recent years on the doctrine of glorification, even though I was beginning to suspect that it had tremendous ramifications for a person's faith and hope. I was not alone in this assessment. Millard Erickson commented over two decades ago, 'The topic is one which receives little treatment in standard theology textbooks, and even less attention in sermons, yet it is rich in practical significance, for it gives believers encouragement and strengthens their hope.'[4] I am convinced that little has changed since Erickson penned those words.

A decade ago I began to collect information and take note of statements in the Bible which would relate to this topic. I decided that someday I would study glorification thoroughly for the purpose of my own growth and for that of teaching my own congregation. The results of what I have found have had such a profound impact that I decided that I needed to share them with a wider audience. This book is the result.

My prayer for you as you read this work is that your faith in our great Lord and his work in your life will be strengthened, that you will come to see with greater clarity the hope of your calling, that you will be moved to worship our Saviour, and finally that your life will become a billboard for the glory of our sovereign God!

Soli Deo Gloria!

Tom Barnes
Fort Collins, Colorado
September 2004

PART ONE

THE THEOLOGY OF GLORIFICATION

Thine image, Lord, bestow, thy presence and thy love; I ask to serve thee here below, and reign with thee above. Teach me to live by faith; conform my will to thine; let me victorious be in death, and then in glory shine.

— From John Newton, 'Behold the Throne of Thy Grace!', Trinity Hymnal, 627

Chapter 1

WHERE IT ALL BEGAN

I PASTORED A CHURCH in the midwestern United States (Nebraska) for eleven years. Even though I had grown up in rural Indiana, only a few states to the east, there were still some cultural differences, especially in the use of language. Shortly after we moved to Nebraska, my wife and daughter went on a trip to visit relatives. Being left at home by myself, one of the women in our church called me and asked if I would like to come over and have dinner the next day with her family. Where I came from, dinner was either the evening meal or any special meal, so when I accepted the invitation I was thinking that I would be coming over to eat the evening of the next day. At 12:05 p.m. my host called and asked, 'Are you coming over for dinner?' 'Oh,' I said, 'I'm sorry. I was thinking that I was coming tonight.' As I rushed out the door for my dinner I realized I had forgotten about the language difference.

Where did the Nebraska use of 'meal words' begin? Actually, it makes good sense. Because farmers work so hard physically, they normally stop for a 'lunch' mid-morning and even sometimes in the afternoon to give them between-meal energy. 'Lunch' in rural Nebraska came to mean any snack. Dinner was the large noon meal which was necessary to refuel those working in the fields.

As with my education in Nebraska's vernacular, so it is with glorification; we are helped along by learning where it all began. The majority of glorification teaching, and indeed the clearest teaching, is found in the New Testament. Yet why is the final perfection of the believer referred to as 'glory' and God's action of perfecting with the term 'glorify'? It is brought into sharper focus when we look back into the Old Testament. This is where it all began.

Something which sticks out right away is that at the end of the Old Testament era some Jews understood the original state of man as being one of glory because man was made in the image of God.[1] This glory had been tainted, yet there would come a day in the future when it would be restored fully.[2] Is there any warrant for such a conclusion from the Old Testament or were these intertestamental Jews spouting some form of man-made tradition? Upon close scrutiny we find that the Old Testament does in fact equate man being made in the image of God with glory and does speak of future glorification. Let's see how this is developed.

GLORY AND THE IMAGE OF GOD

In Psalm 8, as David worships God for his creation and care of man, he asserts that Yahweh made man just 'a little lower than God'. Though the Hebrew term standing behind this latter word (*elohim*) is tough to translate with certainty in this instance, the evidence is in favour of taking it as 'God' (rather than 'gods' or 'heavenly beings, angels').[3] Obviously, there is an infinite ontological and moral difference between God and man. Yet the reference is to man's dominion in the world. God is the Lord, and yet man has been placed second only to God himself when it comes to ruling the creation.

With regards to such rulership, God has given him glory (*kabod*) and majesty (*hadar*) which are similar to his own.[4] We should note that elsewhere in the Psalter David sees glory that man possesses as inseparably linked to the Creator (Ps. 3:3 [MT 4]). David sets forth God's own glory as a display of his power, strength, works and his very nature (Pss. 24:7-10; 29:1-2, 9; 57:5; 138:5; 145:10-12) and a visible manifestation of his greatness (Ps. 26:8). It is not at all out of the question that David had in mind that man's glory was somehow in connection with God and ultimately found in his ability to display the greatness and acts of God through himself and his life.[5]

In what way would man's glory be in connection with God? The answer lies in what appears to be the background for David's statement. The mention of man's governing other creatures in the world automatically makes the reader think of the words of Genesis 1:26 where we read, 'And God said, "Let Us make man in Our image, according to Our likeness; let them have dominion over the fish of the sea, over the birds of the air, and over the cattle, over all the earth and over every creeping thing that creeps on the earth."'[6] Even though David does not explicitly connect 'glory' with being made in the image of God, he does implicitly connect the 'glory' of man with that Genesis text. Scarcely could David or any other Jew of his day have thought about or read an assertion like we find in Psalm 8:5 and not be taken back to Genesis 1.[7]

In Genesis 1:26, the implication seems to be that man's ability to have dominion is part of what it means that man is made in God's image. Man's glory is connected with being made in the image of God. James R. Tony comments on Psalm 8 and man being crowned with glory and honour: 'This "glory" is the reflected radiation of the presence of God. So when the psalmist writes that God crowned man at creation with glory and honor, what he means is that in humanity the image and likeness of God is revealed.'[8]

If Psalm 8:5 was all we had to go on we might conclude that the evidence for the connection of the *imago dei* (Latin for 'image of God') and glory was less than convincing. Yet when we understand what the Bible teaches about the *imago dei* and also the meaning of glory, the case becomes much stronger.

The imago dei

The views throughout the history of the Church with regards to what the *imago dei* consists of have been divided primarily into three main categories.[9] First there is the substantive view. Millard Erickson describes what has been the dominant stance in this way: 'The common element in the several varieties of this view is that the image is identified as some definite characteristic or quality within the makeup of the human.'[10] Some sects (such as Mormons) have argued for physical similarity, asserting that God has a body. Most Christian advocates of the substantive view have argued that the characteristics involved in the *imago dei* include knowledge and the ability to think and reason,[11] the ability to will and make moral decisions,[12] and also moral purity or original righteousness, that is, holiness.[13]

Second, there is the relational view. '[Advocates of this position] think of the image of God as the experiencing of a relationship. Man is said to be in the image or to display the image when he stands in a particular relationship. In fact, that relationship is the image.'[14] Emil Brunner and Karl Barth were proponents of this approach.

Finally, there is the functional view. '[This assessment] has had quite a long history and has recently enjoyed an increase in popularity. This is the idea that the image is not something present in the makeup of man, nor is it the experiencing of relationship with God or with fellow man.' Instead, the image consists of something man does. 'It is a function which man performs, the most frequently mentioned being the exercise of dominion over the creation.'[15] Some have argued that the functions carried out through man's body (seeing, working, etc.) resemble God.[16] Others have argued that the functions include man's ability to relate,[17] his ability to create,[18] his ability to have dominion over the rest of creation[19] and his ability to communicate.[20]

It is true that the Bible never explicitly defines what the *imago dei* is. Yet I agree with J. I. Packer that we need to look no further than Genesis 1 to discover a clear picture.[21] In Genesis 1:1-26 we see God creating, governing creation, relating within the Godhead (in community) and exercising rational abilities. In that context he says, 'Let Us make man in Our image.' Immediately following that statement humans are said to be both male and female and are called to have dominion over creation. Additionally, in Genesis 5:1-2, the fact that humans are made in the image of God is also followed by the truth that they were made male and female. When we bring all this together it seems as if view one (the substantive view) and view three (the functional view) both are true. In other words, man resembles God in his creativity, in his rationality, in both his typical characteristics of maleness and femaleness, in his ability to have dominion over creation and in his ability to create.

One aspect of the *imago dei* as revealed in Genesis needs to be highlighted before we move on since it will play a significant role later in the book. The reality that God made humans male and female in the image of the triune God strongly suggests that we are social beings. Though individually we are created in God's image and can reflect that same image, it is only in our relationship with God that we fulfil the image completely. This not only lays the groundwork for the importance of the church, but it also prepares us for the discovery that the ultimate restoration of the *imago dei* in the future will not only consist of a restoration of individuals but also a restoration among God's people in community.[22]

In the New Testament we gain further commentary as we find out that redemption in Christ involves a progressive restoration of the full image of God and this new man includes righteousness and holiness (Eph. 4:24). In other words, man must have originally resembled God in both his moral purity and his ability to make moral decisions. This implies that the image, though not totally lost (Gen. 9:6), nevertheless was twisted and in need of restoration.[23]

I agree with those who suggest that man resembled God in all that he originally was and was able to do, and still does (Gen.

9:6; James 3:9). Yet because of the fall, the resemblance has been twisted.

Included in this resemblance are the functions of his body. John Frame agrees and calls attention to Psalm 94:4 which reads, 'He who planted the ear, shall He not hear? He who formed the eye, shall He not see?' This suggests that what we accomplish through our body parts does resemble the functions of God.[24]

There is also support for this approach to the understanding of the *imago dei* from the meaning of 'likeness' (*d'muth*) and 'image' (*zalem*) (Gen. 1:26). These terms '...refer to something that is similar but not identical to the thing that it represents or is an "image" of'.[25] Though not identical to God, man does resemble God. Even if we must not affirm that our bodies themselves resemble God (knowing that he does not have a body), the implication is strong throughout Scripture that man resembles God in the functions he carries out through his body. We must take in context the entire teaching of the Scriptures which make it clear that God is a Spirit (John 4:24) as well as what we have seen in Genesis 1 and Ephesians 4:24.

Finally, it seems that being made in the image of God, man not only resembles God substantively and functionally in all he is and does, but he also represents God. Craig Smith provides help in this area when he comments:

> To be made in God's image means that we are physical beings created to be His representatives in creation ... Support for this position comes from various biblical evidences. Among them is the fact that the Hebrew word rendered as 'image' in Gen. 1:26 (*zalem*) is used frequently in the OT canon to refer to idols – physical representations of pagan deities [2 Kings 11:18; 2 Chr. 23:17; Ezek. 16:17]. It is my contention that pagans of the Ancient Near East did not believe their idols to be literal gods and goddesses. Rather, they saw such idols as representing the deities they worshipped. Hence, the Hebrew use of the term in

reference to man implies a notion that human beings represent God in the physical creation, bearing His image so that he might be glorified throughout the universe He made ... Therefore, to be made in God's image is inescapably tied to being physical beings and it is for this reason that human life in the eschaton is carried out in resurrected physical bodies [1 Cor. 15].[26]

In affirming that we are made in the image of God, the Old Testament Scriptures teach us that we both resemble and represent God.[27] We are like him in a way that none of the rest of his creation is and we portray him in the creation as nothing else does. The heavens may declare the weight of the greatness of God (Ps. 19:1), but not to the extent that mankind does. As we will see shortly, this sounds much like what we mean when we speak of man possessing glory from God and glorifying God.

Glory

When we understand how the Old Testament uses the *kabod* (glory) word group, the connection between glory and the *imago dei* will be clarified that much more. John Oswalt writes of the term *kabod*,

The root is a common Semitic one, occurring in all except Aramaic where *yaqar* seems to take its place. The basic meaning is 'to be heavy, weighty', a meaning which is only rarely used literally, the figurative ... being more common. From this figurative usage it is an easy step to the concept of a 'weighty' person in society, someone who is honorable, impressive, worthy of respect.[28]

By far the most prominent connotation of the word has to do with a manifestation of the full weight of who God is. The closest English word in this sense is gravity, which signifies both weight and importance.[29] It is associated with his name or reputation (Ps. 102:15 [MT 16]; Isa. 59:19; Neh. 9:5), his holiness (Isa. 6:3), his ways and great acts (Ps. 138:5), his judgement (Ezek. 39:21; Hab. 2:14) and even the very essence of his nature[30] which is manifested in his mercy, grace, patience, goodness, truth and justice (cf. Exod. 34:6-7 in light of Exod. 33:18ff.), that is, his very attributes.[31]

Another very prominent use has to do with the visible radiance, a manifestation of the presence of God – also designed to show the full weight of who he is (cf. Exod. 16:10; 24:16-17; 29:43; 40:34, 35; Lev. 9:23; 1 Sam. 4:21, 22; 1 Kings 8:11; 2 Chr. 5:14; 7:1; Pss. 26:8; 102:16 [MT 17]; Ezek. 9:3). There seems to be a connection between God's glory of his essence, character and works and that of the visible manifestation of greatness. That connection seems to centre on his presence.

> The several references which speak of God's glory filling the earth and/or becoming evident are instructive. On the one hand, they quite legitimately refer to that reputation for greatness which God alone deserves, not only because of His natural position as King, but also because of His unsurpassed activity as Deliverer and Savior. However ... it is not merely God's reputation which fills the earth, it is the very reality of his presence.[32]

God is able to be glorified among certain men to a fuller degree because he is present among them in a more realized fashion.

John Piper captures the essence of the Old Testament use of glory in reference to the Divine when he writes:

> God's glory is the beauty of his manifold perfections. It can refer to the bright and awesome radiance that sometimes breaks forth in visible manifestations. Or it can refer to the infinite moral excellence of his character. In either case it signifies a reality of infinite greatness and worth.[33]

Finally, the term is also used to refer to man. *Kabod* ('glory') has to do with man's wealth, that which shows his prosperity, honour or a special place – making him praiseworthy (cf. Gen. 31:1; 45:13; Exod. 28:2; 1 Sam. 2:8; Ps. 49:6-7; 1 Chr. 29:28). With regards to man, it is also instructive that with '[*kabod*] there is also the notion of number. The numerous soldiers of an army are the [*kabod*] of the nation and the great number of trees in a forest is the [*kabod*] of the forest'. Bernard Ramm also asserts that the term 'refers to that which is fundamentally perceptible or ostentatious … A man's wealth, the insignia of his wealth and the pomp of his surroundings were called his *kabod*'.[34] In Isaiah 16:14 and 17:4 the 'glory of a people' (Moab and Jacob respectively) includes their prosperity and blessing. For that glory to depart is to see them face judgement, calamity and hardship.[35]

At this point I do not want to be guilty of the exegetical fallacy of reading into the word 'glory' all of its possible meanings each time it is used just because examples of each of the meanings can be found. The present point is simply this: each of the uses of 'glory' (*kabod*) in the Old Testament have a systematic bearing upon man. The threads (the glory of God's being and works, the visible manifestation of God's glory, and man's glory) are brought together to form a tapestry in the development of the theology of the Old Testament. This happens in three different ways.[36]

As we have already alluded to, the threads are brought together in the teaching of the *imago dei*. Man is God's resemblance and representative upon the earth. This is what gives man his dignity and his value (Gen. 9:6). Os Guiness puts it this way: 'Human nature was … considered to have dignity and weight because humanity was the glory of God and made in His image (dignitas being Latin for glory). As Rieff writes, "The true self derived from the one self, self-disclosed in Exodus 3:14…"'[37]

Man's glory is truly and ultimately derived from God's glory. To put it another way, man has glory because he is in God's image. Psalm 16:3 even refers to those who know God as 'glorious ones' (*'addiyrey*). This term refers to that which is majestic, noble, mighty, principal or glorious, especially those who are nobility (Judg. 5:13; 2 Chr. 23:20; Neh. 3:5; Ps. 136:18; Jer. 25:35, 36;

Nahum 3:18; Zech. 11:2). In fact it refers to the might and glory of God (1 Sam. 4:8; Pss. 8:1, 9 [here clearly it is connected with God's excellent name]; 76:4; 93:4; Isa. 33:21). It seems that the meaning is parallel to 'the saints', yet it is not simply equal to it. It does seem to carry the connotation of being separated and chosen, special unto God. Yet it also seems to suggest that the majesty, excellence and the glory are present because they are part of God's people and he himself is glorious, excellent and majestic.

The second way in which these threads are brought together is by means of the Old Testament emphasis on the reality that man's chief purpose in life is to glorify God, which consists of displaying through his life and works the full weight of God's greatness, beauty and magnificence (see Josh. 7:19; 1 Sam. 6:5; 1 Chr. 16:24, 28, 29; Pss. 50:15; 96:3, 7, 8; 145:10-12).[38] Man is made in order to glorify God (Isa. 43:7). We should not be surprised to find that the very makeup of mankind especially equips him to carry out that task. Man was designed to be a God-glorifier!

The third and final way that we know the threads of God's glory, the glory of his visible manifestation and the glory of man are brought together into one fabric stems from the reality that Jews at the end of the Old Testament era and the inspired writers of the New Testament understood these different strands to be interconnected.

When we look at all the evidence, we conclude that the Old Testament does teach that when God created man, he crowned him with glory and honour. This involves man being made in the image of God – to resemble and represent God as none of his other creation could. Man was to display God-like character and functions which would display to the universe the greatness of God in a splendid and full way. He could do so because of how God made him. Though this image and glory have been twisted through the fall, they have not been altogether lost (cf. Gen. 9:6).

It is important for us to note at this point that no mere man has been a God-glorifier in the originally-intended way. Only Jesus Christ has accomplished this. This seems to be one of the implications intended by the author of Hebrews 2:5-8, who applied Psalm 8:4-6 specifically to Jesus Christ. He who never sinned (Heb. 4:15) and who always did what the Father desired (John 8:29; Rom. 5:19) displayed the image of God and glorified him as no other man ever did, even with regards to his manhood. '[Christ] was the "Second Adam", that is, the perfect example of all that humanity was meant to be.'[39]

This is a truth that must be remembered later on as we find out how we also can be restored to well-functioning God-glorifiers.

The display of the artist's work

Even though American artist Norman Rockwell was often not accepted by art critics, he is one of my favourite painters. You may have seen reprints of the hundreds of works which graced the cover of The Saturday Evening Post from 1916 through 1963. His illustrations are easily recognizable – so much so that most Americans would not need his signature to know that 'this is a Rockwell'. He had an uncanny ability to depict people involved in relationships and day-to-day life realistically and with a touch of humour. Every time I see one of his works, whether it is people praying at a table, a boy with trousers ready to be pulled down checking the credentials of the doctor about to insert the needle, two childhood 'lovers' watching the sunset with their dog in tow or youngsters ready to play baseball, I can relate to the figures. I am often left with feelings of honour, duty, patriotism, nostalgia, and a heart-warming feeling of life as we enjoy it and would like for it always to be.

From my perspective and the outlook of many observers, every Rockwell illustration honours the artist. Not only do we conclude, 'That's a Rockwell', but also, what an ability this New Englander had for illustrating life and warming our hearts. In a sense, each Rockwell work glorifies the hand behind it.

So it is with man with regards to his Creator, God. Particularly when we experience the best aspects of mankind, such as his creativity, his love and courage, the soft touch and care of a mother for her baby, a dad's ability to instil courage in his son, the way that mankind has bettered the environment and life with reservoirs, weather forecasts, medical breakthroughs and sacrificial love, we are to be drawn back to the Creator, to give him praise for how he has made man. And when a man, woman, boy or girl is reconciled to God and thus can display his image in a fuller way, this becomes even more of a source for God's honour. How do we explain young women leaving the comforts of home to go into the heart of an inner-city to better the lives of children? How do we account for families leaving jobs and relatives to go to far-off lands, learning new languages and ways of life and often placing themselves in danger, all to share the good news of eternal life in Jesus Christ? The answer is found in the ultimate Artist. We have been made to be God-glorifiers, works of art that display the magnificence, power, holiness and love of our sovereign God. And when we (or angels) see displayed the genius of the Creator in mankind, we are left saying, 'Ah, that's a work of God. We praise you Lord!' Such is the *imago dei* and man's God-given glory!

What a privilege it is for us to be God's cover illustration, his canvas that surpasses the most breathtaking sunset, the majestic snow-capped mountains of the Rocky Mountains, the lush green rolling heights and valleys of the Appalachian Mountains in the eastern United States and the soft fragile artistry of a flower.

Until we understand that this was the beginning and the desired end for man and that every human being comes into the world with this ability twisted, we will never understand who we are and who we are intended to be![40]

OTHER OLD TESTAMENT TEACHINGS THAT CONTRIBUTE TO A THEOLOGY OF GLORIFICATION

Even though the Old Testament never uses the terminology of God glorifying saints in the eschaton, it does have many other strands of teaching which lay a foundation for the doctrine. It is to this teaching that we now turn our attention.

The presence of God's glory leads to man's display of that glory
Few Old Testament texts lay a greater foundation for glorification than that of Exodus 33-34.

The main purpose of the book of Exodus is to reveal the nature of God to the reader, and particularly three characteristics about God. First, God is a God of deliverance. Exodus recounts the plight of Israel in Egypt and how God saved them in a glorious way (1:1 – 15:21). This saving work becomes the backdrop for God's salvation in both the Old and New Testaments. It shows his grace and his power.

Secondly, God is a God of direction. God directed Israel away from Egypt, to Mt Sinai and to water, and he also gave them direction for living in his covenant and his law. God wanted Israel to know how they were to live now that he had graciously saved them (15:22 – 24:18).

Thirdly (flowing out of the second revelation), Exodus shows to the reader that God is a God who deserves and demands due devotion. God revealed to Israel how to construct the tabernacle so that he might visibly dwell among them (25:8) and teach them the need for atonement in the right worship of him (25:1 – 40:38).

Placed right in the midst of the third section of Exodus are three chapters dealing with Israel's rebellion, judgement upon her and restoration (32-34). Moses had been upon Mt Sinai receiving the law and instructions for the tabernacle for forty days and nights (24:18). Growing restless, the people did not know if he was coming back or not. They wanted leadership and provision. Even though they had worshipped the true God as part of their heritage, nevertheless all of them had grown up in pagan, idolatrous Egypt where they were accustomed to man fashioning idols to represent gods who would provide and lead. They wanted some physical representation, some supposed security, assurance that they had divine help and guidance. So they resorted to what was familiar to them and asked Aaron to make an idol (32:1). They did not trust in God to be their provision and direction and very quickly disobeyed him. By this impotent, degrading representation, they disobeyed God's law and belittled who he really is. They sinned out of lack of faith and disobedience to God's law. The accounts of the making of the golden calf, Moses coming down out of the mountain and judgement taking place at the hands of the sons of Levi (about 3,000 died that day) are found in Exodus 32:2-29.

In Exodus 32:30-35, Moses informs the people that they have committed a grave sin and that perhaps he can make atonement for it. Moses prays to God and the LORD responds by saying that he will judge those who have sinned.

Exodus 33 continues with the LORD's response to Moses when Moses interceded for Israel. God tells Moses to depart from Mt Sinai and to go to the Promised Land. He promises to send his angel before them and to drive out the present inhabitants. However, he drops a bombshell upon Moses: because of their idolatry, God will not go up in their midst ('lest I consume you on the way') for they are a stubborn, rebellious people (33:1-3). The people mourn and the LORD sets before them the possibility that he would judge them further or turn away his wrath – depending on their response (33:4-6).

Moses' intercessory ministry on behalf of the people and God's presence among them (albeit outside the camp) are parenthetically introduced in preparation for Moses' following intercession with regards to God's presence with them or his absence from them (33:7-11).[41]

This brings us to the heart of the text which has bearing upon glorification. In Exodus 33:12-23 the results of one of Moses' meetings with the LORD are recorded. Yahweh will be present with his people as they go to the Promised Land. This is developed as follows.

First, Moses makes a request. He recollects to God that he has told Moses to bring up this people to the Promised Land (which was a major endeavour), yet God has not let Moses know whom he would send with them. Yes, the angel would go before them, but Yahweh had said he would not be present (33:2-3). So Moses is unclear as to who will go with him – just an angel or the presence of Yahweh himself? He is concerned that it will not be Yahweh, even though God has said that he knows Moses intimately (by name) and also that Moses has found favour in the LORD's eyes. These divine assertions seem not to square with the lack of God's presence. After all, how can Moses lead these people by himself? Hence, Moses makes the following request (v. 13): 'Now if, I pray, I have found favor in Your eyes, make known to me, I pray, Your ways that I may know You in order that I may find favor in Your eyes and see that this nation is Your people.' It seems that Moses' desire is to understand what Yahweh is like and what he is doing among them. Moses sees this understanding as crucial to knowing how to relate to and serve God[42] that he might find more favour in God's eyes – mainly for the great task at hand. Also, Moses pleads for God's grace based upon the reality that the Israelites comprise Yahweh's covenant people.

In verse 14 Yahweh responds to Moses' request. The text reads, 'And He said, "My presence will go and I will give you rest."' It is crucial to understand this answer because it also helps us understand what Moses was asking and it helps explain the context. The hiphil consecutive perfect first person verb *nuach* ('give rest') needs to be understood as follows: 'I will give rest to you' (singular). Moses' concern in verses 12-13 had been with the fact that God had called him personally to lead Israel and yet had not revealed to him who he was, his ways or who would accompany them. The reader cannot conclude that Moses is not concerned about Israel as a whole (cf. v. 15). Yet at this point in the text, the focus seems to be on Moses as leader, and the second person masculine singular ending on the preposition in this verse certainly has its normal significance. As such, the 'rest' has to do with what God will do for Moses. Probably the rest is that which deals with the 'psychological-spiritual', as 'the absence of trouble or internal conflict' and is exemplified in other Old Testament texts. Job 3:26 reads, 'I am not at ease, nor am I quiet; I have no rest, for trouble comes.' Proverbs 29:17 connects it with delight: 'Correct your son, and he will give you rest; yes, he will give delight to your soul.' Isaiah 14:3 associates lack of rest with sorrow and fear.[43] God will give a sense of assurance, security and delight to Moses as he leads Israel. Moses is not going to have to do this alone or in the dark. The rest is directly related to Yahweh's presence which he has not promised will go with Moses and Israel.

In verses 15-16 Moses responds to Yahweh and shows that clearly what he longs for is his presence. The leader believes God's presence and provision are absolutely mandatory for the trek to the Promised Land and the conquering of it. These verses read:

> And he said unto Him, 'If Your presence is not going, do not bring us up from here. For by what then will it be known that I have found favor in Your eyes, I and Your people, unless You go with us – so that we, I and Your people, may be distinguished from all the peoples who are on the face of the earth?'

There are a number of things we need to take note of in these verses. To begin, Moses makes it clear that Yahweh's presence is essential. He has heard the LORD say that his presence[44] would be with him (v. 14), yet he seems concerned that the presence will not go with them all. If the LORD will not continually be with them, then Moses would rather stay right where they are.

Next, we must see that what Moses is concerned about with the lack of God's presence among the people as a whole is not only the resultant inability to lead the people and the threatened failure of the entire endeavour (seemingly implied in vv. 12-14), but it is also that other peoples will not see that Israel has a special place with Yahweh: 'For by what then[45] will it be known that I have found favor in Your eyes, I and Your people, unless you go with us...?'[46]

Finally, we must notice one of the ways in which God would be glorified through his presence with Israel. A purpose of God's favour being with Moses and the people was that they 'may be distinguished, I and Your people, from all the people who are upon the face of the earth'. The niphal consecutive perfect first person plural verb *wᵉniphleynu* denotes being 'separate' or 'distinct from'.[47] Particularly in Exodus it refers to God distinguishing between the world at large and his people such that the former are under his judgement for sin and the latter are under his gracious protection. This is born out in its occurrences in this book. It is a verb that is not used often (only seven times, four in Exodus and three in the Psalter), however,

> in the fourth plague on Egypt of flies (8:22), the Lord 'sets apart' the land of Goshen from the

plague which infests the Egyptian houses. In the fifth plague, the death of the Egyptians' livestock, the Lord 'discriminates' between the cattle of Israel and Egypt (9:4). When Moses announces the death of the firstborn (Exod. 11:1ff.), he says again that the Lord will 'discriminate' between Israel and Egypt (11:7).[48]

Hence, Moses wants Yahweh to distinguish between Israel and the peoples around them by means of his presence with them, provision for them, and direction of them, so that these peoples can see his grace upon them. Moses wants God's presence and his blessing so that others will see they are his covenant people. This ultimately will bring glory to God among Israel (cf. Exodus 14:30-31) and among the world at large (cf. Exod. 7:5; 14:18; 15:14-16; Josh. 2:10-11).

In verse 17 Yahweh responds to Moses that his presence will go with them all to show they have found favour in his eyes and to distinguish between them and others, ultimately for God's glory. The reason? Because Moses has found favour in Yahweh's eyes and Yahweh has known him by name. God's blessing is graciously upon Moses and with Moses he has entered into a special, intimate relationship. Yahweh will grant the request because of Moses.

Now that Yahweh has announced his presence and his special favour upon Moses, Moses longs for a fuller revelation of God, so he requests, 'Show me Your glory' (33:18). Moses demonstrates understanding that God must be the one who causes another to see his glory. Also, God's glory (at least in this sense) is not always seen by the individual unaided; rather, it must be revealed. The request was a heartfelt one; it was very important to Moses – an intense request. The succeeding context suggests that God's glory here is not only a physical manifestation (33:22 ['while My glory passes by']; v. 23 ['you shall see My back; but My face shall not be seen']; 34:5 ['Now the LORD descended in the cloud and stood with him there']), but it is also an unveiling of God's attributes (33:19 ['I will make all My goodness pass before you, and I will proclaim the name of the LORD before you. I will be gracious to whom I will be gracious, and I will have compassion on whom I will have compassion.']; 34:6-7 ['merciful and gracious, long-suffering, and abounding in goodness and truth, keeping mercy for thousands, forgiving iniquity and transgression and sin, by no means clearing the guilty, visiting the iniquity of the fathers upon the children...']).

God begins his response by revealing his glory (vv. 19-23). Notice what takes place. In verse 19 we read, 'And He said, "I Myself will make My goodness pass before your face and will proclaim the name of Yahweh before your face and I will be gracious unto whom I will be gracious, and I will have compassion on whom I will have compassion."'[49] Then, in verses 20-23 the LORD tells Moses that he cannot see his face (his full presence or glory) but only his back and then makes provision for that.[50]

After the LORD instructed Moses to take two more tablets and go up into the mountain to receive the ten words again (34:1-4), thus setting the stage for the subsequent revelation, he showed Moses his glory – that of both visible manifestation and his attributes (34:5-7). Such a revelation led Moses once again to bring before God the request that stands at the centre of chapters 33-34 – that God's presence would go with them (34:8-9).

After the covenant is renewed (34:10-28) – which confirms God's presence and working among Israel, Moses comes down from the mountain to the people and we are told that 'the skin of his face shone, and they were afraid to come near him' (34:30). The following verses let us know that the face of Moses would shine with God's glory whenever he would go into the tabernacle of meeting and so he would veil his face while speaking to the people (34:32-35). The point we need to realize is that being in the presence of God and his glory leads to reflecting the glory of God. Such sets part of the backdrop to the full doctrine of glorification taught in the New Testament. R. C. Sproul summarizes this when he writes:

> When God told Moses that he could see His back, the literal reading of the text can be translated 'hindquarters'. God allowed Moses to see His

hindquarters but never His face. When Moses returned from the mount, his face was shining. The people were terrified, and they shrank away from him in horror. Moses' face was too dazzling for them to look upon. So Moses put a veil over his face so that the people could approach him. This experience of terror was directed at the face of a man who had come so close to God that he was reflecting God's glory. This was a reflection of the glory from the back of God, not the refulgent glory of His face. If people are terrified by the sight of the reflected glory of the back parts of God, how can anyone stand to gaze directly into His holy face?

Yet the final goal of every Christian is to be allowed to see what was denied to Moses ... This hope, crystallized in the benediction of Israel [i.e. Num. 6:24-26], becomes more than a hope for the Christian – it becomes a promise ... 1 John 3:2 ... Theologians call this future expectation the beatific vision.[51]

The contribution that Exodus 33-34 makes to the doctrine of glorification is not only to remind us that God's glory consists of both a visible manifestation as well as his character (emphasis upon grace and mercy), but it also demonstrates that God's presence is absolutely necessary for living a life in covenant with him. In that presence we learn of his character and see his glory displayed, which strengthens us for obedience and ministry. Yet what also results is that man can reflect the very glory of the presence of God. Though this was temporary in the Old Testament, we do learn that it can happen – and this sets an all-important foundation for the New Testament teaching on glorification.

As the sun is the source of light and power for all luminaries on earth and the latter radiates the power and effulgence of the former, so God is the source of all beauty, holiness and power for the child of God, who has been called to reflect his presence and glory. What's more, the longer we are in the presence of God, the more we become like him and thus display his glory.

Some time ago I had lunch with a friend at his job site. While we were visiting he mentioned the tendency for spouses to begin to resemble each other the longer they are together. They often begin to develop similar worldviews, political views, to speak alike, to mirror each other's facial expressions and sometimes even to look alike. This is similar to what the Bible asserts with regards to God and man. Man was made in God's image and this image was twisted, its effect diluted. Yet the Scriptures establish the principle that in God's presence we can begin to reflect his glory again. As we will see later, this is not only likeness in character, but it also can and will be reflecting his likeness in all aspects – even visible glory someday.

But as we will see, our internal desires also reflect God-given glory and the future of glorification. This leads us to the next area of Old Testament teaching.

God has placed a desire in man for glory, which can be realized as a believer

The first place this appears in the canon is in Judges 5:31, which closes the 'Song of Deborah'. This poetic work is found within Judges 4-5, the account of Deborah and Barak delivering the Israelites from the hand of Jabin, king of Canaan (4:2). Deborah was a prophetess who was judging in Israel (4:4-5).[52] She called for Barak and told him that the LORD has commanded him and the troops to go against Sisera (commander of the army of the Canaanites) and that he would deliver the enemy into their hands (4:6-7). Barak responded that he would not go unless she went with him (4:8). So Deborah consented and she and Barak led the army to victory. In the process, Sisera died by having a tent peg run through his temple at the hands of a woman, Jael. In chapter 5 Deborah and Barak sing about the victory, giving a poetic depiction of the battle. Judges 5:24-30 focuses upon the death of Sisera. The entire victory was shown to be a resounding defeat for the Canaanites and it was considered a shameful thing to die at the hand of a woman, as Sisera did (cf. Judges 9:53-54).

Having sung of the great victory and the shameful death of Sisera, Deborah and Barak conclude the song with these words: 'Thus let all Your enemies perish, Yahweh, and those who love Him, [let them be] as the sun going out in its might.'[53] The adverb *ken* ('thus') often connotes 'as has been described or commanded, with reference to what has preceded'.[54] What verse 31 calls for then is that all those who oppose God and his people, as well as hate him (implied in 'all Your enemies' – cf. how it is opposed to 'those who love Him') would perish in the same way that Sisera (who represents the Canaanites here) did – namely in shame and dishonour. The jussive third person masculine verb *yo'vdu* ('let all ... perish') shows that the song is making a request. The request is that the enemies would die as a result of their sin – the death being judgement.[55] As can be seen from the uses of the verb elsewhere, it communicates the opposite of long life and prosperity which were to be part of covenantal blessings. Hence, the song opens its concluding double-edged request on a note of soliciting justice from God for enemies, i.e. for the wicked. A parallel passage to the imprecation in this verse would be Psalm 83:9-10: 'Deal with them as with Midian, as with Sisera, as with Jabin at the Brook Kishon, who perished at En Dor, who became as refuse on the earth.'

Conversely to this appeal with regards to the wicked, a request is also offered up on behalf of those who love God. Truly, those who love God are those who, out of their great affections for God, have trusted in him and thus obey him (cf. Deut. 6:5; Josh. 22:5; 23:11).[56] Most versions see the idea of the request being carried over into this second half of the verse and supplying the idea of action in place of a missing verb (common in Hebrew, known as ellipsis). So Deborah and Barak request for those who love the LORD that they be as 'the rising of the sun in its might' (NASB).

The rising of the sun not only marked the boundary of the earth and the direction of the east (Judg. 11:18; 21:19), but it was also seen as a glorious event (Ps. 19:5-6). The sun itself was associated with very good and positive benefits. The sun was considered a blessing in helping the fields bring forth crops (Deut. 33:14). 2

Samuel 23:4 speaks of the just and godly king: 'And he shall be like the light of the morning when the sun rises, a morning without clouds...' The Reformation Study Bible (p.462) says of this idiom, 'The benefits of the righteous rule are enlightenment, fruitfulness, and refreshment.' Psalm 84:11 says of God, 'For the LORD God is a sun and shield; the LORD will give grace and glory; no good thing will He withhold from those who walk uprightly.' Again, The Reformation Study Bible, p.848, comments, 'The metaphor comparing God to the sun praises Him as the source of light and energy. The burning rays of the sun in the dry country east of the Mediterranean make it a suitable portrayal of God's power.' In Proverbs 4:18 it is written: 'But the path of the just is like the shining sun, that shines ever brighter unto the perfect day.' In verse 19 of Proverbs 4 the wicked who stumble and do not know why are contrasted with the just.

There also may very well be an allusion to victory over Israel's enemies. Daniel Block comments:

> Although the idiom derives ultimately from the daily emergence of the sun on the eastern horizon, one may recognize in the present usage a polemic against pagan nations. In ancient Near Eastern thought the sun was worshiped as a deity who rode triumphantly across the sky in his chariot each day. The association of the sun with a chariot derives from the sun's disc-like appearance. The ancients perceived it as a chariot wheel turning through the heavens. Indeed the present image may have been suggested to Deborah by the earlier references to Sisera's chariots. If this interpretation is correct, the prayer now wishes for Yahweh's people continued triumph against their enemies; this military nuance also creates a fitting inclusion with the opening vision of Yahweh coming forth from Sinai ahead of his people (v. 4). No earthly chariots can stand against those who are covenantally committed to God.[57]

In Judges 5:31 this appeal for God's people is contrasted with the desire for judgement on the enemies of God. As such, it also seems to fit the context that what Deborah and Barak are requesting on behalf of those who love God is that they would experience God's covenantal blessings and that these blessings would be displayed to the world, both in benefits, as well as in vindication – i.e. that the world would see who are God's favoured.[58] This also is supported by the fact that in the simile used here the sun is going forth 'in its might' (bigvurato). This feminine noun can refer to 'strength', 'might' and 'valour', all in such a way that it shows forth the glory and greatness of the subject.[59] Such is the thought here with regards to the sun. It is rising in its strength and glory. People see how beneficial and powerful it is. Deborah and Barak appeal to God on behalf of those who love him – that they too would be shown forth in a glorious way with splendour. They desire that the world would see their blessed status before God.

Once the reader understands what Judges 5:31 is communicating, it is seen that the song-ending request becomes a seed for the idea of glorification of the believer in the Scriptures. God has placed a longing in the heart of the believer not only to be blessed by him, but also to experience a glorious existence which is displayed to the world (a vindication of who believers really are). The implication is that this request will be fulfilled in God's blessing of his people. It is this idea that is developed later in the Old Testament and certainly comes to fruition in the New Testament.

There are other places in the Old Testament where the vindication of God's people is set forth as part of his blessing. In Lamentations 2:1-22 the prophet displays God's anger over Judah's sin. The first verse reads, 'How the Lord covered with a cloud in His anger the daughter of Zion! He cast down from heaven to the earth the beauty of Israel and did not remember His footstool in the day of His anger.' If we understand correctly the meaning of 'beauty' here we see that what God has done is destroy the reputation of Jerusalem.[60] Such is part of God's discipline upon sin, i.e. his curse. The converse, his blessing, would then include establishing and preserving the reputation of Jerusalem or his people. In fact, Deuteronomy 26:19 clearly shows that such honouring and displaying of glory (part of vindication) is included in God's covenantal blessing.[61] In Isaiah 46:13 Israel is said to be the glory or beauty of Yahweh. As such, these, his people, display his true beauty, which causes people to acknowledge and admire him. This same idea is found in Isaiah 62:3 and Jeremiah 13:11. God's vindication of his people leads to the glorification of himself.

In Psalm 9:18 David affirms that 'the needy shall not always be forgotten; the expectation of the poor shall not perish forever'. Often in the Old Testament the terms 'needy' and 'poor' refer to actual material poverty, but also often relate to the righteous, who for various reasons are being taken advantage of and thus are in a destitute state. The promise is that someday things will be made right. The righteous shall not always be poor, taken advantage of, persecuted and abused. There will come a day when God shall right the wrongs.

Such a future vindication was also applied to prophetic promises made to Israel in the Old Testament. Zephaniah 3:20 states, 'At that time I will bring you back, even at the time I gather you; for I will give you fame and praise among all the peoples of the earth, when I return your captives before your eyes, Says the LORD.' Vindication, then, is a promise that God has made to his people of all ages.

Bernard Ramm asserts that there are 'some verses in the Psalms ... which speak of glory as something bestowed or given to men ... In other passages glory seems to be the vindication of the righteous man ... The wicked will be swept away into a judgmental flood but with glory shall the righteous be rewarded'.[62] Then he adds, 'In such verses we have only a suggestion ... that in some future day God will reward the righteous man with a final, complete, and perfect vindication, which is described as a bestowal of honor or [glory].'[63]

Throughout history God has promised to his people that he would bless them. Part of this blessing is seen in being vindicated before the world so that the world sees their true standing and significance before God. For this to be a legitimate motivation for man's faithfulness to God (as God often uses it), it must truly be a desire of man. In fact, we could argue that whether or not we seek blessings, vindication and fulfilment in God or elsewhere is what much of life is all about. Will we see God as all-sufficient and the headwaters of blessing – the very source of our life, or will we see self, someone or something else? Lucifer wanted it his own way, on his own terms. Adam and Eve suffered the same downfall. In fact, desiring such pleasure apart from God's plan, timing and means (what we might call covetousness) stands at the heart of all sin (Rom. 7:7-8).

I would like to suggest that our desire for vindication, blessing and fulfilment comes back to the fact that God has made us in his image to be God-glorifiers.[64] And one of the ways we glorify God is in being recipients of his blessings and his vindication someday. In other words, it is in the world someday seeing our true weight and who we really are, and seeing that our love, forgiveness and the way we have raised our children have all been true significant contributions. We may have never won the Tour de France, our face may have never graced the cover of a magazine or shown up in the newspaper and we may have never led a nationally ac-claimed company or pastored a world-renowned church. Yet we will shine like the sun; we will be honoured. And this honour will be designed ultimately to shine right back upon the source, God himself, so that he will be glorified.

When the believer understands this, he now can see why he has the longings for significance he does. But he can also rest con-tent in this life. It doesn't matter whether or not I receive acclaim now. One day I will be glorified, and as a result, my Saviour will be honoured!

This also puts into perspective the promises for blessing which are found in the covenant God has made with his people. Things such as a promised land, dwelling in the promised land safely, be-ing made into a great nation, overcoming enemies, fruitfulness in child-bearing, fruitfulness in harvest and raising animals, being set above the nations of the earth, having a special place before God with a special reputation, establishment as a holy people, serving as the agency for God's blessing to the rest of the world, and an ev-erlasting dynasty (Gen. 12:1-3; Gen. 22:15-18; Lev. 26; Deut. 28; Josh. 23; 2 Sam. 7:12-16) all show great significance and reward to those who are God's people and who are faithful to him.[65] All of these outcomes are not only to benefit saints, but also ultimately to glorify God (Jer. 13:11; Ps. 106:7-8; Ezek. 10:14; 2 Sam. 7:23).

The covenantal blessings pronounced in the Old Testament primarily focus upon God's benefits within this life. However, as the Old Testament progresses, the prophets clarify that these blessings draw the attention of God's people to ultimate rewards and blessings in the eschaton.[66] No prophet focuses upon this any more than Isaiah. Ministering in the last half of the eighth century to Judah, he announces God's judgement upon them for their sin (e.g. chapter 1). He tells Judah to repent and escape the impending judgement (1:18-20), yet God made it evident that they would not repent (6:9-10). With this reality as a backdrop, Isaiah proclaims the necessity of God's judgement so that he could eventually bring true deliverance and ultimate salvation (cf. 4:4-6; 54:7-10). If Judah was to be the people of God out of whom the Messiah would come, punishment was necessary. God's refining of them was actually an indication that he had not given up on this purpose. It is as if the very presence of the impending hard times and coming judgement was to be part of their hope (cf. Prov. 3:11-12).[67] Yes, they would face judgement (1-39), but God would also restore them (40-66).

In the second major section of Isaiah (40-66) God makes it clear that he will restore them after the time of judgement. The way that this is developed is interesting. First there is a funneling down of focus in the four servant songs (42:1-9; 49:1-7; 50:4-11; 52:13 – 53:12). Israel is corporately God's servant and God will work through them for deliverance and restoration (49:3). Yet it is even more specific than this, for it will be the true believing remnant within Israel who will be the real agency for the great and future working of God (49:5-6). But even more than this, it is the individual suffering servant out of the remnant who will be the agent for ultimate deliverance and restoration (cf. 52:13 – 53:12).[68] The reader of these sections of Isaiah gets the idea that the restoration and deliverance are not only speaking of an immediate return to the land after captivity, but also something much more than this.

This something more is also communicated through another development by Isaiah. While the servant songs become more narrow in focus regarding Yahweh's servant, this section of Isaiah broadens its focus regarding those who will be recipients of God's blessings and restoration – to include the Gentiles also (cf. 49:6, 22-23; 51:4; 54:1 – 55:13 [especially 54:3]; 56:1-8 [especially vv. 7-8]). This broadening tendency also pertains to the blessings themselves. The land promises give way to promises of inheriting the nations (54:3; 55:5) and the temporal blessings give way to eternal blessings in the age to come. Consider Isaiah 65:17-18:

> For behold, I create a new heavens and a new earth; and the former shall not be remembered or come to mind. But be glad and rejoice forever in what I create; for behold, I create Jerusalem as a rejoicing, and her people a joy (NKJV).

And then the prophet adds in chapter 66:22-23:

> 'For as the new heavens and the new earth which I will make shall remain before me', says the LORD, 'So shall your descendants and your name remain. And it shall come to pass that from one New Moon to another, and from one Sabbath to another, all flesh shall come to worship before Me', says the LORD.

So Isaiah tells Judah that though you will face judgement, nevertheless God will restore you to the land and from within that land and the believing remnant he will bring forth a servant who will accomplish salvation that will make even greater blessings possible – with worldwide and eternal proportions. Thus the eyes of God's discerning saints were taken from the present to the eschaton. It would be the eschaton that would be the place and time of ultimate reward and glory. This is why the author of Hebrews comments:

> All these died in faith, without receiving the promises, but having seen them and having welcomed them from a distance, and having confessed that they were strangers and exiles on the earth. For those who say such things make it clear that they are seeking a country of their own. And indeed if they had been thinking of that country from which they went out, they would have had opportunity to return. But as it is, they desire a better country, that is, a heavenly one (Heb. 11:13-16b, NASB).

What we find in the Old Testament Scriptures is a clear affirmation running throughout that God has set forth a great reward and glory for man in the future, ultimately in the eschaton. In light of this, he has crafted mankind to desire glory and therefore to find his fulfilment only in what God has to offer. This forms a very important backdrop for the New Testament teaching on the glorification of the believer.

Israel as a light to the nations

In Isaiah 42:6 and 49:6 the prophet writes that God has given Israel as 'a light to the nations'. The latter verse adds that the purpose is so that 'My salvation may reach to the end of the earth'. The way that Israel functioned as a nation, as a collective people, was to have an impact upon the nations of the world for the glory of God (see also Jer. 13:11). It has already been demonstrated that man is a social being. What we will see again and again is that God's people in community, as they reflect the righteous and holy character of God among each other, have a tremendous impact on others for the honour of God's name.

THE OLD TESTAMENT TEACHING ON BODILY RESURRECTION

In light of what we have already seen, we should not be surprised that many intertestamental writers and the inspired New Testament writers believed that part of the glorification process would be the perfecting of the body in the eschaton. After all, we can never become all of what God originally intended for us to be until he has reversed all the effects of sin upon the world. Such seems to necessitate resurrection. We must be made new as God-glorifiers, fully displaying his image.

Because of this we are inclined to ask, 'What did the Old Testament teach about resurrection? Did it lay a foundation for this aspect of the doctrine of glorification?' Some would say 'no'. Yet, we have to disagree. Though we can concur that there may not be a full-fledged body of resurrection doctrine in the Old Testament, none the less, we will see that the foundation is there.[69]

The Old Testament's view towards flesh

Some theologians, such as Oscar Cullmann, have argued that the Scriptures are positive toward the body as a whole, yet negative toward the actual flesh itself, which is the locus of sin and death. As such, there will be no resurrection of a body that would contain any kind of flesh.[70] Yet, such a view is invalid. In the Old Testament we are told that God formed man 'of the dust of the ground, and breathed into his nostrils the breath of life; and man became a living being' (Gen. 2:7). Nothing could be more fleshly than this depiction. This is part of the more detailed account of the creation of man out of Genesis 2. After the more general overview in the first chapter (1:26-30), God 'saw everything He had made, and indeed it was very good' (1:31). Certainly this included man in his flesh. God's view towards man as a total (including flesh) was good. And if we are not convinced yet, we ought to be by the description of Adam and Eve in Genesis 2:25: 'And they were both naked, the man and his wife, and were not ashamed.' J. A. Schep has commented on these texts:

> It is obvious from the narratives of Genesis 1 and 2 that being a creature of flesh belongs to the divinely planned and created structure of man. It was as a creature of flesh that man in Paradise was

> God's very good image. The inference from man's essential and original makeup [is] that our existence of the age-to-come will include flesh ... Nevertheless, we have learned that being a creature of flesh belongs to man's essence as the very good image of God. This leads us to infer plausibly that the final stage of man's development, as it will become real in the resurrection day for those that are Christ's, cannot mean the total abandonment of his flesh, since this would imply that man ceases to be man, or at least ceases to be a complete man. It would amount to the destruction forever of an essential aspect of man's humanity.[71]

Flesh is not the source of man's evil, only the tool or instrument through which sin is accomplished. There are several other Old Testament passages which support the reality that flesh itself is not evil (which, if it were, would necessitate a non-bodily or non-fleshly resurrection). In Psalm 63:1 David addresses God with these words: 'My flesh (*b*ᵉ*sariy*) longs for You.' The term is parallel to *naphshiy* ('my soul') and could refer to David's whole being. However, it is hard to believe that it could be used even in an idiomatic way in this context if 'flesh' was inherently evil. Psalm 84:2b similarly reads, 'My heart and my flesh (*b*ᵉ*sariy*) cry out for the living God.' We also find idiomatic uses of 'flesh' in Ezekiel 11:19 and 36:26 which would call into question any view ascribing inherent evil to flesh.

There is certainly nothing in the Old Testament that would prohibit an actual bodily resurrection that includes flesh. In fact, there is significant support for such an idea.

Support from poetry

While struggling with what appears to be God's unjust treatment of him (Job 19:1-29), Job breathes an affirmation of his trust in God and the fact that he will be vindicated in the end. Part of this affirmation is verse 26 which reads, 'And after my skin is destroyed, this I know, that in my flesh I shall see God.' Job clearly affirms his belief in resurrection.[72] More specifically, it is a fleshly, bodily resurrection that gives him hope.

We also have several statements in the Psalter which deal with resurrection. The first comes from Psalm 16:9-11. Though we don't know the exact situation which the psalmist faced, we do know that it was some kind of crisis which threatened his very life. The psalm itself alternates between affirmation of trust in the Lord (vv. 1-4; 7-8) and the reasons why he trusts in the Lord (vv. 5-6; 9-11). David here affirms, 'My heart is glad and my mouth rejoices'[73] and his 'flesh also will rest in security' (v. 9). Even though he faces danger and death, yet he has contentment in and praise for God and the assurance that his flesh will not be left simply to be destroyed or deteriorate.

Why? Because, as he says to God, 'You will not abandon my soul to *Sheol*; You will not give your holy one to see corruption.' It should be understood that these two clauses are synonymously parallel. In the first David affirms that God will not leave or abandon his soul (which probably stands for the whole being) to the grave (i.e. the abode of the dead). What he is saying is that death will not be the last word about his life. This seems to be a veiled reference to life after death, even if it is not a clear affirmation of bodily resurrection.

The second clause, 'You will not give Your holy one to see corruption', seems to be reiterating the message of the first. The first person common singular ending on 'soul' makes it clear that David is focusing upon what God will do with him in death, so 'Your holy one' also refers to David. The term *chasiyd* connotes 'holy one', 'saint', and 'faithful one'.[74] It is clearly a reference to one who knows God and whom God has justified. This second clause states that Yahweh will not give (i.e. 'give over' or 'abandon') his holy one to corruption, i.e. to the destruction of the grave. God will not just leave a saint in the grave as the final word on his life. Again, we seem to have a veiled reference to life after death. Willem VanGemeren adds, 'The phrase "see corruption" (v. 10) is a metaphor for total isolation and abandonment from God's presence. Though not a clear and inescapable confession of faith in bodily resurrection, "in the apostolic preaching this verse did have a particular apologetic significance, as both Peter (Acts 2:27, 31) and Paul (Acts 13:35) quoted verse 10 as proof of the resurrection of our Lord".[75]

In verse 11 David elaborates upon the essence of his future hope as introduced in verse 10. He first says, 'You will make known to me the path of life'. In this affirmation David expresses his trust in God's transforming grace which will lead to blessings in the life to come. Let's see how this is true by looking briefly at this clause.

When we put together the use of 'path' (Job 6:18; Pss. 25:4; 119:9; 139:3; 142:3; Prov. 2:8, 13) and 'life' (Pss. 30:6; 133:3; Prov. 3:22; 4:13, 22; 8:35; 10:16, et al.), and also consider the other uses of 'path of life' (Prov. 2:19; 5:6; 10:17; 15:24) in the Wisdom Literature, we conclude that the phrase refers to that mode of existence and manner of relating to God and others in which the person experiences God's abundance, blessing and joy. Willem VanGemeren adds, '[It] signifies the way that leads to life. It is a wisdom term for the fullness of life that only the wise could achieve...'[76] It is the result of God's working and it also brings God's blessing. It is chiefly characterized by keeping God's Word, being faithful to his covenant and therefore living righteously.

How then does this whole clause ('You will make known to me the path of life') relate to the context? What is it that David is celebrating and trusting? It seems that in context he is rejoicing in, celebrating and trusting in the glorious blessings that God gives to one who trusts in him. He knows that as he trusts in Yahweh that Yahweh will not abandon him. His soul will rest in hope and he will not be abandoned to death. Yahweh will make known to him how to live such a life that brings God's abundant blessings (cf. v. 7) and God will enable David to experience such abundance that comes from covenant faithfulness and obedience to the Word. Though the focus is primarily blessing in this life (as it usually is in the Old Testament), none the less, this blessing bleeds and overflows into the life to come (cf. vv. 9-10 and 11c).

The psalm ends with these words: 'fullness of joy is in Your presence; in Your right hand there are pleasures forever'. Though there is not clear and explicit affirmation of future bodily resurrection, there is confession that God will enable David to defeat death in some way and to experience pleasures for ever more. Such lays the groundwork for life after death accompanied by pleasure. And elsewhere that pleasure in heaven is referred to as glory (Ps. 73:24). The Old Testament believer knew that he would experience the full weight of who God is and the full weight of his presence, and that this would bring great satisfaction and delight!

Psalm 17:15 clarifies in large part what brings such pleasure to the saint in the life to come. In all probability it is a veiled reference to what has already been called the 'beatific vision'.[77] In this psalm David prays to God and asks for protection from the wicked who are pursuing him. He ends the psalm with an affirmation of the hope that he has because of his God-given righteousness. The text reads, 'Yet I myself in righteousness, I will see Your face; I will be satisfied with Your likeness when I awake.' The juxtaposition of this verse with verse 14 ('From men with Your hand, Yahweh, from men of the world whose portion is in this life, and You fill their bellies with Your hidden punishment; may their children be sated, may they leave their abundance to their babes') suggests that the psalmist is focused upon a reward outside of this life and is best taken as an unhindered vision of God's face at that time. Even Moses was allowed only to see God's 'back' (Exod. 33:23), for 'no man shall see Me, and live' (Exod. 33:20). As a result, the vision described by the psalmist necessarily is one in the life to come. And if this is the case, the awakening of the psalmist must be something similar to resurrection. What can be deduced is that the Old Testament saint expected that he would live in some way and mode after death. And what is more, his reward would be the vision of God as he is!

In Psalm 49 the sons of Korah[78] affirm the futility of wealth and those who trust in it, for it does not last. In verse 15 (MT 16) the text takes quite a turn. So far the shortfalls and folly of those who trust in self and riches have been addressed. It is clear that there is no need to fear the unrighteous rich, because their end is death and hopelessness. Yet now it is added: 'God will redeem my soul from the hand of the grave (*sheol*)'. With regards to 'redeem',

William B. Cooker[79] writes, 'The basic meaning ... is to achieve the transfer of ownership from one to another through payment of a price or an equivalent substitute...' In other words, the text makes the assertion that God will indeed 'buy back' the soul of the saint from the hand of the grave. Such means that God will free him from the grip of the grave as a slave is freed from his slavery (cf. Exod. 13:15; 21:8). The 'hand of *Sheol*' is the 'power of the grave'.[80] We do not know just from this verse how much detail the Old Testament believer knew about future life, but what is reasonably clear is that he did expect God somehow to rescue him from the clutches of death.

We find a similar affirmation in Psalm 73. Here Asaph[81] struggles with the prosperity of the wicked and the suffering of God's people. Verses 1-17 deal with his own experience and the prosperity of the wicked. Verses 18-20 affirm God's justice. Verses 21-28 deal with a more positive message, mainly Asaph's hope in God and God's future for him.

Verses 23-26 are the heart of the psalmist's hope in God's presence, his help in the present and the future. Verse 24 reads, 'You will guide me with Your counsel and afterward receive me to glory.' The psalmist expresses his trust that God will guide him according to his counsel, which is his Word, his revelation.[82] This meaning of 'counsel' is supported by its use in other parts of the Old Testament.[83] Such is crucial in the midst of suffering and the apparent unfair prospering of the wicked. The saint must come back to God's Word, what God says about himself, his faithfulness, his working and his promises. Asaph believes God will enable him to navigate his way through the treacherous waters of this life's difficulties.

Yet not only will Yahweh do this, but afterward (pointing to the end of life) He will also receive him to glory. The verb translated 'receive' is used in Psalm 49:15 to refer to God receiving one into heaven. The sense is the same here. Both the context here as well as parallel thoughts in Psalms (cf. 16:11; 49:15) suggest that 'glory' (*kabod*) is synonymous for heaven. Joseph M. Stowell agrees when he writes that the term refers in this instance to 'home ... an eternity of fulfilled joy and pleasure with Him'.[84]

Again the reader learns that the Old Testament audience of the Psalter had a hope of life after death. And this hope constituted something weighty, significant and even magnificent – it is glory.

Support from the prophets

The first prophetic passage to consider is Isaiah 25:8. After laying a foundation of Judah's sin and hypocrisy along with God's impending judgement upon them (1-5), Isaiah records his own call to the prophetic ministry, which contrasts God's holiness and the sinfulness of his people – and the reality that they will not listen (6). In chapters 7-12 oracles of judgement and hope are pronounced in conjunction with the Syro-Ephramite war (2 Chr. 28). The point seems to be that this is a harbinger of things to come – judgement for sin. In chapters 13-39 pronouncement of judgement is repeated, this time in oracles against the nations (13-23), the pronouncement of apocalyptic judgement over all the world (24-27) and then more on judgement and salvation in chapters 28-39. The events of these chapters relate to 'Sennacherib's attack on Jerusalem during the reign of Hezekiah (701 B.C.)'.[85]

> Isaiah 24-27, sometimes called the Isaiah Apocalypse, is one of the earliest examples of apocalyptic content and technique. According to the prophet, the earth's condition is wretched and, apart from outside intervention, seemingly hopeless. But God is going to rise up and destroy wickedness from the earth and inaugurate a new order.[86]

Even though the chapters are written to Judah facing attack upon Jerusalem and have reference to those events, the language clearly goes beyond that situation to deal with the end times.[87] Interspersed in these chapters are words about judgement upon Judah and the nations, as well as protection of God's people and restoration.[88] The sense seems to be that God will right all things

– bringing judgement upon those who reject him, yet bringing deliverance to those who belong to him. Such not only refers to the immediate situation of facing Sennacharib and perhaps future judgement upon the nation and subsequent restoration (within the sixth century B.C.), but the universal and eschatological terminology takes the focus to the end of time as well. At that time God also will right all wrongs, bringing judgement and deliverance to the wicked and righteous respectively. 'Chapters 24-27 bring [Isaiah 13-23] to a climax. They explain how the final, universal judgment will come upon the world.'[89]

Isaiah's statement in chapter 25:8 is found in a context of the millennium (25:6) and ultimate deliverance and blessing upon saints. God will make a feast for all peoples (i.e. believing peoples from all nations) at Mt Zion – 'a delicious feast of good food, with clear, well-aged wine and choice beef' (25:6, NLT). At that time God will remove the 'veil of mourning and grief ... [a] symbol of suffering and death'[90] figuratively covering everyone (25:7). More specifically, in verse 8, he 'will swallow up death forever', 'will wipe away tears from upon every face', and 'will remove the disgrace of his people from all the earth' (NIV). Though verse 6 seems to be dealing more with the millennium, verse 8 agrees with what is said elsewhere about the New Jerusalem and the age to come (cf. Rev. 21:4). Isaiah is giving the reader an overview of the complex of events at the end of time.

The pertinent clause in this verse for the present discussion is the first one: He 'will swallow up death forever' (NIV).[91] The sense is that God will do away with death for his saints. No longer will they be subject to the state of lacking physical and spiritual life. No believer will die again. What this necessitates is life in the eschaton and the cessation of death. Again, this does not explicitly speak of resurrection, but does strongly imply it. J.A. Schep agrees:

> This prophecy of Isaiah 25:8a does not teach a physical resurrection expressis verbis, but the absolute language employed certainly carries this implication. A world without death and therefore without mourning and grief cannot possibly be a

> world with unopened graves, in which the bod-
> ies of children of God are still in the power of
> death. Only when all deceased saints are raised
> from their graves to immortal life, raised in the
> selfsame bodies that death had laid hold on, only
> then is death 'swallowed up forever'.[92]

What this clause implies, the next relevant statement out of Isaiah explicitly affirms. One chapter later, in chapter 26:19, we read, 'But your dead will live; their bodies will rise. You who dwell in the dust, wake up and shout for joy. Your dew is like the dew of the morning; the earth will give birth to her dead' (NIV).

Chapter 26, like the rest of this Isaiah Apocalypse, refers first of all to events within the day of Isaiah (invasion, along with subsequent captivity and deliverance) and it also contrasts the righteous and the wicked. Judah will face severe times (20-21), yet God will prove himself trustworthy, protect his people and bring down the wicked (1-19), even though Judah has not been faithful and accomplished their purpose in the world (12-18).[93] Again, as with chapter 25, the language here also takes us beyond the events of Judah in the sixth to eighth centuries B.C. to the end times. Like God did then, so in the end times he will graciously right all wrongs, judging the wicked and caring for his children. This is his consistent pattern.[94]

What we have then in Isaiah 26:19 is a promise that has ramifications for the eschaton. Isaiah begins by saying, 'Your dead ones will live'. All throughout this chapter the prophet has been addressing the LORD (e.g. vv. 3, 7c, 8, 9, 11a, 12, 13, 14c, 14, 16, 17c). As a result, the reader must understand that these dead ones belong to Yahweh.[95] These are true believers, the remnant, as opposed to those in verse 14 who are enemies of God and will not rise. The 'dead ones' also speaks of those literally and physically dead, since the term (*mawet*) is parallel to three further statements that clarify that some kind of figurative death is not in view. First, the text says that 'their bodies will rise'. The term for 'bodies' (*n*ᵉ*belah*) refers to carcasses or corpses.[96] What is in view here is a human dying and then that corpse being raised to life again. 'In speaking thus, the prophet makes himself the mouthpiece of the people, and expresses the belief that the actual body that died will be revivified.'[97] This is one of the clearest statements of bodily resurrection in the Old Testament.

The next statement, 'the ones who dwell in the dust, wake up and shout for joy', also clearly refers to those physically dead. It calls to mind the description of death found in the sin curse of Genesis 3:19: 'In the sweat of your face you shall eat bread till you return to the ground, for out of it you were taken; for dust you are, and to dust you shall return'[98] (NKJV). This is also supported by the following and parallel 'and the earth shall cast out the dead'. The imperatives call to mind God's command to rise. The risen ones are called to 'shout for joy'! Such is a reminder that being raised from the dead is a glorious gift that brings great gladness of heart.[99] After all, this is overcoming death and entering eternal life. The biblical teaching is that for the believer death is the gateway to joy. Such forms a foundation for the full-orbed New Testament doctrine of glorification.

The final statement that confirms this verse and deals with physical death and subsequent bodily resurrection is 'the earth will cast forth the dead ones'.[100] The *r'pha'iym* ('dead ones') refers to disembodied persons, and is the name of the dead used often in Wisdom and other late literature.[101] J. A. Schep's words aptly bring the discussion of this verse to a close:

> Whatever changes the body may undergo at the resurrection (a point not under discussion in Isaiah 26), the identity of the body of flesh that was buried will be maintained. So understood, Isaiah 26:19 is a most significant passage: it is the first clear Old Testament prophecy concerning the eschatological, physical resurrection of the individual dead.[102]

The next prophetic text which teaches resurrection is Isaiah 53:10-12. These three verses are found in the fourth and final Servant Song in this Old Testament book. It was Berhard Duhm in his commentary who for the first time set forth clearly the four Servant Songs of Isaiah.[103] These include chapters 42:1-9, 49:1-7, 50:4-11 and 52:13 – 53:12. One of the most difficult issues with regards to the Servant Songs is the identity of the servant. Some have suggested that it is Jesus only, the whole nation of Israel, remnant Israel, Isaiah or various other historical figures.[104] None of these approaches seems to be altogether correct. As was shown above, there seems to be a development from the use of 'servant' referring to Israel collectively, to Israel as the faithful remnant, to finally the ultimate representative of that corporate servant, namely the suffering Servant, the Messiah.[105]

This fourth song clearly speaks of the individual Servant who would suffer and die in the place of God's people to pay their sin penalty and justify them. The individuality of the Servant at this point is evidenced in many ways. He is marred such that his appearance was not like a human (52:14), his growing up years are spoken of (53:2), he is described as a 'man of sorrows and acquainted with grief' (53:3), he is despised and of him people conclude that he is not significant (53:3), he suffers vicariously (53:4-6) and yet he does not open his mouth (53:7), he is imprisoned unjustly and put to death on behalf of God's people (53:8), he is assigned a grave with the wicked (53:9), he did no violence nor spoke any deceit (53:9) and yet he will be vindicated and rewarded as his salvation work justifies sinners and brings forth spiritual offspring (53:10-12). So whatever is said of him, we are not dealing with what a corporate entity does, but rather what happens with an individual. And Isaiah intimates that he would be raised from the dead.

It is clear that this individual would not only suffer, but also die. Verse 8 reads, 'He was cut off out of the land of the living'. This clause suggests 'a violent, premature death ... not simply the oppressive judgment of men'.[106] This is reinforced in verse 9 when it is said that 'and His grave was assigned with the wicked, and with the rich in His death'. Clearly Isaiah was prophesying that the suffering Servant of God would die vicariously in the place of God's people.

This sets the stage for us to consider what is said in Isaiah 53:10-12. Several clauses in these three verses imply life after death for the servant: 'He will see His offspring'[107] (v. 10), 'He will prolong His days'[108] (v. 10), 'He will see that which comes from the suffering of His soul'[109] (v. 11), 'He will be satisfied'[110] (v. 11), 'I will divide a portion to Him with the great ones' (v. 12) and 'He will divide the spoil with the strong ones' (v. 12).[111] The servant will die, yet post-mortem he experiences a number of phenomena (e.g. seeing, prolonging and being satisfied).

Though it is not explicit in affirming bodily resurrection, again we have at least implied the reality of coming back to life in some form. In light of other teachings, the most probable implication we can draw is that Isaiah is revealing that the suffering Servant will be resurrected bodily. This fourth servant song was applied to Jesus Christ multiple times by New Testament writers.[112] In fact, we could say that no more accurate commentary of his suffering, death and resurrection could be found than what we see in these fifteen verses recorded seven centuries before the fact. As such, we find one more text supporting the tenet that the Old Testament did in fact teach the possibility, yes, even the certainty of future bodily resurrection.

Our next prophetic support for resurrection is located in Ezekiel 37:1-14. In this book in which Ezekiel demonstrates the necessity of the Babylonian captivity.(Ezek. 1-32), he turns to the truth that God will restore them (Ezek. 33-48). In the midst of this discussion of restoration, Ezekiel recounts a vision in a valley of dry bones. The bones take on flesh, then become alive. God is representing how he will bring Judah corporately back to life and restore them. What is used to make this point is the figure of the resurrection of individuals. Some commentators have argued that there must have been at least some in Judah at this time who believed in bodily resurrection in order for this vision to be intelligible.[113] By itself, Ezekiel 37 proves nothing conclusively, but along with other texts it becomes one of the pieces of evidence to demonstrate belief in resurrection among the Old Testament canon.

Support from Daniel

Willem A. VanGemeren says of Daniel, 'The message focuses on the sovereignty of the Creator-Redeemer over the kingdoms of this world, on the suffering and perseverance of the saints during the wars among the kingdoms of the earth, and on their final reward ... This revelation is ... to inspire confident hope in the final establishment of the everlasting kingdom of God'.[114] Such a message is unfolded first of all by focusing upon the faithful remnant of Judah in Babylon and how by the sovereign grace of God they overcame their trials by captors who threatened to undermine faith in Yahweh (Dan. 1-6).[115]

Additionally, the work takes the reader into the future, through a number of visions, to offer hope to God's people and the promise that as God triumphed through faithful individuals within the foreign court, so also he will triumph through his people for all time (Dan. 7-12).

It seems most likely that Daniel authored this powerful book (cf. 9:2; 10:2) and that the time of its writing was soon after Cyrus captured Babylon. Judah needed the reminder that God is in control and certainly not done with them. He must be the object of their future hope and faith.

At the end of the hope-producing visionary second half of the book, the text focuses upon how Antiochus IV (175-163 B.C., who took the epithet Epiphanes [He thought of himself as the manifestation on earth of Olympian Zeus.]), the future Seleucid king, would desecrate the temple (Dan. 11:29-35). He tried to increase his empire by annexing Egypt, but was checked by the Romans in 168 B.C. News of the Roman check prompted an attempt in Judea to oust the king's high priestly nominee Menelaus in favour of the deposed Jason. Antiochus looked upon this as an act of rebellion. On his way back from Egypt he abolished the temple operation and set up the abomination of desolation for three years, from December of 167 B.C. to December of 164 B.C.[116]

Daniel 11:36-45 does not seem to recount any known events at the end of the life of Antiochus IV and therefore most probably takes the reader beyond that time in history to a point when the antitype of Antiochus (Antichrist) will be active at the end of this age (cf. Matt. 24:15; Mark 13:14; Luke 21:20).[117]

Daniel takes the reader's focus to the very end of the age in Daniel 12:1-3. He writes that 'at that time' the ruling angel (cf. Jude 9) and one who regularly defends God's people against their enemies (cf. also Rev. 12:7), Michael, will stand up. The implication seems to be that he will stand up in order to bring deliverance to the people of God. This is what the first verse goes on to address. After the great tribulation of the end ('a time of trouble, such as never was since there was a nation') the people of God will be delivered – those who are truly saints of God and who are recorded in his Book. Since this group delivered in verse 1 seems to be distinguished from the group addressed in verse 2 and 3 (and they are dead), it makes sense that Michael is delivering those true saints who are still alive from their enemies.

Then in Daniel 12:2-3 we find one of the clearest statements of resurrection in all the Old Testament. At that time, at the end of the tribulation period, here is what will take place: 'Multitudes who sleep in the dust of the earth will awake: some to everlasting life, others to shame and everlasting contempt' (12:2, NIV). Literally, the first part of the verse reads 'And many from those sleeping in the ground-dust'.[118] Concerning the wording 'many from those sleeping', it could be that the vision which Daniel received did not specify whether or not all would be resurrected. He simply saw multitudes being raised. Though the text could be construed to mean that only some people are resurrected, the overwhelming testimony of Scripture elsewhere is that all people are raised. Yet this verse need not be made to affirm that all will be raised without exception, nor should it be taken so woodenly as to affirm that less than all will be raised. The NIV's 'multitudes' seems to be the sense that Daniel intended. In his vision he simply saw multitudes being raised.[119] It is no more specific at this point in the progress of revelation than that.

Are these ones being raised that Daniel saw truly dead? The answer is yes. The adjective yashen ('sleeping') can figuratively connote death. Though the adjective is never used elsewhere in the Old Testament to refer to death, its cognate verb is (Job 3:13;

Ps. 13:3 [MT 4]; Jer. 51:39, 57). It may be that the Hebrews borrowed this concept of sleep signifying death from the Canaanite fertility cult 'with its notion of the annual death and resurrection of the deity'.[120] Though we cannot be sure of the origin, the use is clear. And the picture is a good one especially when resurrection is also implied.[121] These ones are said to be 'sleeping in the dust of the ground'. This latter phrase denotes the realm in which they are sleeping; it is 'in the dust of the ground'. Such defines the kind of sleep this is – and Old Testament theology demands that this is death. When God pronounced sin's curse upon Adam he stated, 'By the sweat of your brow you will eat your food until you return to the ground, since from it you were taken; for dust you are and to dust you will return' (Gen. 3:19, NIV). Most likely then, Daniel intends that those who are sleeping in the realm of the dust of the ground are those who have returned to the ground; they have died.[122]

Now that we know whom Daniel has in mind (the dead), we are prepared to understand the verb *yaqiyxu* ('will awake'). It is the reversal of the sleep of death.[123] The phrase 'in the dust of the earth' implies that the body is in view (cf. Gen. 3:19). This is not just a reanimation of a sleeping soul; rather it is the rising of a body. This is why Calvin writes, 'This passage is worthy of especial notice, because the prophets do not contain any clearer testimony than this to the last resurrection, particularly as the angel asserts the future rising again of both the righteous and the wicked.'[124]

The end of the righteous is *chayyey 'olam* ('everlasting life'). This is the only Old Testament occurrence of this phrase. The term *'olam* ('everlasting') can mean 'for ever' or 'everlasting', 'perpetual', 'old' or 'ancient'.[125] The fact that it is used to refer to post-mortem, post-resurrection existence (for both righteous and wicked) suggests a reference to existence beyond time as we know it in this world and thus it is without end. The case for this is made even stronger when we recall the affirmation of forever or eternal reward to the righteous in Psalm 16:11 which ends with the words: 'in Your right hand there are pleasures forever' (*nexach*).

Further, there is more than just future for ever existence under consideration for the righteous. We know this not only from the rich Old Testament connotations connected to 'life' (see Psalm 16:11 discussion above), but also because 'everlasting life' is antithetical to the just rewards of the wicked upon their resurrection, stated as 'shame and everlasting contempt'. The former term (*charaphot*) denotes that the wicked will have disgrace and reproach pronounced upon them. They will feel fully the statement and judgement of God that they have acted wrongly.[126] This is the opposite of the honour and significance that we have seen the Old Testament holds out for the righteous. The latter term (*dir'on*) has an even stronger connotation, 'aversion, abhorrence'.[127] This term suggests that God (and perhaps others) will look upon those raised to the everlasting state of judgement as twisted and someone from whom heads are turned. The wickedness repels and separates from God (Isa. 59:2). Again, one could not choose a term that would have any more stark contrast to the blessing, reward and honour bestowed by God upon the righteous. Those who are not part of God's covenant will not only miss out upon the blessings of God in some neutral way, but they will also experience shame and contempt for eternity! It will be clear to all who these people are, the kind of life that they have lived and that they do not deserve the honour of God's presence. They will wear this label without end.

It should not be missed that Daniel 12:2 teaches, by implication, the future honouring (and vindication) of the righteous. Part of their reward of everlasting life, as it will be opposite of the wicked, will be honour bestowed by God. He will acknowledge and reward their true state before him. This is an aspect of glorification which has emerged time and again in the Old Testament and one which we can expect to colour the more detailed New Testament teaching.

Though the New Testament has connotations of the everlasting life being an existence characterized by the eternal and thus an eternal existence that bleeds into the present age and experience,[128] the Old Testament is not that complex or advanced in its personal eschatology. The point here is simply that the righteous will be bodily resurrected and rewarded with existence and the experience of God's abundance, blessing and joy for ever.[129]

This does not mean, however, that the mere concept of ongoing, for ever existence and blessing would not have bearing upon this life. Charles Colson and Nancy Pearcey have astutely captured the present significance of future for ever life when they commented:

> The existentialists pointed out that if there is nothing beyond the grave, then death makes a mockery of everything we have lived for; death reduces human projects and dreams to a temporary diversion, with no ultimate significance. But if our souls survive beyond the grave, as the Bible teaches, then this life is invested with profound meaning. Everything we do here has a significance for all eternity. The life of each person, whether in the womb or out, whether healthy or infirm, takes on enormous dignity.[130]

The present significance is strongly intended by Daniel 12:2. The very discussion of personal eschatology at this point seems to be that of encouraging the righteous with future victory, reward and vindication, as well as motivating the readers to make sure they are part of the righteous remnant in light of the end they will face if they are not. Herein we find helpful direction in what bearing the doctrine of glorification has for the believer now. This is a reality that Paul draws out with great clarity in Romans 8:18ff.

In verse 3, Daniel elaborates upon those who will be raised to everlasting life. He calls them here 'those who are wise'. This hiphil plural participle (*hamaskiyliym*) can mean 'to have insight and comprehension', 'to act circumspectly and prudently' or to 'prosper and have success'.[131] It was used in chapter 11:33, 35 to refer clearly to true believers, saints and those who instruct others (this sense may still be present since the following parallel speaks of turning many to righteousness). This same verb is used of the suffering Servant of the LORD in Isaiah 52:13 to describe how he will act wisely and prosper. The term is found in Jeremiah 9:24 to speak of the true believer, the really wise person, who understands and knows Yahweh. It is enough for our present study to know that those under consideration are believers, ones who have understood the truth of God and acted upon it in wise obedience, which is nothing more than 'conforming one's life to the character of God'.[132]

These wise ones, writes Daniel, 'will shine like the brightness of the sky above' (ESV). The verb *zahar* ('shine') is used only here in the Old Testament and denotes sending out or emitting light. It might be a play on words, since the wise ones are spoken of in Daniel 11:33 as instructing many. The following parallel describes them as turning many to righteousness and a homonym of the word means to 'teach' or 'warn'.[133] These ones will not only discharge wisdom and instruction, but they will also someday radiate great light and splendour.

The comparison of what they will shine like is 'the sky above'. Some translate this as 'the firmament' (NKJV) or 'heavens' (NIV). The term (*haraqiy*) seems to refer to the expanse between the earth and the heavens above (Gen. 1:6-7). When the wise ones, the righteous, are raised, their physical appearance will be changed such that they emit light similar to the brightness of the sun which brightens the midday sky. That Daniel speaks of physical transformation here follows from the thought flow of the text. As we saw in verse 2, the focus is upon the dead and their bodies. These dead ones will be bodily raised and now he writes that they will shine like the sky above. This can only mean that they will be physically transformed such that they emit great light. Any figurative sense given to the text at this point would be foreign to the context.[134]

The subsequent parallel statement affirms, 'and those who turn many to righteousness, like the stars forever and ever'. 'Those who turn many to righteousness' is parallel to 'those who are wise'. The clause speaks of those who show others the way to righteousness for themselves. It can connote both leading by example and verbal explanation.[135] It is interesting that those who know God and are wise have a tendency to lead others to the way of truth also as an almost intrinsic characteristic.

Of these ones the text says they 'will shine like the stars forever and ever'. The figure of speech known as ellipsis is present, in which the thought or action previously stated is to be carried over into this clause. 'Will shine' is not repeated, but it is to be understood. The wise ones who turn others to righteousness will shine like the sky above and like the stars for ever. This is an eternal transformation, one in which they will resemble the brightness of the sun and stars. With this verse we have the first explicit Old Testament reference to the glorification of the believer in the eschaton.[136]

Resurrection hope

The promise held out to the saint in Daniel 12:2-3 (as well as in the other Old Testament teaching on resurrection and glorification) reminds me of a recent box office hit movie, *Gladiator* (DreamWorks, 2000). In this story that takes place at the end of the second century A.D., a victorious Roman general by the name of Maximus is sold into slavery due to the new emperor's jealousy over the war veteran's popularity and power among the people – as well as his designation by the former emperor, Marcus Aurelius, to lead Rome upon his death. Maximus is not only made a gladiator, destined to fight and kill or be killed for the people's entertainment, but his wife and son are brutally murdered by evil thugs under the command of the wicked Roman ruler, Commodus.

Maximus is reduced to a mere fighting slave who at first is ridiculed by the masses. Shame, despair, danger and hopelessness were the daily diet of the gladiators. Yet this man did have a glimmer of hope. What was it? That he would defeat his enemy, Commodus, and be reunited with his family in the next life. The movie ends with Maximus regaining his full honour and glory, taking the life of Commodus, being vindicated in the eyes of the people and being reunited with his family.

The hope that Daniel holds out in Daniel 12:1-2 is very much the same. The prophet writes for a people about to return from seventy years of captivity. They had been through hardships and felt at many times as if they had nothing, as if there was no hope. Yet here God reminds them that there is always hope for the saint. And he gives us the same reminder today. No matter what our difficulties are presently, no matter what are the heartaches or disappointments that have threatened to suck the life out of us, no matter how the world presently views us, there will come a time when we will defeat our last enemy – death, and we will be vindicated before the world as we receive honour from God because we are his. Regardless of our physical condition or lack of resources here, we will be clothed in the glorious, radiant body of One who shines like the sun and stars. We will be billboards (British: advertisement hoarding) for the glorious work that God has done in us and our great delight will be that we are reflecting back to him the honour he has accomplished in us. And all this will be for eternity!

CONCLUSION

We have learned that in the creation of mankind, God crowned him with glory and honour. This means that we are made in God's image, resembling him as nothing else in his creation does, and we represent God, that is, we show to the world the weightiness and magnificence of our Creator through our actions, relationships, accomplishments and moral uprightness. We are God's work of art, which brings the focus of other people and the angelic world back to the Artist himself. We were created as God-glorifiers. Yet, through sin, this initial state and purpose have been twisted. This capacity can be restored only as we are reconciled to him.

Put another way, we carry out this purpose only when we are in covenant relationship with God. After all, God is the source of all beauty, holiness, and power. Such a relationship requires his empowering presence and brings with it promises from God to bless us and shower us with his benefits. As that happens, we bring even more glory to the source of those blessings and benefits. God has created us with a desire for significance and glory, that is, that we might accomplish much and be blessed. This desire can only be fulfilled, both in this life and the life to come, as we fulfil our ultimate purpose as God-glorifiers.

Even though we, as individuals and the collective church, can experience much of God's blessings and benefits and thus carry out our purpose of bringing glory to God in this life, it will not happen in the full sense until the world is changed, sin is no more and we are transformed. Our focus then must be taken to the eschaton and the reality that it will be only in the life to come that our full God-glorifying status will be restored. This is why God promises, even to the Old Testament saint, that he will resurrect him bodily, give him eternal life and grant him pleasures and fulness of joy for ever and ever. It was man, as a physical being, who was meant to reflect the weight and splendour of God. Therefore, resurrection and full transformation are essential.

Likewise, God will often show to the world in this life who his church really is, but even that, what we call vindication, will not happen fully until the eschaton. Shame and scorn, often attached to the lives of believers, will be replaced with God's own revelation of who the saints really are, and thus honour and glory recovered. This honour and glory will bring great pleasure to man because ultimately it will bring the attention and praise back to God. The delight and the pleasure will be so satisfying and intense that it will be even greater than the joy the mute might express who has regained speech or the lame who has recovered use of his legs.

When believers are resurrected, it will not only be their character that reflects glory to God, but it will also be their appearance. Their metamorphosis will include effulgence, a radiation of light so that they will shine like the sun and stars. In light of the example of Moses who reflected a physical manifestation of God's glory when in his presence, this may very well be due to the saint being in the realized and full presence of our glorious and mighty God.

It is no wonder that during the intertestamental period it was affirmed that men would be resurrected (even though not all Jews shared this belief, nor did all those who believed in resurrection agree in the details).[137] Additionally, it was taught that the bodies of the elect would be transformed such that they would radiate a glorious light,[138] and that their presence in heaven would be a sharing in the glory of God and a restoration of the pre-fall glory that was Adam's.[139]

Though the Old Testament does not develop the idea of glorification to the extent that we will see in the New Testament, nevertheless it lays a significant foundation and does say a great deal. Its teaching also should have a vital bearing upon how we live now. For one thing, we must see that we cannot understand ourselves fully unless we see that we were created to be God-glorifiers. An understanding of this ought to permeate all that we do – no less than salt permeating the entirety of a favourite stew simmering in a crock pot. Such sets the stage for the uniting of our vertical relationship with God and our horizontal relationship with others. God-glorifiers, according to what the first two-thirds of the Scriptures have set forth, must honour God by both loving him and loving others.

Is it not also an implication that the more we are in God's presence, the longer we know him and the more that we love him and savour him, the greater should be our reflecting of his full weight and magnificence? Shouldn't this capacity to glorify God grow and grow in this life? Then, one day, having passed from this life into the next and having received our resurrected and transformed bodies, we become full-fledged neon-lighted billboards for the magnificence, beauty and holiness of God!

Oh, reader, what great hope that even the more elementary glorification teaching of the Old Testament gives to us! It matters nothing what your status or accomplishments are or are not in this world. Someday you will be honoured, someday in the very presence of the King of kings and Lord of lords, you will be esteemed and your true nature and identity exposed. What delight we will take that this will do none other than shift the focus upon the true centre, the Artist himself!

But be warned! As magnificent as this great and blessed hope is for the one who has trusted in the Lord for salvation, the converse for the one who never trusts the true source of beauty and blessing is equally horrific. For ever and ever your full identity will be displayed as well. Shame and contempt will be your just deserts. The wickedness of your heart will be exposed, and, alone with the torture of your eternal state and full realization of who you are, you shall be separated from God for eternity. Consider:

He will bring down his anger with fury, and his re-
buke with flames of fire. For with fire and with his
sword the LORD will execute judgment upon all
men...those who rebelled against me; their worm
will not die, nor will their fire be quenched, and
they will be loathsome to all mankind (Is. 66:15-
16, 24, NIV).

Remember that we are made as God-glorifiers. In relation to
those who have never realized that purpose but have sought glory
only for themselves, God will in no way overlook their rebellion
and sin! (cf. Exod. 34:7b). Please do not ignore the choice which
is before you this day, as you read these words. As Joshua, the suc-
cessor to Moses, once said, 'Choose for yourselves this day whom
you will serve ... But as for me and my household, we will serve
the LORD' (Josh. 24:15, NIV).

Join me in this prayer:

> *Lord of all being, there is one thing that deserves my
> greatest care, that calls forth my ardent desires, that is,
> that I may answer the great end for which I am made
> – to glorify thee who has given me being, and to do all
> the good I can for my fellow men; verily life is not worth
> having if it be not improved for this noble purpose ...
> Give me grace always to keep in covenant with thee,
> and to reject as delusion a great name here or hereafter,
> together with all sinful pleasures or profits. Help me to
> know continually that there can be no true happiness,
> no fulfilling of thy purpose for me, apart from a life lived
> in and for the Son of thy love.*

– From 'Man's Great End', *The Valley Of Vision*, p.13.

O Lord, God, Thou hast commanded me to believe in Jesus; and I would flee to no other refuge, wash in no other fountain, build no other foundation, receive from no other fullness, rest in no other relief ... Help me to guide my affections with discretion, to owe no man anything, to be able to give to him that needeth, to feel it my duty and pleasure to be merciful and forgiving, to show to the world the likeness of Jesus.

– From 'Jesus My Glory', *The Valley of Vision*, p.24.

Chapter 2

THE HEART OF THE MATTER

For years I have wanted to take up bow hunting. Seasons would come and go and I would still be no closer to my goal, because I never acted. Finally, this past year I took the plunge and purchased a wonderful and sleek 'arrow-launcher'. Excited about my new toy, I asked a friend if I could go out shooting with him some time and he said matter-of-factly, 'No, not until you have practised for a few months.' I guess he did not want to be carted home to his wife with an arrow lodged anywhere near where he kept his wallet. 'Ah, there are some preliminaries to this thing of hunting', I said to myself. 'You have to learn first what you are doing.' Of course, I did not realize how many prerequisites there were! The state of Colorado not only requires a hunting license, but also prior to this a hunter safety course for those who are new to the sport.

I was not looking forward to spending fourteen to fifteen hours worth of instruction in a two week span of time – especially since it was only a couple of weeks prior to Christmas. But, I told myself to suck it up, get this out of the way, and I will be one step closer to the real thing – going out next year and bringing home the meat!

I have to tell you that I was pleasantly surprised about the classes. Rather than being bored, I found myself looking forward to them, not to mention coming away with some valuable advice. I learned a great deal about hunting, survival skills, and even how to clean an animal once he is killed (something that the deer, elk and antelope of our area probably don't have to fear from me for a while). Yet, as helpful and necessary as the classes were, I have to be honest. I am glad I'm past them and now looking at getting out in the plains and mountains and hunting – after all this is what it is all about.

I have found my study of glorification to be a little like my hunting prep. I knew that the preliminary step was to delve into the Old Testament to discover how the doctrine developed and what was taught there. I must admit that initially I did not expect much from these more ancient pages of the sacred text. But, as we saw in the last chapter, there was much more there than what you or I expected. Yet, as helpful as the Old Testament was, as foundational and indispensable as we found it to be, the New Testament still remains as the main source of glorification teaching. Here is why we signed up for this adventure, and here will be the main dividends for why you purchased the book. For it is here that we come to the heart of the matter.

We're now prepared because we have examined the foundation and source of the teaching about believer's glorification. So, let's turn our focus upon what the New Testament teaches about this final stage of our sanctification, which is the goal of our very existence.

'GLORY' IN THE NEW TESTAMENT

Students of the New Testament have long been aware that the

Bible the New Testament authors read and in which they were immersed was the Greek translation of the Old Testament, often called the Septuagint (abbreviated LXX).[1] This late third century B.C. translation is what largely shaped the language of the New Testament. In fact, one author has stated that 'the total impact of the LXX on the New Testament writers is so great as to defy measurement'.[2] Having soaked themselves in these Scriptures, the authors of the last twenty-seven books of the Bible regularly chose their words and attached meanings and theology that find their root there. As such, we should not be surprised that the uses of 'glory' (*doxa*) and 'glorify' (*doxazo*) are a continuation of how they were employed in the Septuagint, which mostly reflects the original Hebrew Scriptures.[3] Yet, as with many biblical subjects, we do find a progression, a development and an enlargement in the last third of the Scriptures. Let's take a brief overview of glory from Matthew to Revelation.

The use of the terms

It was Millard Erickson who said, 'To understand the doctrine of glorification, we must first know the meaning of the term glory...'[4] Like with the Old Testament, we see that glory refers to the display of God's character, power, and greatness – not exhaustively – yet with a sense of fulness. Just before Stephen became the first martyr of the New Testament he 'gazed into heaven and saw the glory of God' (Acts 7:55, NKJV). In other words, the witness witnessed a full weight of the power and presence of God. When Lazarus became sick and died, Jesus affirmed that this sickness was not going to end simply with death; rather, it was for the purpose of 'the glory of God' (John 11:4). Raised from the dead, men witnessed in Lazarus a fuller sense of the power, ability and life-giving nature of God.

At times this full weight of God is visible. When Jesus was transfigured before Peter, James and John, there was a visible manifestation of greatness and divine presence seen in Jesus, as well as in Moses and Elijah. With regards to Jesus, 'the appearance of His face was altered, and His robe became white and glistening' (Luke

9:29, NKJV) and this is referred to as 'glory' (*doxa*, v. 32). And of the other two men, we are told that they 'appeared in glory' (*doxa*, v. 31). Such visible glory belonging to the Father will accompany Jesus when he returns again (Matt. 16:27), it was present when the angelic announcement of the birth of the Saviour was made to the shepherds (Luke 2:9) and it will provide the light for the eschatological New Jerusalem (Rev. 21:11, 23).

Again, like with its more ancient cousin, the New Testament also shows that the natural and expected response to this manifestation of God's power, character, work and visible greatness is to worship God, to recount back to him, to delight in him and to give adoration for his magnificence – his all-together 'otherness'.[5] Hence, we have instances of giving glory to God and glorifying him. In no way can any creature give some essence or glory to God that he does not already possess. This simply signifies one acknowledging the glory God has. Angels gave glory (*doxa*) to God for the salvation and peace he brought into the world through the birth of the Saviour (Luke 2:4). A healed Samaritan leper does the same in response to his divinely accomplished recovery (Luke 17:18). Abraham trusted God's promise to him and, as a result, gave glory to God (Rom. 4:20). Visions of heaven often include angelic and saintly giving of glory to God (Rev. 4:9, 11; 5:13). And the biblical writers themselves sometimes cannot contain their praise of the Redeemer as they write of such wonderful salvation and grace (Rom. 16:25-27; Gal. 1:5; Eph. 3:21; Phil. 4:20).

The verb 'glorify' (*doxazo*) is used frequently to communicate the same idea: 'The shepherds returned, glorifying and praising God for all the things they had heard and seen' (Luke 2:20, NIV), Paul speaks of Gentiles glorifying God for his mercy as they come to know him (Rom. 15:9) and a woman healed from her crippling disease glorified God (Luke 13:13).

The Holy Spirit upped the ante regarding man's obligation to respond in faith and worship the full weightiness of God, for in these documents of the early church man is not only described as giving glory to or glorifying God, but also it is made clear that this is man's chief purpose. God has ordered all events such that they show forth his glory and elicit response from creation (Eph. 1:11-

12). This includes his gracious, salvific dealings with man (Eph. 1:4-12), but also the converse judgement and damnation of the wicked (2 Thess. 1:9; Rev. 11:13; 14:7). The chief sin of mankind is not glorifying God (Rom. 3:23; Rev. 16:9) and giving the glory that is meant for God to self or another (Rom. 1:23).[6] In fact, a Jewish king was even put to death for this atrocity (Acts 12:23). Man is commanded that every aspect of his life and all he does is to result in showing forth the greatness of God: 'Whether therefore you eat or drink or whatever you do, do all things unto the glory of God' (1 Cor. 10:31).

There are two categories of people in the world, says the apostle Paul: 'those who are perishing' and 'those who are being saved' (1 Cor. 1:18). The deciding factor is whether or not man trusts in God and acknowledges him as the only hope for salvation. Paul finishes out that chapter by paraphrasing Jeremiah 9:24: 'The person who wishes to boast should boast only of what the Lord has done' (1 Cor. 1:31, NLT). In other words, life comes down to this – either glorifying or not glorifying the glorious God!

To summarize, the New Testament presents God as one who is glorious and worthy of being glorified beyond all creatures and things. Man is a God-glorifier, and thus, is to fulfil his God-given purpose of honouring God. Such is the substance of life and man's problem is that he falls short of this design. Two questions immediately arise. By what manner specifically does man glorify God? By what means does man overcome his unwillingness and his selfish spiritual inability to glorify God? The New Testament, in large part, is about responding to those two inquiries.

Glory in Jesus Christ

Both questions find their solution in the Son of God who becomes the chief instrument of glorification in the last twenty-seven biblical books. How does man overcome his inability to glorify God? The answer, simply put, is through Jesus Christ. Here is where the Old Testament is superseded by the New Testament. The former spoke of God's glory and of men worshipping and honouring him. Yet with the progress of revelation, we discover that God has ordered things such that his glory is now chiefly manifest through the Son, Jesus Christ, and that men glorify him only in union with the same. We need to see how this is so.

God called his people under the Old Covenant to keep the law because he had delivered them (Exod. 20:2ff.). Such obedience was towards the end of honouring him. Jeremiah 13:11 reads, "'For as the sash clings to the waist of a man, so I have caused the whole house of Israel and the whole house of Judah to cling to Me,' says the LORD, 'that they may become My people, for renown, for praise, and for glory; but they would not hear'" (NKJV). Addressing corrupt priests who had disobeyed God and broken his covenant, Malachi 2:1-2 reiterates this purpose of obedience: "'And now, O priests, this commandment is for you. If you will not hear, and if you will not take it to heart, to give glory to My name,' says the LORD of hosts, 'I will send a curse upon you, and I will curse your blessings. Yes, I have cursed them already, Because you do not take it to heart'" (NKJV).

Yet, Israel demonstrated that man, left to himself, is not able to keep the law unto God's glory, as God desires. Such empowerment unto righteousness had not been given to man on a permanent basis (Deut. 5:29; 29:4). This is why the prophet Jeremiah often emphasizes Judah's inability to repent and obey God. With a strong word picture, Jeremiah asks a rhetorical question that implies their spiritual impotence (13:23): 'Can the Ethiopian change his skin or the leopard its spots? Neither can you do good who are accustomed to doing evil' (NIV). Paul even makes this point with greater clarity in Romans 7:1-13 where he teaches that when the good, holy law comes into contact with man's sin nature, disobedience is even exacerbated. This reality is what makes the promise of the new covenant so appealing as we see in Jeremiah 31:31-33 (NKJV):

> 'Behold, the days are coming', says the LORD, 'when I will make a new covenant with the house of Israel and with the house of Judah – not according to the covenant I made with their fathers in the day that I took them by the hand to lead

them out of the land of Egypt, My covenant
which they broke, though I was a husband to
them', says the LORD. 'But this is the covenant
I will make with the house of Israel after those
days', says the LORD: 'I will put My law in their
minds, and write it on their hearts; and I will be
their God, and they shall be My people.'

This new covenant, says the author of Hebrews, has been
made with God's people; it has been fulfilled through the salvific
work of Jesus Christ as we see in Hebrews 8-10, which harkens
back to the words of Jesus himself during the institution of the
Lord's Supper: 'This cup is the new covenant in My blood' (1 Cor.
11:25). It is through the death and resurrection of Jesus Christ that
man is forgiven of his sins (Eph. 1:7), reconciled to God (2 Cor.
5:18-19; Eph. 2:16-18) and thus changed and empowered to bring
honour and glory to God (Phil. 1:6, 9-11; 2:12-13). More specifically, the active righteousness of Jesus Christ who never sinned
(Heb. 4:15; 7:26) and always did the will of the Father (John 8:29),
along with his passive righteousness whereby he paid the perfect
and complete penalty for sin (2 Cor. 5:21; 1 Peter 3:18) is imputed
to those who receive this gracious gift by faith alone (Rom. 3:21-
26; Eph. 2:8-9). This forensic justification of man by God removes
the sin barrier (Isa. 59:2) between God and man, thus paving the
way for God's Spirit to indwell permanently, guide, lead and instruct (John 16:5-15; Rom. 8:9).[7] The result is that the regenerate,
saved man grows in holiness, becoming more like Christ and thus
is able to bring glory to God (2 Cor. 3:16-18; Heb. 12:14).

What we see is that man's ultimate purpose (functioning as a
God-glorifier), and in fact the purpose of the world, is made possible and realized in Christ. God has orchestrated all of time such
that all hope, the solution to man's dilemma and the chief purpose of all beings all come together in Jesus Christ. Paul writes in
Ephesians 1:9-10: 'God's secret plan has now been revealed to us;
it is a plan centered on Christ, designed long ago according to his
good pleasure. And this is his plan: At the right time he will bring

everything together under the authority of Christ – everything in heaven and on earth'[8] (NLT).

We should not be surprised that this brief sketch of biblical theology brings us to the place where God is chiefly glorified, through the life, death, resurrection and ongoing work of Jesus Christ. And man must regain his original design as a God-glorifier in and through him. Yet, what is it that qualifies Jesus Christ to be the chief instrument of the glorification of the Godhead? In addition to his work as Saviour, the answer lies in the understanding that the very essence of the Son, Jesus Christ, displays the full weight, identity and magnificence of God as no one and nothing else can.

In the prologue to his gospel, John commences with the well-known words: 'In the beginning was the Word, and the Word was with God, and the Word was God' (John 1:1). This is to say that when time, space and history began, the Word (*logos*) already was. At that same beginning that commences the Hebrew Scriptures (Gen. 1:1), the Word was and had already been in eternity past. The clear implication is that the Word is eternal. We know from the context of the prologue that the Word is Jesus Christ. As the Word, Jesus Christ is the ultimate communication from and about God. In other words, the inference is that since he is the 'ruling fact of the universe' and 'the self-expression of God',[9] if we want to know who God is and what he is like, the best place to look is to Jesus Christ.

Of this Word John says that when God spoke all things into existence, he was already 'with God' and he 'was God'. The first clause shows that Jesus Christ was and is, in some way, different from God the Father. As the sixth century Athanasian Creed affirms: '...we worship one God in trinity, and trinity in unity. Neither confounding the persons nor dividing the substance. For the person of the Father is one; of the Son, another, of the Holy Spirit another'. The Son is different from the Father in that he is a different person within the Godhead. Yet, at the same time, John 1:1 also affirms that the Word, Jesus Christ, is in essence, God. The phrase 'the Word was God' is grammatically similar to saying that the ocean is water. In other words, the Word has always been and is and will always remain of one substance with the Father. This is affirmed in both the Nicean and Chalcedonian creeds. It has been foundational to orthodox Christianity for its entire history.[10]

Of this Word, who is the ultimate self-expression of God, John goes on to say in John 1:14: 'And the Word became flesh and tabernacled among us, and we beheld His glory, glory as the only begotten from the Father, full of grace and truth.' The Word (Jesus Christ) became flesh (*sarx*). No more graphic term could have been chosen to correct readers dabbling with an infant form of an anti-material philosophy – known as Gnosticism – than this. Jesus Christ, as God, did not merely appear to become man. He entered into the world and became human in the fullest sense.[11] The second person of the Trinity, the God-revealer, became the God-man.

And what was the result? 'We beheld His glory'. Some commentators suggest that this has specific reference to John witnessing the transfiguration. I believe that is part of it, but not all. Certainly, the transfiguration was that instance in which the veil was pulled back so that in a fuller sense the weightiness of Christ's deity could be seen. In many ways, this was a benchmark to put the rest of the life of Christ in perspective. Yet, I believe that John also has in mind here the manifold other ways the glory of Christ was manifest. We will look at these shortly. Before we do that, however, we want to feast upon John's more specific description of the glory that he sets on the table before us.

This glory was 'glory as the only begotten from the Father'. The display of who Jesus really was and is and the spilling forth of his true identity, character, power and eminence was all unique to the one who is 'the only begotten from the Father'. There has been disagreement in recent years over how the term *monogenes* ('only begotten' or 'only child') should be rendered. On the one hand some think that it simply means that Jesus Christ is, in some sense, the only Son of the Father.[12] On the other hand are those who believe that the term has reference to the doctrine known as the eternal generation[13] of the Son.[14] Since this description of the Word is so important to the present discussion, we need briefly to look at what it means.

Without a doubt, the term refers, at least, to an only child. Most probably, it is used because it is literally the 'only one born'.[15] It is used with either 'son' (Luke 7:12; 9:38) or 'daughter' (Luke 8:42) to describe that child further as the only one. Also, in the texts in which it is used, it typically connotes the special view of the parent toward the child because he or she is the only one and greatly loved.[16] In this light it also comes very close to the use of *prototokos* ('firstborn'), because this latter term originally had numerical reference – the one who was born before any others. However, the true significance of 'firstborn' is seen in the evolution of the term, namely, the one who has the birthright, the double portion, who has preeminence over the others. And of course a *monogenes* would, in this fuller sense, also be a *prototokos*.

Monogenes also sometimes stands alone, not to describe further a son or daughter, but simply as something close to a technical term: 'an only child' or 'the only one born'. This is true of Hebrews 11:17 where it refers to the only son of Abraham whom he was willing to offer as a sacrifice to God. Behind this text stands the original account (Gen. 22) where in three different instances (vv. 2, 12, 16) we read the following description of Isaac: 'your son, your only son' (*binka 'et y'chiydka*). Yes, Isaac was the son of Abraham, but the Hebrew text clarifies he was not simply a son, he was the only one born to Abraham at the time and very special, beloved of him.[17] So, it seems that the term has reference to one being the only child, the only one born to a parent and, as such, is uniquely loved. In these instances the sense of 'begotten' may very well be retained.

When we come to the Johannine corpus we find the term used only five times in three different passages to refer exclusively to Jesus Christ and his relationship to God the Father. In the passage under consideration John has said that many rejected the Word (vv. 10-11), yet to those who do receive him, they are given all the rights and privileges of the children of God since they are born (*gennao*) of God (vv. 12-13). In the paragraph running from verse

14 through verse 18 John speaks of the incarnation of the Word. It seems most reasonable to assume that the *monogenes* of verse 14 is, in some sense, contrasted with those born (*gennao*) of God (v. 13). The one who has special son status, the unique son status, is the one who makes possible the sonship of those adopted by God, those who receive the Son. This line of thought in the context suggests that the aspect of begetting is implied in *monogenes*. The specially begotten makes possible the begetting of the others. It is interesting that in the only other passage in John where the term occurs (John 3:16, 18), it also is preceded by a discussion of believers being born (*gennao*). Again, the only begotten makes it possible that man can be born of God. And again, it seems reasonable to conclude a sense of begetting is retained in the term there.

At the end of the John 1:14-18 paragraph we actually find our most conclusive evidence that monogenes not only means 'only Son', but also carries a sense of 'begotten'. This verse reads, 'No one has seen God at any time (i.e. not fully). The *monogenes* of God, the one who is continually in the bosom of the Father, He explained Him.' One of the keys to this verse is the clause: 'the one who is continually in the bosom of the Father'. The present, active substantival participle, translated 'the one who is continually', suggests an ongoing, continual relationship. We already know from John 1:1 that when time, space and history came into existence the Word already was. Hence, this phrase is most likely implying an eternal, ongoing relationship between the *monogenes* and God the Father. Of this clause Timothy George writes, 'This connotes an intimacy, a relationship, a unity that a mere "alongside" comes nowhere near. John is saying that Jesus Christ, the one who has come to make God known to us, has shared with the Father an eternal life of intimacy and intercommunication, a life of mutual self-giving and love "in the bosom" of the Father from all eternity.'[18] And we need to notice that *monogenes* occurs without any further designation such as 'son'. We saw above that in such a scenario it most likely retains its sense of 'begotten'.

It must be admitted that the case for the sense of 'begotten' in the John 1:14-18 uses of *monogenes*, though strong, is not beyond doubt. However, even if the term means 'only Son', the main idea behind eternal generation is still present. Verse 18 makes it clear that the 'only Son' (or 'the only begotten') has been in this close relationship with the Father continually (in context, eternally).

Lest we are not convinced that John 1:18 must mean an eternal on-going relationship of the Father begetting the Son, we can look to 1 John 4:9, the last Johannine passage with the term. Here we read, 'In this the love of God was manifested in us, that God has sent the only begotten Son into the world in order that we might be saved through Him.' John writes that God the Father sent into the world the one who was, who already had status as 'the only begotten Son'. In other words, this implies that status prior to the incarnation and thus places it in the realm of his pre-existence, which extends into eternity past.[19]

John Piper aptly summarizes what John is teaching about Jesus Christ when he writes of the Father-Son relationship in the Trinity:

> No other relationship comes close to this one. It is utterly unique. The Son is absolutely unique in the affections of the Father. He is the 'only-begotten' ... There is the Son, by eternal generation, and there are other 'sons' by adoption ... Only in receiving Jesus as the Son are others empowered to become 'children of God' (John 1:12). The relationship between God the Father and his eternal Son is utterly unique.[20]

The point of this discussion about the eternal generation of the Son, Jesus Christ, can be seen in a discussion I had with an eight year-old boy at our congregation's children's club one evening. Our leader had asked me to speak to the children. In the course of my talk I made the statement that Jesus is the only Son of God. Stephen latched on to this phrase right away. He raised his hand and asked, 'How can Jesus be the only Son of God when the Bible says that we are children of God?' That is very perceptive for a second-grader . Many times adults aren't even thinking enough to ask the right questions. Yet, Stephen knew the right question to ask which puts him well on the way to finding the right answer. My response to him and the other children was that Jesus Christ is the Son of God in a special and unique way. He has been part of the Trinity for all eternity. He is the only one who is 'Son' in this sense. The rest of us are adopted as children into God's family because of what the Son did.[21]

What those children learned that evening is our present eureka. The Word, Jesus Christ, is in a unique relationship to God the Father. All through eternity he has continually been in the most intimate relationship with the Father. All through eternity he has been of the same essence with God the Father. This very one, Jesus Christ, became flesh and took up residence among mankind for a time. He was qualified to show us who God is as no other man could do. Why? Because, as the begotten, he is God.[22]

Yet, let's take this even further. Why does the Son of God, who is of the same substance as the Father, make a difference in revealing the glory of God? Because this is, in large part, what he came to do. Returning to John 1:18, we read that 'No one has seen God at any time. The only begotten of God, the one who is continually in the bosom of the Father, He explained Him.' The term translated 'explained' is *exegesato*. Like with *logos*, John chooses a term which is full of meaning for both the Greek and Jewish reader. It is 'a technical term in Judaism for making known interpretations of the law ... and a term in Greek religion for making known divine truths...'[23] As a capable teacher would make clear the understanding of an obscure, previously misunderstood truth, so Jesus Christ reveals and explains God so that man can know the Creator and Saviour as he has not been able to formerly. The author of Hebrews captures the superiority of the revelation of God through the Son when he writes, 'God, after speaking long ago in many fragmentary parts and by means of many different ways to the fathers in the prophets, in these last days spoke to us in a Son, whom He appointed heir of all things, through whom also He made the worlds' (Heb. 1:1-2).

So the weight of his power, wisdom, love, holiness and the fulness of all that God is has been unveiled and explained through Jesus Christ as nowhere else and through no one else. Yes, God displayed his glory in the Old Testament through his works and his visible shekinah glory in the tabernacle. But these revelations always had a veiled quality about them. As Moses saw the hind parts of God, so man caught only a glimpse of the shadow of the glory of Yahweh. Yet, now, in the God-man, God has been revealed in an unprecedented fashion. He is 'the radiance of the glory and the exact representation of His [i.e. God's] nature' (Heb. 1:3). He is the 'image of God' (2 Cor. 4:4).

Jesus Christ reveals God in his essence, but there is more. He also reveals him through his works. He seeks to honour God in all he does (John 5:44; 8:49-50). He raised Lazarus and healed a leper and paralytic to the glory of the Father (John 11:4; Luke 17:18; Matt. 9:8); this is why he taught and ministered (John 7:18). He answers prayer to glorify the Father (John 14:13), and the future recognition Jesus Christ will receive from all men (saved and un-saved) as Lord will result in the glorification of God the Father (Phil. 2:10-11).

Yet, without question, Jesus Christ glorifies the Father to the greatest degree through his salvific work. The verb *doxazo* ('glori-fy') was sometimes used as a technical term in the New Testament for the complex of events including Christ's death, burial, resur-rection and exaltation (John 7:39; 12:16, 23; 13:31-32; Acts 3:13). The full, complete and magnificent purpose for which Christ came, that purpose which brought him greatest honour, was re-vealed in these events. And, as Jesus Christ was glorified in his death, resurrection and exaltation, so also was the Father glorified. Consider the opening words of Jesus' high priestly prayer in John 17:1-5 (NKJV):

> Father, the hour has come. Glorify Your Son, that Your Son also may glorify You, as You have given Him authority over all flesh, that He should give eternal life to as many as You have given Him. And this is eternal life, that they may know You, the only true God, and Jesus Christ whom You have sent. I have glorified You on the earth. I have finished the work which You have given Me

to do. And now, O Father, glorify Me together
with Yourself, with the glory which I had with You
before the world was.

In these short intra-trinitarian requests we learn that Jesus
viewed his earthly life as a mission to glorify God through his
work. At this point, on the night of his betrayal and eve of his crucifixion, that work was completed. Now there stood before him
an even greater work. It was a work in which men would see in a
fuller way the identity and purpose of Jesus Christ (he would be
glorified) and, as a result, he would glorify the Father by bringing
men to a true and full knowledge of the Father and Son. And the
epilogue to this great work would be the reacquisition of the glorious status the Son had before the incarnation. His suffering, then,
would lead to glorification of the Son and Father.

It was the apostle Paul who clarifies for us just how Christ
further revealed and glorified the Father through his death, burial
and resurrection. In Romans 3:21-26 Paul writes:

But now apart from Law, righteousness of God
has been manifested, being witnessed by the Law
and the Prophets; even the righteousness of God
through faith in Jesus Christ for all those who
believe. For there is no distinction. For all have
sinned and fall short of the glory of God. These
are justified as a gift by His grace through the redemption which is in Christ Jesus; whom God
purposed as a propitiation through faith in His
blood unto a demonstration of His righteousness
because, in the forbearance of God, of the passing over of sins previously committed. This is all
for the demonstration of His righteousness at this
present hour that He might be just and justify the
one who has faith in Jesus.

After building his case to the Romans that all men are sinners
in need of salvation and that God is justified in bringing his wrath

upon them, Paul now turns to the solution, beginning with this paragraph. The righteousness of God has to do both with his act of saving man as well as the resulting righteous status that man has before God.[24] Paul says that God has now provided apart from law for man to be saved and to be righteous before him. This is not a new idea; the Old Testament Scriptures had alluded to a way in which man's sins would be dealt with such that he could be forgiven and righteous before God (cf. Gen. 15:6; Ps. 32:1-2; Isa. 52:13 – 53:12). This righteousness comes through faith in Jesus Christ for anyone who trusts in him (after all, all are in need since all have sinned and fallen short of their original purpose of glorifying God).

The way that man is declared righteous through Jesus Christ is by means of his sacrificial death. In this death and the subsequent imputation of righteousness unto the elect, two things are shown about God. First, God saves man. In other words, he is a merciful God who has not left all men to suffer in their sin and misery. Secondly, God has saved in such a way that he remains just (he operates always in accordance with his own character) and does not overlook sin. If God had merely overlooked the sin of mankind and somehow declared, 'You are forgiven', he would have ceased to be just. He would no longer be acting in accordance with his perfect, good, and holy character. What is more, he would have left man in a state of not knowing what is right and wrong and whether or not consequences for sin would be faced. Such would be a horrible existence where pain, hurt, abuse, persecution and death all were belittled as unimportant. Yet, at the same time, if God had merely left all mankind to suffer in the condition of sin and misery, and ultimately to face eternal damnation, then he would not have displayed to the fullest his mercy and grace.

In the salvific work of Jesus Christ God is revealed as a gloriously gracious God who loves mankind and at the same time will not overlook sin. Divine love is the headline, but the sub-heading reads that death, pain, abuse and evil will not be merely winked at! In this glorious work the triune God takes man who was made in God's image as a God-glorifier and restores him to the 'classic' that was his original design.

The Christ-centred means and manner of glorification

So, we asked two questions earlier in the chapter about the New Testament's teaching with regards to the means by which man can glorify God and the manner in which he does this. The answer to the first question has been shown to be this: by means of the sacrificial death and resurrection of the ultimate God-Glorifier and Revealer Jesus Christ. The answer to the second question is also located in Jesus Christ – man glorifies God by appropriating what Jesus Christ has done in him. This is why Paul writes in Galatians 2:20, 'I have been crucified with Christ; now I no longer am the one who lives, but Christ lives in me; now the life I live in the flesh, I live by faith in the Son of God who loved me and gave Himself in my behalf.' This is also why Paul wrote in 2 Thessalonians 1:12 that we are glorified 'in Christ'. Perhaps this preface to glorification teaching in the New Testament can be best understood with something that we can relate to off the street.

The 'Goat'

Back in the late seventies my brother-in-law bought a 1968 GTO from his cousin. Blue with a white hardtop, this long stylish machine looked like the Pontiac version of something we might see bounding after its prey on the Serengeti. The model was introduced in 1964, having borrowed the name from Ferrari. The 'Grand Touring Homologated' (or more affectionately called 'Gas, Tires and Oil') was designed in large part by Pontiac chief engineer John DeLorean. Since there was not a large number of GTOs manufactured (e.g. only 3,140 of the 1968 two-door hardtop, 400 cubic inch, 360 horsepower versions), this car draws stares from car enthusiasts when sitting at a stoplight or resting in a parking lot. I know because for a few months it was our job to keep the 'Goat' (as it has been affectionately called by GTO enthusiasts) for Dan when he and his family went back to the Democratic Republic of the Congo where he is a missions pilot. The thought was that it would stay in better running condition than if it were stored away for four years.

Eventually Dan decided that he would sell the car. With a family of nine, this four-passenger machine was not very practical. So, he handed over the keys to his cousin, a younger brother of the owner of the car from whom it had been purchased in the first place. It had made the full circle and stayed in the family.

Lovers of old cars will quickly tell you that this GTO is a classic, a rare jewel. But time has not been friendly to this roaring, fast-moving attitude on wheels (Motor Trend, February 1968 says 0 to 60 miles per hour in 6.5 seconds!). The seats and dashboard are cracking, the exterior needs painting and the heater doesn't work. The list goes on and on. Truly, it is only a memory of what it once was. But here is where the human interest enters. You see Tim, the cousin, took the car home for his son to restore. Wow! What a great ride for someone in high school! I can easily imagine what it will be like when the 'Goat' is on the road with its overhauled engine, re-upholstered interior and refurbished glistening blue coat. It will make grown men stop in their tracks to watch it go by. Some will merely be silent. Others may let out a 'Whoa!' A few might turn to their sons and say, 'That's a '68 GTO with a 360 V-8 under the hood. That thing will move! What a classic!'

But for those friends and family who will know the story, they will not only see a classic rebuilt, they will exclaim, 'What a great job Jared did restoring that car!' As people see the real machine emerge from the rust, cracks and flat tires, the son will be honoured for his work. He pulled it off. But the work he has done will ultimately shine forth to honour the father. 'Tim', some will say, 'You did a great job with Jared. It looks great! We haven't seen one of these look this good for years.'

And so it is with glory in the New Testament. What this latter third of the Bible does is to take the true story of God and man to its climax and its eternal end. The Old Testament told of how the classic, whose original shine and horsepower (the *imago dei*) truly displayed the great work of the Designer, had been dented, twisted, torn and dulled. He just doesn't run, nor does he shimmer as was the original intent. Yet a great number from among the masses have been redeemed. They have been purchased from the junkyard of sin. It has happened through the work of the Son, the one who reveals and represents the Father (the original Designer) as no one or nothing else can. After all, he is the only begotten Son; he is God. He has saved the classic from one day providing only scrap metal or spare parts in the eternal garbage dump and has restored him. As the process continues some will stop in their tracks and exclaim, 'Wow, did you see that love, that sacrifice, the humility, the forgiveness? How does he do that? It must be Jesus Christ!' And as the Son is honoured for restoring the glory, the Father will ultimately be honoured.

It is in this context that we must understand the teaching of the glorification of man in the New Testament. If we keep in mind that man is being reclaimed and his original glory restored through justification, sanctification and ultimate glorification, to reflect the glory of Christ and God the Father, then and only then are we ready to hear what these pages have to say about this amazing purpose for the church!

SPECIFIC NEW TESTAMENT GLORIFICATION TEACHING

Now that we have set forth both the Old and New Testament theological soil in which glorification is sown, we can consider how this doctrine is developed.

The imago dei and glory

The sole time that the *imago dei* is closely aligned with glory is in 1 Corinthians 11:7. What Paul is doing in chapters 7-15 of this letter is addressing issues about which the Corinthians had inquired (cf. 7:1). In chapter 11 he takes up the topic of whether or not women should have their head covered in their assemblies. The context speaks of behaviours which are lawful, yet may need to be avoided in certain circumstances (8:9-13; 9:8-18; 10:23) in order to love and serve others (8:11-13; 9:19-27; 10:24, 33), as well as glorify God (10:31-33). This, along with certain indicators in the text, suggests that the head coverings in Corinth are not to be taken as normative for all time.[25] Yet, they served a particular purpose in that cultural milieu, namely to help the Corinthians preserve and honour the different God-given roles among men and women (cf. 11:3).[26]

1 Corinthians 11:3 forms the theological foundation for the passage. It reads, 'Now I want you to know that the head of every man is Christ, the head of woman is man, and the head of Christ is God.' Wayne Grudem has demonstrated that the term 'head' (*kephale*) has reference to authority and not source.[27] This verse, then, sets forth different roles. The Father is the authority over the Son, who is the authority over the male (and by implication, women also), and the man is an authority over the woman. We know that Paul is not arguing for a difference in value, worth or that of innate ability. The Scriptures are clear from the beginning that men and women are equal in value and significance, even though they possess differing roles (Gen. 2:18).[28] This is also supported by the reference to the Father and Son which deals with the economic aspect of the Trinity rather than the ontological aspect of the Trinity, which shows that each person is the same in substance and equal in power and glory.[29]

Based upon the theological foundation of the difference in roles, in verses 4-6 Paul makes it clear that within that culture men dishonour their heads when they pray or prophesy with heads covered and women dishonour their heads when praying or prophesying with heads uncovered. The verb 'dishonour' (*kataischuno*) means here to bring to a lesser view or status than is appropriate. In other words, it leaves the man or woman in such a state that the adornment of their head is not in keeping with the full weight of who they really are. Regarding the use of *kephale* ('head') as the direct object of *kataischunei* ('dishonours'), it seems to be a figure of speech known as synecdoche of the part. The part ('head') stands for the whole (man or woman). The focus, the head, is the source of the dishonour in either case and as such represents the whole person. Yet, it is the whole person (and the God-given role) being dishonoured.

Beginning with verse 7 Paul offers another reason why the man's head should be uncovered and the woman's covered: 'For on the one hand man should not cover the head since he is the image and glory of God; yet on the other hand, the woman is the glory of man.' The possible interpretations are as follows: Males are made in the image of God and are the glory of God, while females are the glory of males, without being the image and glory of God. Another possibility, recognizing that the focus here appears to be on the word 'glory' and that Genesis 1:26-27 clearly shows woman are also created *imago dei*, is that Paul does not mean that women are not made in God's image by his omission of that term in speaking of them. But, since the focus is upon glory, that is what is mentioned again with regards to women and what they lack with regards to God. Therefore, men are the glory of God; women are not. They are only the glory of man.

I find neither of these understandings of the text to be adequate. The first interpretation is clearly wrong for the reasoning the second states. Women are made in God's image, so Paul, by the omission of 'image' regarding women is not denying the *imago dei* to women. Yet, the second interpretation also falls short for a similar reason. In Psalm 8 we have already seen that God crowned mankind with glory and honour and that this has reference to the fact that mankind (male and female) is made in God's image. As such, women too are the glory of God in that they resemble and represent him – they reflect his glory.[30]

It seems most likely that what Paul is saying is that men are made in the image of God and honour[31] him in a way that women do not. And women honour men. It seems that Paul sees 'image' and 'glory' as very closely connected. Man is God's glory because he is made in God's image. Yet, when it comes to women, women are not made in the image of man, at least in the technical sense that mankind is made in God's image. Yet, Paul's point is to show that men are made to honour God in a special way and women are made to honour men in a special way (without denying that they also honour God).[32] The reasoning is found in verses 8-9: man was the source of woman and woman was created for man, to be his helper. In other words, creation order and role distinction lies at the bottom of Paul's reasoning.

What is important from this passage for our present purpose is the close connection between 'image' and 'glory'. Certainly men (and by implication, we could also argue women) are made in God's image and thus glorify and honour him. They resemble him and represent him to the world in a way that causes others to honour the Creator. Though the *imago dei* is not explicitly connected with 'glory' anywhere else in the New Testament, nevertheless we find the same starting point here that we did in the Old Testament. Man, through creation in the image of God, has a glory that shines forth with the weight and magnificence of who God is.

We must remember, however, that this glorious image has been twisted through the fall of mankind. This is why Paul speaks of the new regenerated man as 'the new self, which in the likeness of God has been created in righteousness and holiness of the truth' (Eph. 4:24, NASB). The Christian is being remade into the fuller image and likeness of God as he becomes more like Christ (Eph. 5:2). The need for this makeover stems from the twisting of the original *imago dei* and the result is that man now falls short of glorifying God (Rom. 3:23).

So, the New Testament clarifies the reality that sanctification is, in large part, about the process of man recovering his original design and intent and thus reflecting in a fuller sense the glory of God. Let's turn to the specifics of how this is done.

Glorification is a future eschatological reality for the justified alone

Romans 8:17-18 is our first stop. In the magisterial epistle to the Romans Paul explains the gospel with detail unmatched anywhere else in the New Testament. He does this in order to lay the foundation for the reconciliation of Jews and Gentiles in that congregation.[33] Their disunity had, in all probability, resulted from the five year absence of the Jewish Christians by the edict of Claudius in A.D. 49 (cf. Acts 18:1). When these believers started returning to their home at the beginning of the reign of Nero in A.D. 54, they were dismayed to find such a Gentile flavour within the church. This division was not only unbecoming of Christians, but it posed a threat to their partnership with Paul's desired future missions trip to Spain and his relief work in Jerusalem (cf. 15:22-33).[34]

As Paul expounds upon the gospel, one of his desired purposes is to show the practical outworking of the salvific work of Christ in one's life. Such is largely what he does in chapters 5-8. Certainly in these chapters the main group of people he is addressing is the redeemed (cf. 8:1).

The subject inhe first seventeen verses of chapter 8 is primarily the Spirit of God. The Spirit of God applies the work of Christ and enables us to fulfil the Law (vv. 1-4). The presence of the Spirit is important because he enables the saint to set his mind on things of God and please God (vv. 5-11). Then, in vv. 12-17 Paul draws an inference: if one has the Spirit, he need not be enslaved to the unregenerate desires and actions. As Paul explains the outworkings, he speaks of the Spirit's ministry of verifying that we are sons of God, but not only sons, also heirs, and not only heirs, but also joint heirs with Christ. Verse 17 reads, 'Now if children, also heirs; heirs on the one hand of God, but on the other hand joint heirs with Christ, provided that we suffer with [Him] in order that we might also be glorified with [Him].'

To understand the verse, we need to see it in light of the analogy Paul is utilizing. If a Roman lad was adopted into a family, the sequence was this: he was adopted, he became a full-fledged son and as such he became an heir with the other sons. This was a logical order that Paul says is also true of the believer. The believer is an heir of God, meaning that he is entitled to all future blessings and benefits which God has promised to his children. Yet, it is not just that he is an heir of God, he is a joint heir with Christ (and the plural denotes joint heir with all other believers). In other words, all the things which God the Father has promised the beloved Son, these also belong to the saint. And the saint is reminded that all he has and all which awaits him is because he is in union with Christ.

Chiefly what does the Son have in his glorious inheritance? First, God the Father has exalted him because of his finished work of redemption (Isa. 53:13; Phil. 2:9; Heb. 2:9). In part, this consists of being restored to the status he had before the incarnation (John 17:5). Yet, there is something added – not to the essence of the Son himself who is the same yesterday, today and forever (Heb. 13:8). However, he is now shown to be the saving, redeeming Son of God, the one who has conquered sin and death (Acts 2:36; Rom. 1:4; Heb. 1:4; 2:10). In short, the fulness of his identity and character are displayed for all to see. This is why Paul writes that God 'gave to Him a name' (i.e. encompassing all he is – his reputation), 'which is above every name, in order that at the name of Jesus every knee will bow, of those in heaven and upon the earth and under the earth, and that every tongue will confess that Jesus Christ is Lord unto the glory of God the Father' (Phil. 2:9b-11). Included with this exaltation would be the placement of all enemies and all things under the feet of Christ (1 Cor. 15:25-27). Additionally, he will have the perfect and intimate love of the Father as he has had through eternity (Ps. 18:50; John 10:15, 17; 14:31; 17:24; Eph. 1:6). It is also true that in the resurrection, ascension and exaltation of Christ he is vindicated (Isa. 53:10-12; John 2:18-21; Acts 2:22-36; Rom. 1:4). In other words, it is validated that he is not a criminal or impostor, but truly the Messiah, the Son of God. Another aspect of Christ's glory is a special place beside the Father – he is at his right hand (Heb. 1:3; 12:2). Finally, he will judge the world (Acts 17:31).

Since believers are joint heirs with Jesus Christ, we too can expect to be exalted and our true identity and honour displayed to the world (1 John 3:1-2). This manifestation of true identity will include God's praise of saints (Rom. 2:29), the transformation of our body to be like the resurrected body of Christ's (Phil. 3:21) and vindication (Matt. 13:43; Rom. 8:19).[35] The church will sit with Christ at the Father's right hand and judge the world (Matt. 19:28; Luke 22:30; 1 Cor. 6:2; Rev. 3:21).[36] And we will have the blessing of God's presence, love and the eternal expression of his gracious kindness (Phil. 1:19-26; 1 Thess. 4:17-18; Rev. 21-22; Eph. 2:7).

What we see here in Romans 8:17 is that glorification is a future reward only for those who are in Christ. Man's restoration to glory takes place only in and through the Son. In fact, one can say that it is because he is in the Son, the one who fulfils ultimately and completely the original design for man (Heb. 2:6-11), that he will be glorified. Our glorification is a sharing in the glory of Christ. Consistent with what we have already seen, glorification for the believer will involve vindication, as well as revelation of the true identity, character and adopted status of saints. We also see implied that it will involve great intimacy with God the Father and Son.

There is a condition placed on this promise, however. The inheritance of God and with Christ is ours, if we suffer with him. Paul does not mean here that our suffering with Christ earns the inheritance. That would contradict his theology elsewhere, especially in this epistle (cf. 3:19ff.; ch. 4; 5:1). The suffering is a by-product of the deportment that flourishes from our being saved by grace through faith (cf. 2 Tim. 3:12). As such, if we do not suffer with him, then it shows that we may have not been justified, adopted, reconciled and initially sanctified in the first place.

What is our motive for suffering with Christ? Certainly, it is manifold. We could answer, 'Because we love him and because we want to honour God.' Yet, one motive is that we might also be glorified with him. Our view of things as a believer ought to be in large part a future view. God rewards those who seek him (Heb. 11:6) and we seek him because of the joy set before us (Heb. 11:24-26; 12:2).

Since Paul has brought up the issues of suffering and glorification, as well as the implication that future glorification encourages a believer through suffering, he decides that he needs to elaborate upon these subjects in verses 18-39. This section is giving assurance of future glory in the midst of suffering. So, the connection between verses 18-39 and the preceding context is one of explaining the suffering and glory towards the purpose of assuring the reader of the future glory. With this in mind, the conjunction in verse 18 ('for', gar) is explanatory.[37] Thomas R. Schreiner agrees: 'The prospect of suffering seems to dampen hope, so Paul explains ... in the rest of Romans 8 why suffering actually furthers hope instead of suppressing it...'[38] An example may include a man who suffers the loss of a wife he deeply loves. He may have not been drawn to consider the future glory, had it not been for the difficulties through which he is passing.

The thesis of this section is found in verse 18: 'Now I reckon that the sufferings of this present time are not worthy to be compared with the glory which will surely be revealed in us.' Paul has determined that as bad as the sufferings are that we experience here and now, they pale in comparison with the future glory we shall experience. Such a truth puts in perspective the sufferings and glory that he has mentioned in verse 17.

More specifically, Paul writes 'I reckon' (*logizomai*) that this is true. In other words, Paul makes it clear that he has thought about sufferings and glory and he has drawn a sound and well-reasoned conclusion. This is how he uses this verb elsewhere (Cf. Rom. 2:3; 3:28; 6:11). Paul asserts that he has been engaged in careful, deep theological thought and now is sharing God-given reflections. The reader ought to believe strongly that what Paul is about to say is authoritative and important. It is not only within the canon of inspired inerrant Scripture, but Paul also highlights its veracity and completeness.

The first subject that Paul draws a conclusion about in his strong theological thinking involves 'the sufferings of this present time'. The noun *pathemata* ('sufferings') refers to 'That which is suffered or endured, suffering, misfortune, in our lit. almost always in [the] pl[ural]...'[39] The sufferings spoken of are those 'of this present time'. John Murray clarifies the time reference:

> The 'present time' is stated to be the period within which these sufferings fall. This is a technical expression and is not to be equated with our common phrase, 'the time being'. The present time is 'this age' or 'present age' in contrast with 'the age to come' (cf. Matt. 12:32; Mark 10:30; Luke 16:8; 20:34, 35; Rom. 12:2; Gal. 1:4; Eph. 1:21). The age to come is the age of the resurrection and of the glory to be revealed.[40]

The sufferings under consideration include general trials that are the opposite of being honoured (1 Cor. 12:26; 2 Cor. 1:6). They could include disease, loss of loved ones or status (Rev. 21:4), agitators who oppose sound teaching (Gal. 3:4), persecution for the sake of Christ (Phil. 1:29-30; 1 Thess. 2:14; 2 Thess. 1:5ff.; 2 Tim. 1:12) and any of the aspects of the curse upon us and nature that are present because of sin (cf. Rom. 8:19ff.; Rev. 22:3).[41] These are all the things which shall cease when we are glorified and enter into the New Jerusalem (cf. Rev. 21-22). These are all the things with which we so struggle in this life: the death and the incapacitation of limbs and minds, the loss of our possessions (especially those with great sentimental value such as a family farm) and the effects of the sin of others (divorce, family splits and feuds). All of these things loom very large before us. For many they are all we can see. They hurt and crush our hearts and knock the breath right out of us. Yet, as horrid as they are, Paul says that they lose their punch when we look to something much greater.

Think of being in the midst of mind-boggling pain or loss: the loneliness and heart- crushing experience of a bad marriage or being hurt by children. These things can be life and mind-consuming, all we think about. How can we go on? Yet, Paul says that as bad as they are, they are not even worthy to be compared to the sure glory in the future.

Let me help us capture this elusive truth before we move on by telling of two athletes. My favourite baseball player weighs in at a whopping sixty pounds and is about four and a half feet tall. At nine years old, you can guess that it is none other than my son, Jeff Barnes. Believe it or not, Jeff has some features in common with the world renowned Barry Bonds of the San Francisco Giants.[42] After all, they both play baseball, they both wear baseball uniforms, they both run the bases after hitting the baseball, they both throw and hit left-handed, and they both play the same position. Now, of course most sane readers will immediately object, 'Tom, that is nice that you love your son so much and attach such great sentiment to him, but really, Jeff is not worthy to be compared to Barry Bonds when it comes to playing baseball!' And you would be right. On some inconsequential points a comparison may be drawn. But where it really matters when most speak of sports comparisons – ability, accomplishments and impact upon the game – there is no comparison. After all, Jeff has played only three years and is presently working on how to throw a baseball and how to hit one. Bonds, on the other hand, is undoubtedly one of the best who ever played. At over 700 career home runs and with the single season record for home runs (73 in 2001), he will undoubtedly be inducted into baseball's 'Hall of Fame' in Cooperstown, New York.

Paul's point when it comes to present sufferings of life and future glory is that it is just as inappropriate (in fact more so) to equate our present difficulties with the magnificent glory we will share with Christ. Automatically, some will say, 'Hey, wait a minute! With death, disease, paralysis, starvation, divorce, abuse, injustice, persecution, psychological anguish, war, rape and so many other hardships, surely we cannot downplay their impact on us!' And that is true. Life is often very hard. Just ask Job! In fact, ask Paul. Certainly, Paul's experiences would not lend to his owning a 'pie-in-the sky', 'hide-your-head-in-the-sand' denial about hardships. Listen to his own resume. In 1 Corinthians 4:9-13, 2 Corinthians 11:23-33 and 2 Corinthians 12:7-10, we see that he has been considered as a fool, weak and dishonoured, defamed, lacking respect from others, beaten – three times with rods, whipped with thirty-nine lashes five times, stoned once, imprisoned at least three times, homeless and often hungry and thirsty and shipwrecked three times. He has regularly faced the natural and human dangers of travel in that day, has often gone without sleep and been cold and has a chronic physical problem.

Yet, this man who has suffered so much affirms that as hard as these things are, they cannot be compared to our future glory any more than Jeff Barnes can be compared to Barry Bonds as a baseball player. Though some less significant areas might show similarities – both will impact each saint personally, both cannot be ignored, both are significant – yet where it really matters, there is no comparison. And where does it matter? At the point of the sadness and pain caused with suffering versus the joy and delight in our future glorification.

Every Christian will, in the eschaton, share in the glory of Jesus Christ. The assurance of this future eternal reward so overshadows our present trials that the trials seem like a beginning baseball player; yet the glory is a seasoned veteran destined for the 'Hall of Fame'! If Paul said that the glory is as great as the sufferings are hard, then we would conclude that the future glory is wonderful and a boost to our present psyche. But he does not say that. The future glory is so great that the present sufferings are not worthy to be compared to the future glory! Such a statement takes us out of our league. How can we describe a future glory that dwarfs our present pain?

To those of us who will want to compare the experiences (and that would be all of us because we are all looking to cope with the present suffering), Paul says that what we will experience in the future when the glory of Jesus Christ becomes our glory should give us much joy and hope right now. Our glory becomes the honour placed at the feet of the eternal triune God, and that honour becomes our ever increasing delight and satisfaction and ecstasy for eternity – infinitely beyond all the triumphs and accomplishments and joys and victories and satisfactions and peace of this life. It should give us so much joy and hope right now as we anticipate it that the present anguish seems to be almost like nothing!

It is similar to the thoughts that a woman has about her pregnancy, labour and childbirth. For nine months she suffers through gaining weight, sickness, swelling and losing her figure, and then she goes into an excruciating, exhausting labour. Yet, when it is all said and done, most women comment that the pregnancy and labour pale in importance compared to having that precious beautiful baby. It is as if they forget about all the pain. It is the sensation of the great player just inducted into the hall of fame who says that all of his work from little league on was worth it, or the joy of the Olympic athlete who has just celebrated on the top step of the awards podium, saying, with gold medal dawned, that all the 5:00 am practices, the countless hours of training and the lost opportunities with friends, were all nothing compared to this moment. Yet, the difference is that we don't have to wonder whether or not the triumph will come. Paul says that we will be glorified with Christ and the glory will be revealed in us![43] That certain future must colour and shape how we receive what comes our way each and every moment of every day!

> Heaven is one of the greatest assurances for be-
> lievers ... I believe that there is a direct relation-
> ship between our confidence in this reality and
> our obedience to His Word. What a man believes
> about the future always shapes how he lives in
> the present. This certainly marked those disciples
> who were there as [Jesus Christ] disappeared into
> the sky.[44]

Christian, is your spouse taking advantage of you and are you discouraged because what you want to do is divorce, yet you know that the will of God is to remain in the marriage? How do you find the motivation? Look at your future glorification! How about you, saint, flat on your back with racking pain that you cannot get rid of and which is leading you down that path to death – albeit too slowly? Are you tempted to bicker and complain? How can you find the motivation to remain steadfast and to thank God? Look at your future glorification! Persecuted Christian, remain faithful. You will be a pillar in the temple of God, dressed in white robes with God's name written on you, in a place of prominence, serving him for eternity. You will never hunger or thirst, tears will be no more and the Great Shepherd will shepherd you and lead you to fountains of the waters of life (Rev. 3:12; 7:9-17). All that you suffer is worth it.

However, if we are to approach suffering and future glory as does Paul, there are some things that must be true of us. First, we must be disciplined to meditate upon God's Word enough that when we come face to face with suffering we are able to remember that there is another perspective. This means that we must be so in tune with God and his ways and so enraptured with him that we long to see his loving hand in all this and to know that his promises of future glory hold true. That is hard to do when the weight of pain and evil threaten to weigh us down and leave us virtually unable to see anything else. Such an outlook takes faith in God and also practice. Paul said of himself that he 'learned' to be content with whatever state he faced (Phil. 4:11).

Second, we must learn about and value the certain future glory that is promised to us. We must learn what the Scriptures teach and meditate upon them often. This book is designed to help us with that part.

Finally, we must tune out, ignore and refuse to be sucked into how most people around us face suffering. The world, indwelling sin and demonic influence will coax us to grumble, complain and find acceptable the excuses we have for being upset, hopeless and angered at God. Yet, the great apostle, missionary, and theologian tells us here that when we have things in the right perspective, we will find the present pain and evil a small thing. Oh, how appealing is that kind of mindset, sovereign Lord. Help us develop that!

Paul moves on in the subsequent verses (19-25) to prove how appealing and beautiful our future glorification is. His argument centres around the truth that even the creation earnestly expects and eagerly awaits the time when it will be revealed who the sons of God truly are and their full weight.[45] For the creation also will be restored. If the creation awaits this, how much more ought we, when we are the central figures!

In verses 26-27 Paul shows one of the ways the Holy Spirit is employed in assisting us through hard times. When in the midst of pain and sorrow – so much so that we don't even know how to pray – he helps bring our groanings before the Father, to translate them to him as just what we need. Paul's point seems to be, in part, that God has forgotten nothing when it comes to assisting us in hope and in looking forward to our future glory.

With verse 28, however, the whole discussion is turned up just a notch. For in the next three verses (28-30) Paul argues that all things work together for the benefit of the elect, i.e. toward the goal of their sanctification and glorification. In these verses Paul also proves that glorification truly is a certainty. I am convinced that Romans 8 is the locus classicus ('the classical text' or the key passage in the Bible) on glorification. We have already seen how verses 17 and 18 are important. Yet, in many ways we could argue that verses 28-30 take us even further to the heart of the matter since their content is so crucial and so well-known. Let's take a closer look.

Romans 8:28 must be understood in its context to capture the full impact. Paul is speaking about the work the Spirit does in our life and this often includes suffering (8:12-17). Yet through the suffering, God continues to work in us. One of the ways he assists us through such times is by showing us our future eternal reward and end of glorification (8:17-18). He calls our attention to nature's expectation of that time and the Spirit's help in prayer (8:19-27). But, now Paul lets us know that God orchestrates together all events in the world so that they will benefit the saint in her sanctification.[46] It is only the saints (those who are effectually called by God and love him) who can claim this promise. But claim it we must. All things that happen in the world are decreed by God (Eph. 1:11-12) and one of his purposes, in addition to glorifying himself, is that they might all work together to help saints mature and bring about their benefit of growing in grace.[47] The reason Paul brings this up is to prove that the saints' end and future glorification is for sure. How could it not be? God is orchestrating all world events such that they further sanctification and assure the preservation of all saints and their future glorification!

Verses 29-30 take the argument a step further and make it clear that God will complete the entire work of salvation in each of the elect. Here we find the golden chain of salvation. 'For those whom He foreknew, He also predestined to be conformed to the image of His Son, in order that He might be the firstborn among many brothers; those whom He predestined, these He also called; and those whom He called, these He also justified; and those whom He justified, these He also glorified.' The unbreakable chain in these verses is formed by the repetition of the plural relative pronoun 'whom' (*hous*). The group represented in this term that serves as the object of God's varied saving actions is the same throughout. The same group whom God foreknew, he predestined. The same

group that he predestined is also the same that he called, justified
and glorified. This group is comprised of those who are the called
according to God's purpose and who love God (v. 28), the same
group whom God is for and for whom God delivered up his Son
(vv. 31-32). It is none other than the 'elect' (v. 33). God will, in
other words, complete the entire work of salvation in his saints,
the elect.

In verse 29 Paul writes that God 'foreknew' (*proegno*) these persons. In other words, he determined beforehand (i.e. in eternity
past) that he would enter into an intimate saving relationship with
them.[48] These same persons God also 'predestined' (*proorisen*). This
verb is similar to 'foreknow'. It denotes the act of designating beforehand (in eternity past).[49] In the rest of Romans 8:29 Paul gives
the end or purpose unto which God designated beforehand the
elect: 'to be conformed to the image of His Son, in order that He
might be the firstborn among many brothers'. God's eternal plan
for the church collectively has been and remains that they would
be like his Son, Jesus Christ.[50] Both in character and in appearance we will resemble him (Phil. 3:21; 1 John 3:1-3ff.). Thomas R.
Schreiner helpfully explains:

> The 'good' of v. 28 now receives further defini-
> tion; the good is achieved when believers are
> conformed to the likeness of Jesus Christ ... This
> does not mean that all reference to the present era
> should be excluded, for the genius of Paul's theol-
> ogy is that the eschaton has invaded the present
> evil age. The transformation into the image thus
> begins in this age (cf. 2 Cor. 3:18; Col. 3:10) but
> is completed and consummated at the resurrec-
> tion.[51]

God's eternal purpose for the elect is not only to save them,
but also that they would mature and become like Jesus Christ.
The result of this is that Jesus Christ is the firstborn among many
brothers. In other words, we become like him and, as such, he is
honoured as having a place of pre-eminence among those whom

he redeemed and made his brothers. John Piper agrees: 'God aims to surround his Son with living images of himself so that the pre-eminent excellency of the original will shine the more brightly in his images. The goal of predestination is our delight in becoming holy as he is holy and his delight in being exalted as pre-eminent over all in the midst of a transformed, joyful people.'[52]

It is imperative that we understand the connection between this purpose as stated in verse 29 and glorification in verse 30. In verse 29 the purpose of redemption is stated as conformity to the image of the Son; in verse 30 it is glorification. The result is that glorification, in large part, is the process of saints being ultimately and completely conformed to the image of Jesus Christ, both in appearance and character. This is the purpose and end that God has had for the elect through all eternity. They will be restored to glory such that they resemble and represent Christ. They will be like him and bring him glory for what he has done in them.

In verse 30 Paul also makes it clear that between the eternal decree and the ultimate end, there are some all-important steps. He says that this same group of people also will be called (effectu-ally) and justified.[53] This does not mean there are no other effects in the order of salvation. Paul picks out some important ones to imply what he teaches more explicitly elsewhere (Phil. 1:6): 'And I am sure that God, who began the good work within you, will con-tinue his work until it is finally finished on that day when Christ Jesus comes back again' (NLT). Of course in Romans itself, Paul is clear that sanctification necessarily follows justification. That whole process takes place between justification and glorification.

The verse ends by saying, 'those whom He justified, these He also glorified'. This is a dramatic aorist, which states a future reality as if it had the certainty of a past event.[54] We might also refer to this as a 'prophetic past tense'. In the same way that the proph-ets of the Old Testament stated future events as if they were past realities (cf. Isa. 53:4-10) in order to emphasize the certainty of the events, so here Paul speaks of the believers' future glorifica-tion with the dramatic aorist, emphasizing that it is as sure as if it had already happened.[55] This seems to be the whole point of this short paragraph – the certainty of God completing his work. This certainty gives strength to the assertion in verses 26-28 that God is working all things together for our good, even in the midst of redirecting our prayers. We can be assured of this, because he will carry out his work in us and complete it. This means that God has ordained events in our lives such that they enable us to grow and progress. 'Being "glorified" means coming to the final, everlasting experience of seeing God work everything together for our good ... It is our final likeness to Christ which brings him glory ("the first-born among many brethren") and brings us unspeakable joy.'[56]

With a force that is unequalled elsewhere, Paul affirms in Romans 8:29-30 that only those chosen, called and justified will be glorified. Yet, he also makes it clear that all of those who are chosen, called and justified will be glorified. It is a certainty. And, he introduces the truth that glorification has been part of God's eternal plan and purpose for the elect and that it largely involves conformity to the physical and spiritual image of the Son. Thus, the New Testament theme is reiterated and grows stronger: as we are glorified, Christ is glorified, which, in turn, glorifies the Father.

Before we leave Romans we need to make two more stops. We must visit two more passages which strengthen the case that glorification is a future certainty for the saint and also is only for those who are justified. The first is Romans 2:6-10.

This paragraph is found in the midst of the apostle's expansion upon the theme of God's righteousness revealed in the gospel (1:17) which runs from chapter 1:18 – 3:20. God's righteousness in Romans communicates that he always acts in accordance with his nature and the subsequent standards which emerge. As such, he saves and rightly deals with those who are saved, and he also judges the unrepentant ('by no means clearing the guilty', Exod. 34:7b, NKJV). He is certainly just to judge the unrepentant as Paul makes clear in this entire section. Both Gentile (1:19-32) and Jew (2:1-29) are guilty before God and deserving of punishment. In fact, all men are guilty and deserving of God's wrath (3:9-20).

In Romans 2:1-5 Paul is making the point to the Jewish reader who may think himself exempt from such scandal that they too will be judged for the same sin because, as he argues in Romans

2:6-10, God will repay men according to their works, regardless of nationality. One cannot bring a typical simplistic understanding of grace to this passage that is often taught in evangelicalism today. Frequently, we will hear a preacher or teacher say, 'God will not consider our works when we stand before him. He will only look at what we have done with Jesus Christ.' Though the commitment to grace and to the centrality of Christ is appreciated, such does not square with New Testament teaching. Jesus Christ himself made it clear in Matthew 7:21-27 and Matthew 25:31-46 that one's deeds and how one lived will be one of the chief focal points of judgement. And they will not only be considered for rewards. These texts, along with Romans 2:1-10, make it clear that the person's deeds will be considered with regards to whether or not one has eternal life. Does this mean, then, that works save a Christian? Absolutely not. However, as the Reformers argued, even though we are saved by grace alone through faith alone, that faith does not remain alone. Given the opportunity (i.e. you are not converted just prior to death), faith will produce a changed life; it will produce works (cf. James 2:14-24).[57]

In verses 6-7 Paul says that God will repay each man according to his works. What works will receive eternal life? Paul answers that it goes 'to those who according to perseverance in regard to good work seek glory and honor and immortality'. These three terms form a hendiadys, which 'occurs when two or three terms are added to one another to express the same thing...'[58] In support of this being a hendiadys is the fact that *doxa* ('glory') and time ('honour') have overlapping fields of meaning and often are used as synonyms by Paul (1 Cor. 11:14, 15; 15:43). Of most importance is Paul's use of *atimia* ('dishonour') and *doxa* ('glory') in the eschatological context of 1 Cor. 15:43. In this text Paul speaks of the believer's body dying in dishonour (the lack of honour), yet opposed to this it is raised in glory (in a state in which honour is ascribed to it). Additionally, the term *aphtharsia* ('immorality') is used by Paul in 1 Corinthians 15:53 to refer to that which the righteous put on in the resurrection body (translated as 'imperishable' by the NIV and NASB). As such, 'immortality' helps further describe part of why the believer in the eschaton has honour or glory – part of it is immortality. John Piper is going the right direction when he affirms that 'Glory is the main thing to seek and honor and immortality are simply aspects of it.'[59] In light of teaching in the rest of the book of Romans, we have already discovered that what Paul is most likely referring to is seeking the honour of God through the glorification of the believer. Again, Piper brings perspective:

> To be glorified, or to share in the glory of God, and yet not be God is to be fitted by God in mind and spirit and body to know the glory of God and enjoy the glory of God and thus display the glory of God with the very energy of God. What this does is keep the meaning of glorification radically God-centered. Even though we are being glorified, every aspect of our sharing in his glory is a fitting of us to know or enjoy or display his glory. Which is the same as to say: our glory is to know his glory. Our glory is to enjoy his glory. Our glory is to display his glory. And our glory is to do all of that not in our own strength, but in the strength that God himself supplies so that our joy may be full and his glory fully shown.[60]

When we understand what Paul says is being sought in this text, we now realize that Paul is teaching that eternal life is given to those whose goal is to glorify God and share in the fulness of who he is, i.e. to radiate his glory in themselves for eternity. Such an ultimate goal is in keeping with what Paul says elsewhere in Romans as to the chief end of man and the gospel (cf. 1:5, 21, 23; 3:23; 16:27). Such seeking also seems to be synonymous with faith for Paul when this text is compared with Romans 3:25, 26, 28, 30; 4:3, 5, 11, 16; 5:1, 10; 8:29-39. After all, Paul says in those texts that we are justified by faith, which results in ultimate salvation and eternal life.

In Romans 2:1-10 it is made clear that those who come to value the kindness of God and seek his honour in their own honourable changed life and future glory will live a new life, one of obedience to God and practising good. Verse 10 affirms that the reward for this grace-wrought obedience and righteousness will be 'glory, honor, and peace'. Hence, glory and honour are not only what the saint is to seek, but also his reward.

So, to summarize we can affirm that glorification takes place in the eschaton. Glorification is both the goal and the reward of the believer. Glorification entails finding honour in the honouring of God. And, glorification is the reward of the believer alone.

Towards the end of Paul's argument that Jews also are under the judgement of God he also reveals in our next Romans text that even circumcision does not profit unless one has been inwardly changed and thus obeys God (Rom. 2:25-29). In verse 29 he concludes: 'But he is a Jew who is one inwardly, and circumcision is of the heart in Spirit, not by the letter, the praise is not from men but from God.'

It is likely that *epainos* ('praise') introduces a play on words since there is a connection between 'Judah' and 'praise' in Hebrew.[61] In other words, Paul is teaching that man should not seek his praise and ultimate fulfilment from his nationality or from what others think of him. His focus should be upon God's view of him and the fact that, if a believer, God shall acknowledge his true status and call attention to who he really is in the age to come.

What we see here is that part of our trust in God is that our fulfilment and joy will be found completely in him, and he will reward us. The life in Christ, regardless of material losses or pains, is the life that is truly worth living. He does reward those who diligently seek him (Heb. 11:6). And a great part of that reward is hearing the words, 'Well done, good and faithful servant' (Matt. 25:21) which shall echo off the walls of the great heavenly judgement room for all to hear. Yet, even in those words our joy will not be found in what we have produced or accomplished but in God. All the praise will be given to him, since all that we have we have received from him (1 Cor. 4:7).

The one who has truly been converted by the Spirit can look forward to an adulation which is from God and not from men. We shall share in God's glory and be commended by him. When we realize that God is the ultimate beauty and source of glory in the universe, we will long for that time that we shall share in his glory and be lifted up by him as his prize!

Before we conclude our discussion of the fact that the justified alone are glorified in the eschaton, we want to hear from the Lord himself on the subject out of the Gospels. In Matthew 13:43 Jesus is explaining the parable of the wheat and the tares to his disciples. In verses 40-42, he is speaking of judgement in the eschaton, i.e. of those who commit lawlessness (v. 41) and who are sons of the evil one (v. 38). In verse 43 he turns to the righteous and says, 'At that time the righteous ones will shine as the sun in the kingdom of their Father.'

The 'at that time' (tote) refers to the 'harvest' (*therismos*) at the end of the age (v. 39), the time when the unrighteous are thrown into the lake of fire (v. 40), which most likely refers to the second death of Revelation 20:14-15. What Jesus has in view is the complex of events at the end of time wherein the righteous and wicked are judged and enter into the eternal state. The group Jesus speaks of in verse 43 are 'the righteous ones', that is, the sons of the kingdom (v. 38 [cf. Matt.. 25:37, 46]), those whose righteousness exceeds that of the scribes and Pharisees (Matt. 5:20) since they have responded in faith and been justified by God (cf. Matt. 7:24; 25:46; John 3:16) and, as a result, hunger and thirst after righteousness in practice (Matt. 5:6).

Of this group Jesus says that when they enter the eternal state they 'will shine like the sun'. This is the only time this clause (as well as this concept) appears in the New Testament. It seems to be a clear reference to Judges 5:31 and Daniel 12:3 – both texts we looked at in chapter one. This statement also seems, by implication, to suggest physical transformation.

So, in this short statement, again it is confirmed that only the justified are glorified, glorification proper will take place within the complex of events at the end of time and that physical transformation and vindication are part of that future hope.

Conclusion

What should strike the careful student regarding the New Testament glorification teaching is how much agreement there is with the Old Testament. Glory, in this last third of the Scriptures, connotes the full weight of who God is. God's glory, in both testaments, refers to the manifestation of his power, magnificence, grace, love and holiness. As this is displayed, men and angels recount back to God how great he is in worship. In other words, they glorify him.

The New Testament emphasizes even more, however, just how important it is that men glorify God – not only in recounting back to God in praise and delight who he is, but also living a life that displays the divine glory – that causes others to worship him. This is man's main purpose and its lack is his chief sin.

We also find in the last twenty-seven books of the Bible the focus that man is made in God's image, which means that he was made to resemble and represent him. Yet, this capacity has been twisted through sin. God's redemptive work with man consists in large part of restoring him and enabling him to honour his Creator through life change. Such a work will be completed in the life to come when man is glorified, i.e. his transformation will be complete. At that time, it will be revealed more fully who the redeemed really are. God will praise and vindicate the church. And, yes, he will completely transform them spiritually and physically. Man's glory and God-glorifying capacity will be fully restored and, in some ways, surpassed as then he will display God's mercy that much more. Both individually and in community the *imago dei* will be restored.

Yet, there are very significant ways in which we are taken beyond the teaching of the Old Testament. The most important has to do with the revelation that God is chiefly glorified through his Son, Jesus Christ, and that man's capacity as a God-glorifier can be restored only through him. Christ is qualified for this special role because, as the God-man and only-begotten Son, he reveals God as no one and nothing else can. He accomplishes this through his works, especially the work of salvation. Through his saving work he shows that God is both just and merciful. He also redeems, reconciles and sanctifies men, enabling them to be renovated as God-glorifiers. Because this is the means, Jesus Christ is glorified, which ultimately brings glory to the Father. In union with Christ, man is renewed more and more after Christ's own likeness. And in the age to come, because he is a joint heir in Christ, man will share in his glory. It is only those who are justified by faith in Christ who will be part of this future reward.

The New Testament has also made it clear that the glorification of the church is a sure thing, as much so as if it had already happened. The entire process involves Christ-likeness, both in character and appearance – which also includes immortality. And this end for the saint has been part of God's eternal purpose since it will honour Christ and show forth the greatness of God and his grace. The fact that glorification awaits us should have a strong bearing upon our present experience. We should be encouraged to persevere through trials, to obey God and to love one another in unity, since we have a glimpse of our prize.

Though we now have a good understanding of glorification, there are still some unanswered questions, some itches that have yet to be scratched. How important is this doctrine? What is the specific timing of this ultimate transformation? More specifically, what does the transformation involve? So, we need to keep digging – something we will do in the next chapter.

Chapter 3

GETTING THE 'TALK' RIGHT

I AM FASCINATED WITH THE WAY that God has wired children to learn the language of their parents. I have been told that even in infancy those beautiful little cooing, smiling, flailing charmers are picking up the different language patterns and intonations of those around them.[1] The Japanese infant is latching on to different sounds and inflections than the Swedish baby, the Brazilian than the French, the Chinese than the American, and so on.

Even though this is true, how many of us have not laughed at a child who has picked up patterns and what he thought was the right way to say something, yet it really was not? For example, many of us have heard of the child who thought God's name was Harold. When probed further by his parents as to why he had drawn this conclusion, the little guy replied, 'Well, you know in

the Lord's prayer, it says, "Harold, be Thy name"!' Ah, we smile
– 'Sounds close, little friend, but not quite.'

Then there is the following example I received a couple of
years ago by e-mail:

> While walking along the sidewalk in front of his
> church, our minister heard the intoning of a prayer
> that nearly made his collar wilt. Apparently, his
> five year-old son and his playmates had found
> a dead robin. Feeling that proper burial should
> be performed, they had secured a small box and
> cotton material, then dug a hole and made ready
> for the disposal of the deceased. The minister's
> son was chosen to say the appropriate prayers and
> with sonorous dignity intoned his version of what
> he thought his father always said: 'Glory be unto
> the Faaaather ... and unto the Sonnn ... and into
> the hole he gooooes.

Lest we think that children are the only culprits, we need to
admit that adults are also known to misunderstand certain words
or phrases. This happened once with a man who was visiting me.
This gentleman, not accustomed to all the jargon of Christianity,
heard that I pastor a congregation which is part of the Evangelical Free Church of America. He asked me, 'What is this angelical
free church you pastor, anyway?' I suppose this difficult name
had conjured up pictures in his mind of each meeting place for
Evangelical Free churches being equipped with a sign by the front
door – you know the type – a circle with a diagonal line through
it and the word 'ANGELS' written inside it. This must be posted
on these buildings, thought the inquirer, to let these spirit beings
know that they were not allowed! I am glad that is not what the
name of our association means!

What a keen reminder it is that we do often misunderstand
biblical and theological concepts. Like the child who has the basic
pattern and inflection down, we may be close, yet when it comes
right down to it, we just don't quite have it right.

Such can easily be the case with the doctrine of glorification, especially at this point in our venture into the realms of this teaching. We have the basic ideas down and we have heard the intonations, the patterns. Yet, we want to zero in further and make sure that we are hearing specifically what the Scriptures say about this future and ultimate reward for the believer. We want to consider some questions that may still lurk in the back of our minds.

THE ETERNAL IMPORTANCE OF GLORIFICATION

I assume that a question has been raised in the mind of some readers: 'How important is glorification, anyway?' It is a fair query. After all, the likelihood is strong that very few have ever read anything of length on the subject. Doesn't that suggest that it is of secondary significance at best? I hope that we have sensed from the first two chapters that this future hope of the saint is like the team that comes from out of nowhere to make it into the Olympic basketball finals and the next thing you know, in spite of the commentators forecasting their doom at each turn, they have won the gold medal. I am convinced it receives far too little respect in theological circles. After all, even to this point in our study of glorification, we have learned much about man's origin, his purpose in life and eternity, his identity and what full-orbed salvation is. Yet, there is one other way that the magnitude of this teaching can be felt. That is by looking at the part it has played in God's eternal plan.

Going back to a text which we dealt with in chapter two, Romans 8:29-30, there is a stone that we peered under, but now need to expose fully to the light. Verse 29 affirms that God determined in eternity past that he would enter into intimate knowledge of and relationship with a group of people, and that he would work in this same group so that they would become like his Son, Jesus Christ. It has always been his purpose that he would redeem the elect, sanctify them and bring them to the point that they resemble Jesus Christ. We saw that the glorification of the believer (v. 30), in large part, consists of the ultimate restoration of man into the image of Christ. In other words, it is a parallel concept with conformity to the image of Christ in verse 29. What this means is part of God's eternal decree, that the elect would be glorified. Certainly he decreed the preceding steps, many of which we more frequently speak of – things like justification, regeneration and sanctification. Yet, think about what it is that has eternally been at the bottom of God's 'to-do list' for the church. Oh yes, there are all the Old Testament preparatory events, the virgin conception and birth of Christ, his perfect life, his death, burial, resurrection and exaltation; there is effectual call, regeneration, justification and sanctification for each believer. But right at the very end, with goal written by it, is glorification.

Think of the way that God has been glorified in every aspect of the process – both in redemption accomplished and in its application to each saint. But the end, purpose and goal seems as if it has special significance. It promises to honour God and display his mercy, grace, power, love and holiness (especially among the saints in community) as nothing else ever has. 'Man Fallen, Yet Reclaimed' will read the heavenly headlines. 'God shows unparalleled mercy, grace and love in taking rebellious man, making him like the Son himself and uniting them all together – read all about it!' If man was the crowning creation of God, how much more will his crowning recreation serve as a billboard for his praise?

And this is not the only place in the New Testament that we find this emphasis. Paul also mentions it in 1 Corinthians 2:7. In the first four chapters of this epistle written to the church at Corinth Paul deals primarily with congregational division which had arisen from factions following different personalities (cf. 1:10-13). Such had been reported to him by those belonging to Chloe's household (1:11).[2] He turned in 1 Corinthians 1:14-17 to show the folly. After all, he and the other leaders are not the central point in salvation. Regarding himself, he didn't even baptize many. What Christ sent him to do was preach the gospel so that they would understand that the cross is central and that Christ is the focus. In 1 Corinthians 1:18 – 2:5 he elaborates upon this gospel and how he preached it – namely, not with the rhetorical style recognized as successful in his day.[3] He did not want to leave Corinth focusing upon his ability. He wanted them to hear and understand the gospel and see that the power is in the Spirit working through that message. He wanted their faith to be in the power of God and not in man's ability or wisdom (2:5).

With 1 Corinthians 2:6 – 3:4 Paul turns to the true wisdom that he and others preach (in distinction from the so-called wisdom of the world) – the application and understanding of which comes through the Spirit. In 1 Corinthians 2:7 he gives a synopsis of the message, that is, the wisdom they proclaim. He writes, 'But we speak wisdom from God in a mystery, which has been hidden, which God predestined before the ages unto our glory.' The 'but' (*alla*) shows that the wisdom Paul speaks (and which is received as wisdom by those who are regenerated)[4] is far different than that which the world and rulers view as wisdom (v. 6). In the context Paul uses *sophia* ('wisdom'), first, to refer to the world's way of thinking about meaning, purpose and relating to God, making sense of the world (1:19, 20, 21, 22; 2:1, 4, 5, 6) that is self-generated, man-centred and not from God (1:20, 21, 25, 26, 27, 29; 2:4, 5, 6).[5] Paul says that this is not the wisdom he preaches. Instead, he preaches wisdom from God,[6] which is God's revelation concerning meaning, purpose, right relationship with him and how to get along in this life. And it is centred in Christ and his salvific work, the cross (1:18, 21, 23, 24, 30; 2:2).

The phrase, 'in a mystery', most likely displays the manner in which the wisdom is manifested.[7] The term *musterion* ('mystery') does not refer to a unique form of knowledge that only the specially initiated could acquire. Instead, it denotes that which had been more hidden in the past, yet now has been revealed in a fuller way.[8] In other words, Paul uses 'mystery' to speak of truths under the Old Covenant which were opaque, yet now, under the New Covenant, are made clear. Sometimes it has to do with the extent to which Gentiles are included in the New Covenant and 'sharers together in the promise of Christ Jesus' (e.g. Eph. 3:6, NIV). Other times, as here, it refers to the specifics of the plan of redemption. Though the Old Testament had foretold much about the work of redemption (e.g. Isaiah 52:13 – 53:2), the exact identity of the Messiah and details involved in his salvific work had not been revealed. Now they have been: 'The mystery that has been kept hidden for ages and generations, but is now disclosed to the saints' (Col. 1:26, NIV). Paul's point, therefore, is that God's perfect insight on life and the true way of salvation have been revealed in the gospel, now fully revealed in and through Christ. This is the message that Paul says he and the other apostles preach.

Specifically of this mystery, that is, the gospel of Christ, Paul writes, 'which God predestined before the ages'. The term 'the ages' (*ton aionon*) refers to the present era or age.[9] As a result, it often comes to signify the way of thinking represented by people of this age who do not know God (cf. 1 Cor. 2:6).[10] Paul says that before time began and, yes, long before the world came up with their version of wisdom, God had (in eternity past) determined beforehand certain things about this gospel mystery. He determined that it would be accomplished, proclaimed and applied. Such is necessarily implied in Paul's statement in verse 7.

And what was the eternal purpose of the accomplishment, proclamation and application of the gospel? It was 'unto our glory' – i.e. the glory of believers. Because of the adversative relationship between verse 6 and verse 7, 'glory' has the opposite sense of 'who are coming to nothing' (v. 6) which describes rulers of this age who follow man's wisdom. The 'coming to nothing' seems to communicate something similar to the participle in 1:18: 'those who are perishing'. Those following their own wisdom come to a dishonourable end, one of judgement. Yet saints, those who embrace the gospel, come to an end of honour, one of great reward. Such a use of 'glory' (*doxa*) is consistent with how Paul uses it in other epistles (Rom. 2:6-10; 8:18) and how he uses it in 1 Corinthians 15:43.

What we have in this verse, then, is a clear statement that God's eternal purpose for the gospel and saints is that he would work through Christ and in them in such a way that the end result would be their glorification.[11] It has always been true that God has determined that all the elect would be glorified. This suggests that his greatest purpose and most complete end for saints is that they would be glorified in the age to come. This ultimate purpose has been that which has given direction to all that God has done for the church.

On the window ledge over the desk in my study sits my long-time friend, Tex. This six-inch (15.24 cm) little guy was birthed in 1987 out of a block of wood by my uncle Bob. With a thick moustache that covers part of his mouth and reaches almost to the back lower edge of his jaw line and a worn and turned up cowboy hat, Tex looks every bit the part of a ranch hand. I am amazed at the detail given to the bust. This wooden sculpture was done with the same care as hundreds of similar busts, ducks and geese that graced the workshop of my dad's oldest brother. I was given this particular work after his death because I spent a good deal of time visiting with my uncle Bob while I was on breaks from college and seminary. We would discuss God and life, and talk about the Scriptures. And I would admire his artwork.

Hundreds of carving knives and other tools adorned his bench where he gave expression to his ideas. The joy of the process was a big part of why he carved. Yet with each creation, every step of the process was shaped by the anticipated finished product. Which block of wood would work best for that creation? What about the grain? As the shape emerged, countless decisions must be made. Which knife will work best for that groove? How much wood should I shave off for that curve? How should I represent this cowboy's shirt? His moustache? What about this duck's feathers? The process was enjoyed, but only in light of the emerging finished product. It was the countless shapes sitting in Uncle Bob's shop, and Tex now sitting on my window ledge, that comprised the glory of this woodcarver. The finished product was the goal that defined what was done along the way and what was important in the process.

No one would conclude that the completed work of a wood carver, painter, furniture craftsman or sculptor is insignificant, a mere after-thought of the artisan. Of course, it is what the process is all about. It shapes all that precedes. And though the master no doubt may enjoy the task from beginning to end, what gives him the greatest joy is to stand back and to admire what has been done – to see that every brush stroke, shaved piece of wood, chipped-away stone or sawed board, has come together to form a piece fitting of the master – a masterpiece. And certainly, this also brings him the greatest honour!

The future glorification of the believer comprises the 'masterpiece' for the Sculptor of all sculptors, the Master of all masters, the Artist of all artists. The display of saints, who, in Christ, have been conformed to the image of the perfect man, reclaimed from sin and perfected, will be the crown of God's work. Such will make the glory of the creation of his 'shop' and even its future recreation (as glorious as these are: see Rev. 21-22) pale in comparison. This future, living and breathing eternal art gallery has always been part of the eternal divine blueprint. When God wills something it is so sure that it is as if it already exists and then he creates it (Rev. 4:11). Such is the sure end of the saint.

Is glorification an important aspect of salvation? Absolutely! It is the end towards which God is effectively moving in his work of redemption! In fact, it is one of the key deciding factors in why all the events of history have been orchestrated as they have (Rom. 8:28).

Because God is working towards that end, it is not incorrect to say that those Christians who are faithfully serving him to win others to Christ and disciple them are working for the purpose or end of those believers' glory. This is the point that Paul makes in Ephesians 3:13. There he writes, 'Therefore I ask you not to become discouraged at my tribulations for you, which is your glory.'

In this third chapter of Ephesians, Paul is bringing this doctrinally rich first half of the letter to a close. From Ephesians 1:3 on he has shown the great spiritual blessings that his readers have in Christ. He has already digressed into one prayer aside (1:14-23) and now he enters another (3:1-21). Paul shares much with churches about themselves and God's grace in his revelations of what he prays for them. He introduces his prayer for the Ephesians in Ephesians 3:1 and then does not pick back up on the subject until verses 14-21 where he actually shares his prayer for them.

What this means is that verses 2-13 form an extended parenthesis wherein Paul discusses his mission and present situation. Of this parenthesis, verses 2-12 deal with God's bestowal of the grace and ministry of preaching the mystery of Christ upon Paul, the gospel upon the Gentiles and how this falls in line with God's eternal purpose which he has carried out in Christ and made known through the church. Then in verse 13 Paul draws a logical conclusion ('Therefore' [*dio*]). Based upon these realities and the truth that these present Gentile readers have such tremendous blessings upon them as a result of the gospel and gospel ministry, Paul gives them the exhortation of verse 13.

What is the exhortation? 'I ask you not to become discouraged at my tribulations for you.' The infinitive *egkakein* ('to become discouraged') most likely connotes these believers coming to the conclusion that the Christian life may not be worth it – after all, look at where it landed Paul; he was currently writing from confinement in Rome![12] Paul implores them not to come to that conclusion and not to lose hope because of his tribulations. Paul affirms that his overall tribulations, including his present incarceration, are 'for you' – i.e. for Gentiles (see the preceding context), which includes his current Asia Minor readers.[13] His reasoning has to do with the fact that most of the persecutions and difficulties he has faced have resulted from preaching the gospel to Gentiles. Certainly the church in Ephesus would have been familiar with how the world often responded negatively to Paul from the riot that occurred in Ephesus when Paul ministered there (Acts 19:21-41).

Why does Paul implore the readers not to be discouraged? The preceding context has spoken of the blessings and riches that these readers have because of the gospel and gospel ministry. Paul wants them to see the great and mighty way that God has been there for them and given them all that they need (cf. Rom. 8:31-32). Certainly, if that has been the case, then whatever God brings their way will also be for good. But Paul does not stop here. He adds that this whole thing of his tribulations 'is your glory'.

Now, since Paul's main line of thought has been that of the great blessings, benefits and riches that have accrued to the readers because of the gospel and gospel ministry, and because now he says that all of this 'is your glory', it seems that what Paul is saying is something similar to what he had penned a decade and a half earlier to the Romans when the thought of all things being orchestrated for good was in connection with the glorification of saints. In other words, the good was toward the goal of glorification.[14] Here the same is true. Only it is Paul, as the instrument of God, who is working such that the readers benefit and are glorified. The idea that Paul communicates is parallel to his purpose statement to the Colossians (1:28): 'Him we preach, warning every man and teaching every man with all wisdom, in order that we might present every man perfect in Christ.' Paul wants to tell as many as he can about Christ, warn as many as he can about the consequences of life without Christ, and do all this so that he can present as many as he can someday before Christ in the eschaton as perfect, mature and complete in him.[15]

It is clear that for the apostle Paul, the purpose of ministry is the same purpose that God has in redemption. The ultimate goal is the glorification of the believer. In such a statement, we not only learn of the importance of glorification, but we also come to understand that the reality of this future reward is to motivate Christians from two perspectives. It should motivate us to keep going as we serve others – after all, we are God's instruments towards the goal of their glorification. Second, it should motivate Christians not to lose heart at difficulties. After all, God is using hardships to sanctify us, preserve us and move us towards the goal of conformity to Christ and ultimate transformation.

Before we leave the topic of ministry's purpose being found in the glory of saints, we need to answer a nagging question. In what way does a saint have any bearing upon the glorification of another saint? After all, we might reason, if our salvation and future glorification are secure, what bearing would another have upon this process? The answer will be found as we recall what we said in chapter two when looking at Romans 2:6-7. Sanctification necessarily follows justification. Given the opportunity, a true saint will display a changed life and will mature at some rate. The perseverance of saints does not merely suggest that a saint will remain forgiven and keep eternal life. It also involves God working in him to will and to do for his good pleasure so that the saint can work out his salvation (Phil. 2:12-13). The Scriptures are clear that without sanctification, a person will not realize the promise of eternal life. Hebrews 12:14 reads, 'Pursue peace with all people, and holiness, without which no one will see the Lord' (NKJV). If a person is not pursuing holiness, then it is an indication that he has never been justified. As such, he will not see God and will not be glorified.

Both as the fruit of salvation, as well as part of the perseverance of one's life, i.e. remaining in grace, God uses means. He chiefly uses his word (John 17:17), prayer (John 14:12-14; 17:6-26; Phil. 4:6-7); and the church (Heb. 10:23-25).[16] And of course, we have also seen that he even uses events (Rom. 8:28). As such, when we teach, encourage, love, pray for, mentor and warn others that they might grow, we are doing this ultimately that they might one day share in the glory of Christ!

WHAT IS INVOLVED IN GLORIFICATION AND WHEN

Two related questions are typically batted around in discussions of glorification. When does glorification take place? And what is involved? Regarding time, Millard Erickson argues that glorification includes both what happens with the believer at death (the perfection of his soul) and what happens at the time of his resurrection (the perfection of his body):

> Glorification is multidimensional. It involves both individual and collective eschatology. It involves the perfecting of the spiritual nature of the individual believer, which takes place at death, when the Christian passes into the presence of the Lord. It also involves the perfecting of the bodies of all believers, which will occur at the time of the resurrection in connection with the second coming of Christ. It even involves transformation of the entire creation (Rom. 8:18-25).[17]

Countering this is John Murray, who, with great conviction, says that glorification only involves the transformation of the believer at the times of Christ's coming and the resurrection of the believer. He writes:

> Glorification does not refer to the blessedness upon which the spirits of believers enter at death. It is true that then the saints, as respects their disembodied spirits, are made perfect in holiness and pass immediately into the presence of the Lord Jesus Christ ... 2 Cor. 5:8 ... Heb. 12:23 ... Yet, however glorious ... this is not their glorification ... It is to dishonour Christ and to undermine the nature of the Christian hope to substitute the blessedness upon which believers enter at death for the glory that is to be revealed when 'this corruptible will put on incorruption and this mortal will put on immortality' (1 Cor. 15:54).[18]

It seems beyond question that glorification proper will take place at the coming of Jesus Christ and the resurrection of believers. Creation groans in its earnest anticipation of the revealing of the sons of God that it too might be transformed (Rom. 8:18-22). Certainly, that is not at the time of the perfection of each person's soul. That this ultimate transformation of the believer will take place at the coming of Christ is made clear in many texts. Consider:[19] 'The Son of Man will send out His angels, and they will gather out of His kingdom all things that offend ... and will cast them into the furnace of fire ... Then the righteous will shine forth as the sun in the kingdom of their Father' (Matt. 13:41-43). 'When Christ who is our life appears, then you also will appear with Him in glory' (Col. 3:4). 'When he comes, in that Day, to be glorified in His saints and to be admired among all those who believe...' (2 Thess. 1:10). 'God ... has begotten us again to a living hope through the resurrection of Jesus Christ ... to an inheritance incorruptible and undefiled ... reserved in heaven for you, who are kept by the power of God ... ready to be revealed in the last time' (1 Peter 1:3-5). 'In this you greatly rejoice ... that the genuineness of your faith, being much more precious than gold that perishes, though it is tested by fire, may be found to praise, honor, and glory at the revelation of Jesus Christ' (1 Peter 1:6-7).

There is no question that the climax of God's transformation of believers in Christ, to be like Christ, to radiate his glory through spiritual and physical perfection, to radiate an effulgence of visible glorious light and to be vindicated and praised by God – all rebounding to honour the Creator and Saviour – will be at the coming of Christ and the resurrection of saints. It will involve the bodily resurrection of the believing dead (1 Cor. 15:12-58). And yet, there is much to commend the thinking that this ultimate event will have precursors which bleed into both the present life of the saint and into her intermediate state.

To begin with, those who are in heaven now are spoken of as 'just men made perfect' (Heb. 12:23).[20] We cannot deny that this is part of glorification. We have discovered this from our overview of biblical theology and from learning that salvation, in large part, consists of God restoring to man the glory lost in the fall. In other words, man is enabled through Christ to become a God-glorifier again. Such demands transformation of the soul. Such is evidenced in Jesus' high priestly prayer when he avers, 'And the glory which You gave Me I have given them, that they may be one just as We are one' (John 17:22, NKJV). The context (cf. 17:17-18) is heavy with sanctification. The glory is being shared, at least in part, as saints are sanctified.

There are also many texts which seem to draw a connection between the process of growth in this life and the perfection realized in glorification. Colossians 1:28 demonstrates that the proclamation of Christ, along with warning and teaching, are necessary so that men may be presented before God as perfect. Additionally, the promise of such future perfection is to have a profound effect upon life now (Rom. 2:6-7; 5:2-10; 8:25; 2 Cor. 4:7 – 5:10; Phil. 3:20-21; Col. 3:3-4).

What we are saying is that the future and ultimate transformation found in glorification at the resurrection has bled into the present. The glory, in part, is emerging now in the church as she is sanctified. The souls of believers will be made perfect at death. Yet, the process is not complete until men are resurrected. For it is as a whole person that man stands in God's image and as such man must be reclaimed to bring God the greatest glory. Yet, we should not assume that nothing is happening prior to resurrection. Thomas R. Schreiner has commented, 'The genius of Paul's theology is that the eschaton has invaded the present evil age. The transformation into the image thus begins in this age (cf. 2 Cor. 3:18; Col. 3:10) but is completed and consummated at the resurrection.'[21]

Glorification is a great deal like marriage for a couple who will not consummate their relationship fully until the wedding night. Beginning with the engagement they start making plans for life together. They have now determined that they are right for each other, so they enter counselling to make sure that they are prepared emotionally and spiritually. The closer the wedding day comes the more the marriage bleeds into their experience. They may rent an apartment or purchase a house together. They may even buy furniture and open a joint checking account. More and more life becomes joint. Marriage is seeping into the cracks and crevices. Yet, they have not fully consummated their marriage until that day. At that day, the climax of it all, they are now fully married – husband and wife. Yet, it has been a process which, in one instant, took a major leap to completion.

And so it is with glorification. From the time that redemption is applied into the life of the elect God begins to transform her that she might reflect the glory of Christ. As Paul affirms, 'Though our bodies are dying, our spirits are being renewed every day' (2 Cor. 4:16, NLT). The more that she grows, the more she comes closer to perfection. At death, the process is complete in the soul, and yet the consummation still awaits the 'marriage day' when the bridegroom comes for his bride and crowns her with the glory of full eternal life and the resurrection body. What a glorious wedding dress the church will have! And in that complex of events the bride and bridegroom will move into their new home – an entire creation transformed and glorified to complete the glorious event.

In summary, then, glorification is fully completed at the time of the resurrection of believers and followed by the vindication and praise of saints, along with the glorification of the creation. It is preceded by the perfection of the soul at death.[22] In the following four chapters we will examine in more detail each of the aspects of glorification, as revealed in the New Testament: transformation of the soul, transformation of the body, transformation of the reputation and transformation of the environment.

PART TWO

THE TRANSFORMATION IN GLORIFICATION

Hallelujahs sing ye, ye redeemed oh, bring ye hearts that yield him glad behavior. Blest are ye endlessly; sinless there forever, ye shall laud him ever.

– Joachim Neander, 'Wondrous King, All Glorious', Trinity Hymnal, 166

Chapter 4

SPIRITUAL TRANSFORMATION

In the first three chapters of this work we have focused upon the general teaching of the Scriptures regarding glorification. We have set forth the underpinnings for a theology of our ultimate sanctification. In part two we now zero in on what the different aspects of glorification will involve more specifically.

We begin with a discussion Christians frequently overlook. Often when we think of glorification, the focus is upon the changes that occur in the body at resurrection. Yet, as God restores men to God-glorifiers, one of the most striking areas of change is that of the spiritual. In fact, we might say that though the absence of death, sorrow, crying and physical infirmity will be wonderful, there is also great comfort and hope to be found in the more spiritual changes. We can argue that these will be as cherished by us as the physical, if not more so.[1]

By 'spiritual' I mean that which has to do with the realm of the spirit, how one thinks, loves, wills and primarily relates to God.[2] The word in this chapter also will include conformity with God's will. For the sake of our discussion, it does not include any changes that are mainly located in the resurrection and deal with the body. Nor does it deal with one's reputation (how he is viewed by others) or God's more open praise of him that accompanies eschatological reward. Finally, in this discussion, it will not encompass any change of location (from this earth to heaven or the new heaven and new earth).

With definitions out of the way, we can now state that the future glorification of man will involve his whole and complete spiritual transformation.[3] In other words, man will be made perfect morally. No longer will he sin and fall short of God's glory (Rom. 3:23).

SPIRITUAL TRANSFORMATION AND THE INTERMEDIATE STATE

We will find out over the next several pages that spiritual transformation takes place at death for all believers who pass away before the coming of our Lord. If that is the case, we need briefly to say something about the intermediate state in which the justified find themselves after death.

Paul offers instructive comments in Philippians 1:21-23. The reason Paul wrote the epistle was to address the anxieties of the Philippian believers over false teaching and conflict in their own congregation. Mainly, he is encouraging them to look beyond circumstances to find joy in Christ, which will also buoy their relationships and set the right direction for avoiding false teaching. In Philippians 1:12-26, Paul tells about his own present situation to provide an example to the readers as to how they can properly handle such difficulties.

After Paul explains how his imprisonment has actually helped spread the gospel (1:12-18), he then avers that even though he is convinced he will live, be released and continue to be of benefit to the Philippians, nevertheless, whatever happens – live or die – he is fine with it. He wants, by example, to bring them to the same point. The reason that he is not anxious about the possibility of death is that death is gain (v. 21), since it means he will be with Christ: 'Indeed, I am hard-pressed between the two, because I have a desire to depart and to be with Christ, which is far better' (v. 23). Elsewhere he tells the Corinthians, 'We are confident, yes, well pleased rather to be absent from the body and to be present with the Lord' (2 Cor. 5:8, NKJV). Paul makes it clear that a believer, at death, is immediately in the presence of Christ.

Jesus himself affirms the same truth when he gives the reassuring words to the thief on the cross beside him: 'Assuredly, I say to you, today you will be with Me in Paradise' (Luke 23:43, NKJV).

When we consider these comments, along with the clear teaching of the New Testament that our bodies will not be resurrected until the return of Christ (cf. 1 Thess. 4:13-18), what we conclude is that saints who die prior to the coming of the Lord will enjoy his presence in a disembodied condition which theologians have termed the intermediate state.[4] Our position in this chapter will be that the soul is perfected at death, in the intermediate state. In this we are following solid historical precedent. The Westminster Confession of Faith, in chapter 32, paragraph 1, states:

> The bodies of men, after death, return to dust, and see corruption: but their souls, which neither die nor sleep, having an immortal subsistence, immediately return to God who gave them: the souls of the righteous, being then made perfect in holiness, are received into the highest heavens, where they behold the face of God, in light and glory, waiting for the full redemption of their bodies. And the souls of the wicked are cast into hell, where they remain in torments and utter darkness, reserved to the judgment of the great day. Besides these two places, for souls separated from their bodies, the Scripture acknowledgeth none.

The intermediate state is also affirmed by the Heidelberg Catechism, question and answer 57: 'What comfort does the "resurrection of the body" afford thee?' The answer: 'That not only my soul after this life shall be immediately taken up to Christ its head; but also, that this my body, being raised by the power of Christ, shall be reunited with my soul, and made like unto the glorious body of Christ.'

HOW WE KNOW THE BIBLE TEACHES SPIRITUAL TRANSFORMATION

The first way in which we see that complete moral change will be part of glorification stems from the realization that this is part of the ultimate purpose of Christ's salvific work.

Ephesians 1:4

In this verse Paul writes, 'Just as He chose us in Him before the foundation of the world in order that we might be holy and blameless before Him'. The terms 'blameless' (*amomous*) and 'before' (*katenopion*) are terms that are often cultic in nature and used to speak of the person who is presented as a pleasing sacrifice before God in the eschaton (cf. Col. 1:22; Jude 24). In this text where Paul is using them in a purpose clause, we find out that God's ultimate design in electing persons in Christ is that they might be holy and blameless before him someday. 'Holy and blameless' in this context refers to moral perfection in the age to come.

Ephesians 5:25-27

Later on in Ephesians we see the same point made; only here Paul uses the metaphor of marriage. Comparing the church to a bride, Paul writes:

> Husbands, love your wives, just as Christ loved
> the church and gave Himself in behalf of her, in
> order that He might sanctify her by cleansing her
> with the washing of water by the word, in order

that He might present her unto Himself a glorious church, not having spot or blemish or any such thing, but that she might be holy and blameless (*hagios kai amomos*).

Christ did not die merely to accomplish forgiveness and to bestow eternal life. His salvific work had as its purpose also the purification and cleansing of the church, that someday saints would stand before the triune God as holy and blameless. Sanctification takes place in this life (Rom. 8:4ff.; 2 Cor. 3:18; Phil. 1:6; 1 Thess. 4:3; 2 Thess. 2:13; Heb. 12:14), however, not completely (Eccles. 7:20; 1 John 1:8). As these texts intimate, it will be complete only after death.

1 John 3:8-9

Even thinking about how Christ's work impacts a person in this age, we see that part of the purpose has to do with spiritual transformation. John writes, 'Unto this end the Son of God was manifested, in order that He might destroy the works of the Devil. Everyone who has been born of God does not continually practice sin...' We see that Christ came into the world to destroy the works of the deceiver. And, as a result of the application of Christ's work (new birth) in a person, she does not remain under the dominion of continual defeat by sin or practice of the same.

Titus 2:11-14

Paul puts it this way to Titus:

> For the grace of God appeared [bringing] salvation unto all men, training us that, after denying ungodliness and worldly desires, we should live soberly and righteously and godly in the present age, waiting expectantly for the blessed hope, even the appearing of the glory of the great God and our Savior Jesus Christ, who has given Himself in behalf of us to redeem us from all lawlessness

and to cleanse for Himself a people for His own possession, zealous for good works.

God, by his unmerited favour (grace), not only forgives, but also empowers and transforms. Moreover, Christ gave himself on behalf of the church to redeem us from sin, to cleanse a people for himself, and to make us zealous to practice those deeds that are good, that are according to his will. The whole work of redemption (of which glorification is the ultimate step) is very much inclined towards spiritual transformation.

2 Corinthians 3:12-18

In 2 Corinthians 3:4-11 Paul makes it clear that the new covenant ministry is superior to the old and to Judaizing tendencies. In 2 Corinthians 3:12-18 we read that because of this superiority, Paul and other new covenant ministers speak boldly. Why? Unlike Moses, we have a glory that does not fade. Paul makes it clear in this text that the Old Covenant is inferior to the New Covenant. One who turns to the Lord has the veil taken off his heart (thus understanding God's will, God and the gospel), has liberty in the Lord (thus is enabled to live for God's glory) and is being transformed into the image of glory he beholds (thus he is transformed into the image of Christ, i.e. the image of God is restored). Herein we see that the New Covenant does what the Old Covenant never could.

What is pertinent is that Paul asserts that unlike the divine glory that radiated from Moses when he had been in the presence of God, the glory that is present in the believer as a result of the gospel is unfading. As we live in the presence of God, in relation with him through Christ, his character and glory are being radiated through us as we are transformed.[5] This is another way of saying that we are being remade into the image of God.

Verse 18 summarizes with these words: 'But we all, with unveiled face, beholding as in a mirror the glory of the Lord,[6] are being transformed into the same image, from glory unto glory, just as from the Lord, the Spirit.' Here Paul contrasts Christians with unregenerate children of Israel (v. 13), whose minds are blinded; i.e. they are veiled, and they cannot see the need for the gospel (cf. vv. 14-5 and also 1 Cor. 2:14). Yet, Christians are different, for the veil has been taken away because of union with Christ (v. 14). Every Christian without exception has an unveiled face. In other words, each has the understanding to see the weightiness, character and glory of the Lord in Christ himself (like seeing it in a mirror – Christ being the mirror of the Father). In Christ we see who God really is, how he works and how he can be known. And, as this takes place we are continually being transformed (*metamorphoo*) into the same image.[7] We are becoming like Christ, which means we are becoming like God.

Paul's main focus in affirming that we are increasingly displaying the glory of God is regarding our character, our spiritual or moral state. The context confirms this in several ways. First, it seems that Paul is opposing those with Judaizing tendencies (wanting to hold onto a certain view of the Old Covenant), those who are wrongly teaching that one can gain a right standing with God through the Law. In 2 Corinthians 3:6 Paul reminds readers that the law cannot give life of itself. It kills, meaning that one trying to gain right standing merely through law-keeping certainly will be spiritually dead before God. One cannot obey the law (cf. Rom. 7:1-12). Conversely, the Spirit gives life. He regenerates (Titus 3:5) and he sanctifies (Rom. 8:4ff.; 2 Thess. 2:13). Hence, his focus is upon true practical righteousness empowered by the Spirit through the New Covenant.

Second, regarding the Spirit, Paul mentions the Spirit giving life (3:6), the 'ministry of the Spirit' (3:8), and also 'just as from the Lord, the Spirit' (3:18). This latter phrase shows the cause of the transformation under consideration.[8] These statements are key, since elsewhere Paul makes it clear that he believes the ministry of the Spirit is to make one holy and to transform one's character (cf. Rom. 8:1-17; Eph. 1:14; 4:24, 30; 2 Thess. 2:13). This suggests strongly that what he has in mind is spiritual transformation.

Finally, in 2 Corinthians 4:16 Paul writes, 'Even though our outward man is perishing, yet the inward man is being renewed day by day' (NKJV). If Paul had in mind chiefly the transformation of the body in this age (Keep in mind he writes in 2 Corinthians 3:18 that we are presently being continually transformed.), then he would contradict this statement in chapter 4. One of Paul's points there is that in this age the Christian's body is deteriorating, and yet inwardly he is being continually transformed.

What we have, then, in this text, is as strong a connection as we will find anywhere between the present sanctifying work of the Spirit and glorification. As the Spirit changes us, God's glory is being formed in us. We are being crafted into those who are able to display the glory of God. We are remade into God-glorifiers. Philip Edgcumbe Hughes comments:

> This process of transformation into the image of Christ is none other than the restoration of the image of God which was marred through the fall of man ... The image of Christ is the true seal of the Spirit with which the believer is impressed. Indeed, as Calvin explains, the design of the gospel is precisely this, 'that the image of God, which had been defaced by sin, may be repaired within us...'[9]

Yet, we also have an affirmation that spiritual transformation is a large part of Christ's work in us. Though nothing is said regarding future transformation in the eschaton, certainly this affirmation of the present work in the life of a saint lays a strong foundation for what will also take place after death. Also, we find a strong connection between present sanctification and future glorification in that the former is referred to with glory terminology.

This raises a question that we should answer before proceeding. What exactly is the connection between the present aspect of glorification (our ongoing sanctification) and our future glorification (the ultimate sanctification and perfection)? Will the former gradually bring about the state of the latter? In other words, will a saint be so transformed in this life that he will come to the place of perfection as a process or by way of a second work of grace (the Wesleyan teaching)?[10] The Bible is clear that in this life no one will ever be sinless (Eccles. 7:20; 1 John 1:8). Additionally, we see in the New Testament that perfection, a state of sinlessness, does not take place until after death (Col. 1:22, 28; Jude 24).

Rather than the connection centring around present glorification and sanctification progressing bit by bit into ultimate completion, we see that God's purpose for us (as we have already discovered, Eph. 1:4) is that of perfection, likeness to Christ and the restoration of us to God-glorifiers. As such, we should not be surprised that he accomplishes such a work partially in us throughout this age. We ought not to be taken back that God does sanctify us as a necessary result of our justification. What this means is that if a person is not being changed in this life, then he or she will not be glorified in the next, since true spiritual life is not present in the first place. Such is clarified in many New Testament passages. Some examples are: Matthew 5:15-27, Romans 8:29-30, Ephesians 1:14, Colossians 1:22-23, 1 Thessalonians 5:23; 1 Peter 1:3-9 (especially v. 7) and 2 Peter 1:3-11 (esp. 10-11). So, to summarize: if present sanctification is not taking place, neither will future glorification. More about the connection between present sanctification and future glorification will be said below when we examine 2 Corinthians 4:16-18.

It also needs to be noted that after death all saints will be made perfect, though we know that different saints will progress to different degrees in this life (compare the seven churches in Revelation 2-3; see also Hebrews 5:12 – 6:3).

2 Corinthians 4:7-18

Paul was opposed in Corinth by false teachers. This becomes apparent in chapter 4 of this epistle as he seems to answer a series of accusations brought against him: we don't lose heart (4:1), we don't do shameful things or handle the word of God deceitfully (4:2), our gospel is not veiled to all (4:3-4), and we do not preach ourselves (4:5-6). And all these are predicated upon the more excellent ministry of the New Covenant gospel ministry he just described in chapter 3. The glory of the gospel ministry underlines Paul's discussion throughout this section of 2 Corinthians.

One other disparaging word that Paul's opponents may have launched against him in the hearing of the Corinthians had to do with the state of Paul and his co-workers. It seemed like they lived a very difficult life with great suffering. How could this be the case if they were apostles of Jesus Christ, teachers of the truth? Paul turns to address this question in 2 Corinthians 4:7-15. In verse 7a Paul affirms the reality of their state: 'But we have this treasure in clay jars'. In other words, Paul and his companions are like less significant clay jars that hold a valuable treasure. In their case, the treasure is the gospel message and ministry of the preceding context. His point seems to be that the treasure is the message, not the vessel carrying it.

What is the purpose for this phenomenon? In the rest of verse 7 we learn: 'in order that the extraordinary greatness of the power may be from God and not from us'. The purpose clause implies that the disparity between the gospel message and the messenger (Implied is the fact that the jar often gets broken, showing the messenger to be weak.) is divinely designed to demonstrate that the power for salvation is from God and not from the herald. In other words, Paul is arguing that there is a divinely-ordained purpose in all the suffering he and his co-labourers have undergone.

In verses 8-14 Paul illustrates the trials of the apostolic ministry, thus expanding upon verse 7. He first wants to make the point in verses 8-9 that the gospel minister experiences trials on every side, yet also has God's gracious strength and perseverance: 'In every way we are afflicted but not crushed, we are perplexed but not despairing, we are persecuted but not abandoned, struck down but not destroyed.' Paul is clarifying that their suffering does not spell defeat as the false teachers evidently had claimed. In verses 10-12 Paul shows that they face death so that others may have life: 'Always carrying about the death of Jesus in the body, in order that also the life of Jesus might be shown forth in our body. For we who are alive are always being given over unto death because of Jesus, in order that also the life of Jesus might be shown forth in our mortal flesh. So then death is working in us, but life in you.' And then, Paul writes in verses 13-14 that they speak with the strong trust and the assurance that they will be raised with the saints to whom they minister. Thus, they have hope in the future resurrection and eternal reward: 'Since we have the same spirit of faith according to what has been written, we also believe, therefore we also speak, knowing that the one who raised the Lord Jesus will also raise us with Jesus and present us with you.'

Paul concludes this paragraph in verse 15 by affirming that all the things they experience are for the sake of those to whom they are ministering, that the grace which has multiplied among more and more people should increase in more giving of thanks to the glory of God. In other words, all is experienced for the glory of God.

Arising out of this discussion, Paul senses the need to explain more fully how glory arises from suffering in the life of a believer. This he undertakes in 2 Corinthians 4:16-18 where we find strong teaching about glorification and how it includes spiritual transformation.

First, Paul asserts that what is happening to gospel ministers (outward suffering and bodily pain) is not the whole picture, for inward renewal is continually taking place. In verse 16 he writes, 'For this reason we do not lose heart, even though our outward man is wasting away, but our inner man is being renewed day by day.' When Paul concludes that he and other gospel ministers do not lose heart (lose hope and become weary to the point of giving up [cf. Luke 18:1; Gal. 6:9; Eph. 3:13; 2 Thess. 3:13]), he returns to the same affirmation he made in 2 Corinthians 4:1. Often people lose hope and think there is no use going on because of the suffering and worsening of life situations, especially surrounding their physical and mental abilities (or the 'outward man').[11] Yet, for Paul and other gospel ministers, even though their outward man is continually wasting away or decaying (the same for all people, even though for those undergoing persecutions the process is accelerated), yet the inward man (what we here have spoken of as the spiritual) is continually being renewed on a daily basis. This process is what keeps them from giving up in the face of great hardships.

The only other time Paul uses the verb *anakeinew* (renew) is in Colossians 3:10 where he speaks of the new man which is renewed in knowledge according to the image of God. In other words, it is the process of being remade into the image of God – that which was twisted in the fall. The parallel to Colossians 3:10 – Ephesians 4:24 – makes it clear that the renewal also consists of refashioning in righteousness and holiness.

So, Paul is affirming that at the very time that he and other gospel ministers and apostles are undergoing hardships for the sake of the gospel and their bodies are wasting away, they do not grow weary to the point of giving up, but they focus upon what God is doing in them spiritually. He is working in them such that they are being refashioned anew and afresh into the image of God – a process that is happening in all believers (cf. Eph. 4:24; Phil. 1:6; Col. 3:10). From this verse we learn that certainly spiritual transformation is part of God's redemptive work in us.

Yet, in verse 17 we see that there is a connection between the present sufferings, renewal and the future glorification. 'For our momentary light affliction is working on us an eternal weight of glory beyond all measure.' Paul is not suggesting that the affliction which he and other apostles face is insignificant. To the contrary, he says elsewhere that he has been through tremendous suffering (see vv. 7-12; 2 Cor. 6:4-5; 11:22-33). Yet, when compared with the eternal reward awaiting the believer, this life's troubles are like a vapour that appears for a short time and vanishes (James 4:14). So, contrasted with the 'eternal' they are 'momentary' (*parautika*), and contrasted with that which is a 'weight' (*baros*)[12] they are 'light' (*elaphron*). It is also noteworthy that Paul sets 'affliction' (*thlipsis*) against 'glory' (*doxa*). We experience affliction in this life, yet glory in the next.

Where, then, does the connection between the present and the future come into play? It is in the verb *katergazetai* ('is working'). Paul says that the present affliction 'is working in us' an eternal weight (or fulness)[13] of glory. In other words, it is a glory that is substantial, weighty and significant, something that really matters.

How is affliction working in us an eternal weight of glory? Elsewhere Paul gives us a hint. In Romans 5:2-4 we discover that as an effect of our justification and resultant peace with God 'we exult in hope of the glory of God. And not only this, but we also exult in our tribulations, knowing that tribulation brings about perseverance; and perseverance, proven character; and proven character, hope' (NASB). In other words, hardships drive the saint to trust in God because he hurts so much and there is nowhere else to turn. He must learn to endure such times by trusting in the Lord. Such experiences demonstrate to him that he has character that has been changed, and it brings the certainty of future glory. Yet, it is not only certainty of future glory that is affected in suffering. Tribulations also help refine and grow the saint. They are part of the means whereby God helps one persevere in faith. This seems to be part of Paul's emphasis in Romans 8:28 when he affirms that God is orchestrating together all things for our good. And it most definitely is Peter's point in 1 Peter 1:5-7 when he affirms that God guards us by his power through our faith and that he grows that faith, strengthens it and refines it, through trials.[14]

In no way is Paul affirming that we somehow merit future glory by our present actions. Yet, it is a truism that God 'renders to each one in accordance with his works' (Rom. 2:6). Those works, in that context, are more than mere outward deeds. They are works that encompass both action and motive. And certainly they are not man's own doing. They are the effects of God's gracious work in one's life (Rom. 3:19-26; cf. Phil. 2:13). As Augustine has asserted: 'God crowns not our merits but His own gifts, and the name of reward is given not to what is due to our merits, but to the recompense of grace previously bestowed.'[15] We are rewarded in the life to come for what God has graciously effected in this life. As such, there is strong connection between present progressive sanctification and our future glorification. Presently, he is working in us an eternal weight of glory. Though it will not be complete until after death, nevertheless the work is under way now. In this way, the work of glory (the restoration of the fulness of our weightiness, our reflection of God's image and glory) can be synonymous with sanctification. And therefore, if God is working spiritual transformation now, we ought not to be surprised that such is also part of the finished product, our end goal.

There are two other reflections we must make before leaving this text. First, we need to call to our attention that our future glory is 'eternal'. That new and complete restoration of our reflection and representation of God's glory will never cease.[16] Second, we see once again that the certainty of future glory has amazing impact upon present life. In verse 18 Paul concludes: 'So we do not keep our eyes on the things which are seen but on the things which are unseen. For the things which are seen are temporary, but the things which are not seen are eternal.' And the result is that 'we do not lose heart' (vv. 1, 16). A regular consideration of our future glory ought to let us know that whatever we face in this life, however painful, is worth it. In fact, it cannot even be compared to the glory that awaits us! (Rom. 8:18).

Colossians 1:28

Another way in which we know that spiritual transformation, i.e. moral perfection, is part of glorification stems from Paul's expectations regarding the finished product of ministry. In other words, moral perfection is included in Paul's view of what saints will be like in the eschaton. First, he makes this affirmation in his stated ministry purpose in Colossians 1:28. After affirming that 'Christ is in you, the hope of glory' (1:27), Paul writes, 'Him we preach, warning every man and teaching every man in all wisdom, in order that we might present every man perfect in Christ.' Paul tells the Colossians that contrary to the false teachers who were hounding them (2:6-23), he and his co-labourers proclaim[17] Christ. He is the focus of their message. In what manner is this done? They warn every man. The New Testament sense of the present active participle (from *noutheteo*, 'warn') is to confront an individual with his wrong direction for the purpose of correcting the attitude and behaviour – all based upon biblical truth.[18] Paul says that in his ministry he warns as many men as he can[19] regarding the just desserts of those without Christ, so that they might turn to Christ. Additionally, Paul also teaches as many men as he can what it means to live in Christ and to apply God's will in the specifics of life (with all wisdom).

What is the purpose of the warning and teaching in all wisdom? 'In order that we might present every man perfect in Christ'. The aorist, active, subjunctive, *parastesomen* ('we might present') has the sense of presenting a person before God in the eschaton as one would present a pleasing sacrifice before him (cf. Jude 24). The state in which Paul wants to present as many men as he can before God is 'perfect' (*teleion*). What does Paul mean by the use of this term? I believe if one looks at the use of this word group in the New Testament and especially in the Pauline literature, giving particular weight to uses in eschatological contexts or those dealing with salvation's end, it will be apparent that the connotation has to do with moral perfection – the lack of any moral stain. Bernard Ramm offers a good overview:

> The perfection motif can be briefly sketched as follows. God intends a goal (*telos*) for his people. This goal involves the perfection (*teleios*) of the individual believer. But this calls for a Perfecter (*teleiotes*) who himself must undergo perfecting and so become perfect (*teleiotheis*). Thereby he can perfect (*teleoo*) those who come unto God with a perfection (*teleios*). In this life perfection means spiritual, moral, and doctrinal maturity, but in the life to come it means perfection in the sense of the completion of salvation. The divinely intended purpose (*telos*) comes thereby to its consummation.[20]

Paul's goal in ministry, then, is to reach as many as he can so that as many as possible can someday stand before God as morally perfect, as pleasing sacrifices with a sweet smelling aroma to God. Paul affirms that the end and purpose of true gospel ministry is the complete spiritual transformation of the individual.

1 Thessalonians 5:23-24

Paul affirms to the Thessalonians that he prays for and expects their moral perfection: 'Now may the God of peace Himself sanctify you completely and may your whole spirit and soul and body be kept blameless at the coming of our Lord Jesus Christ. Faithful is the one who calls you, He also will do it.' There are a number of things noteworthy in this prayer.

First, Paul refers to God as 'the God of peace'. Paul is fond of this divine appellation, especially towards the end of his epistles (Rom. 15:33; 16:20; 2 Cor. 13:11; Phil. 4:9; 2 Thess. 3:16 ['the Lord of peace']). The term 'peace' (*eirenes*) is an objective genitive, so the sense is 'the God who produces peace'. 'Peace' connotes a lack of conflict with and estrangement towards God, which results in a whole relationship with him and the fulness and blessing that results. It comes as a result of being justified (Rom. 5:1). Paul wants this congregation who, for the most part was doing well (3:6-10), yet also struggled with personal purity and work issues (4:3-12) and anxiety over the coming of Christ (cf. 4:13ff.), to experience a fulness of fellowship with and blessing from God.

It is also true that for Paul when one has peace with God, this leads to peace, i.e. whole relationships, with others that lack division and ongoing conflict (Eph. 2:11-22). This is important because there apparently was some strife in the church at Thessalonica (cf. 4:6, 10-12; 5:12-22). Paul is reminding the readers that God can bring peace with himself and with others.

Second, to this God who brings peace, Paul prays that he may 'sanctify you'. George Eldon Ladd summarizes Paul's approach to sanctification when he asserts that it must be understood in light of the interplay between the 'indicative and the imperative'.[21] The apostle teaches that man has already been set apart as belonging unto God – the sense of *hagiazo*, 'sanctify' (Rom. 15:16; 1 Cor. 1:2, 30; 2 Thess. 2:13). This is why he refers to believers as 'saints', *hagioi* (Rom. 1:7; 2 Cor. 1:1; Eph. 1:1, et al.). Yet, in light of what God has done through his Spirit in the life of the believer, each saint is called to live in keeping with such set-apart status. In other words, they are called to be holy, to be sanctified (cf. Rom. 12:1ff.; 1 Thess. 4:3ff.). And, as we have seen, this is a large part of the end for which God redeems man. Thus, when Paul prays that God would sanctify Christians, he is asking that God would renew them throughout so that they would become more and more like God, saying 'no' to sin and 'yes' to righteousness.[22] Yet, he is also acknowledging the necessary role that God has in this process. God does not justify man and then man sanctifies himself and grows in the Christian life on his own. God is the one who, by his grace, gives us the desire for his good pleasure (Phil. 2:13) and instructs us towards godliness (Titus 2:11-12) through his Spirit (Rom. 8:1ff.).

The third aspect of this prayer worthy of noting is that Paul not only prays that God would sanctify believers; he prays that God would do this 'completely' (*holoteleis*). This word, occurring only here in the New Testament, is a compound, made up of *holos* ('whole') and *telos* ('end', 'completion'). It may very well be that Paul is merely trying to heighten the sense of wholeness or completion by using this term – 'through and through' (NIV). Yet, the immediate context and even the larger New Testament context may also suggest that the compound is to have its full effect. In other words, he is praying for a complete sanctification, one that comes to its intended end.[23] Either way, it is clear that Paul is praying for the complete moral transformation that we now know is part of future glorification.

The fourth point we note out of this prayer of 1 Thessalonians 5:23-24 is this: Paul, as he restates his request, also couches his request in the same cultic terminology that we have now seen so many times. His request is now that the whole person[24] be kept blameless (*amemptos*) at the coming of our Lord Jesus Christ. Synonyms that are translated 'blameless' often suggest a pleasing offering given to God without blemish. The mention of 'the coming of our Lord Jesus Christ' is expected in the Thessalonian correspondence where it is so emphasized. Yet, it also brings the focus upon the eschaton and the fact that Paul wants the readers to be without moral blemish when the Lord returns. This is another way of praying for complete moral transformation. Since the New Testament expectation was that the Lord could return in their own lifetime, Paul was asking God to work in the Thessalonians such that when the Lord returned they would be transformed in soul and body such that they were perfect morally. He was not saying

that moral transformation would not take place for all people until the Lord's coming and their resurrection. The New Testament
is clear that moral transformation, i.e. the spiritual aspect of glorification, will take place at death for those who exit this life before
the Lord's coming.

Earlier in this same epistle, in 1 Thessalonians 3:12-13, Paul
shows even more clearly what is involved in this blamelessness.
A great part of it is love. There he revealed that his desire was
for the Lord to cause the readers to increase and abound in love
towards one another and unto all men, following the example of
the apostles (which had been the focus in chapter 2). The purpose
was so that 'He might confirm your hearts blameless in holiness
before our God and Father at the coming of our Lord Jesus Christ
with all His saints'. In other words, Paul wants the Thessalonians
to love others even more as a result of divine work, and the end
result is that they would, without doubt, be preserved and be able
to be presented before God as a pleasing sacrifice without blemish
when Jesus Christ comes. This implies that perfection in love is
a crucial aspect of that future moral perfection. It also is another
example of the community nature of glorification. Individuals are
remade into the image of Jesus Christ, yet in part, this means that
they are able to love to a greater degree than other saints and to
fulfil the unity for which Christ prayed (John 17:20-23).

The final noteworthy aspect of this Pauline prayer has to do
with his certainty regarding this future complete moral transformation. In 1 Thessalonians 5:24, Paul reminds readers that the
one who has effectually called them (a call that continues to be
effective and to challenge people toward faithfulness to God, emphasized by the present participle) is faithful. In other words, God
always does what he promises and always acts according to his
nature. As such, one can always depend upon and trust in him. He
is trustworthy.[25] Arising out of this faithful nature of God is the
reality that 'He also will do it'.[26] Elsewhere, Paul has said that 'The
one who began a good work in you will bring it unto completion
until the day of Christ Jesus' (Phil. 1:6). God has promised to do
this and he will accomplish what he has pledged.

We have seen that the moral transformation involves love in 1 Thessalonians 3:12-13, but we also discover here in 1 Thessalonians 5 an even more specific picture of what the moral perfection entails. Before sharing this prayer, the apostle exhorted the Thessalonians at length. Leon Morris writes the following regarding the connection between these commands and the prayer of 1 Thessalonians 5:23-24:

> The exhortations are concluded and Paul passes over to prayer for his readers. The way in which he effects the transition (with the use of the adversative conjunction [*de*, 'but']) indicates that it is only in the power of the God on whom he calls that his exhortations can be brought to fruition. 'I have been urging you to do certain things, but it is only in God's strength that you will be able to do them.'[27]

In other words, Paul's prayer for complete sanctification was prompted in the first place by the need for the transformation that lies behind the exhortations of 1 Thessalonians 5:12-22. This suggests that the injunctions of those verses – lived out completely and perfectly – can give us a good sense of what the moral transformation of glorification will look like.

Consider the following. When perfected in glory we will perfectly recognize the contributions of others out of love (vv.12-13), experience harmony and lack of conflict with one another (v. 13), pursue what is good for all (v. 15),[28] be full of continual joy (v. 16), be in continual fellowship with and dependence upon God (v. 17), give thanks to God for all things (v. 18), follow the directing of the Spirit in all things (v. 19), always do the will of God (vv. 20-1) and be free from evil (v. 22). Just as mankind's combative, evil and disunified nature is a testimony to the fallenness of man and the corruption of the *imago dei*, so the glorification of the church in Christ-like community will be a great advertisement for his restoration and for the grace of God.

Jude 24-25

There is one more New Testament author who, in addition to Paul, validates the reality and certainty of spiritual transformation in glorification by means of cultic terminology. That is Jude in his short epistle. After writing to the recipients so that they will not give in to false teaching and false teachers and that they will defend and hold to the true doctrine of the Christian faith, Jude ends the epistle with a doxology designed both to give glory to God and to encourage his readers. 'Jude now assures them of the divine support and protection without which all their efforts will be fruitless.'[29] 'Jude's message of warning and doom might have depressed and discouraged his readers. Beset by so much false teaching and immorality, how can Christians ever reach heaven? The answer lies only in the power of God.'[30]

Jude eloquently writes, 'Now unto the one who is able to keep you from stumbling, and to present you blameless in the presence of His glory with great joy, unto the only God our Savior through Jesus Christ our Lord, be glory, majesty, strength, and authority before every age, both now and unto every age. Amen.'

This construction, 'Now unto the one', along with the later 'be glory, majesty, strength, and authority' shows that these two verses comprise a doxology. It is Jude's way of closing the letter with the desire that people recognize and then recounting back to God the fact that glory, majesty, strength and authority belong to him. Typically in such doxologies the description of God also comprises the reasons why he is to be praised (cf. Rom. 11:36; 16:27; Gal. 1:5; Eph. 3:20-21; Phil. 4:20; 1 Tim. 1:17; 6:15-16; 2 Tim. 4:18; Heb. 13:20-21; 1 Peter 4:11; 5:11; 2 Peter 3:18; Rev. 1:6; 7:12 [note that doxologies are often interwoven with blessings at the end of books and often the reasons attached are found in the blessings, not the doxology proper]).[31] Here, that reason is this: God is 'able to keep you from stumbling and to cause you to stand blameless in the presence of His glory with great joy'. We want to hone in on this reason or description of God.

Jude says first that God is to be praised because he is 'able to keep (*phulaxai*) you from stumbling' (*aptaistous*). To those whom

Jude has exhorted already in verse 21 to keep themselves, (*tereo*) and to those who have already been kept (*tereo*) by God in Jesus Christ (v. 1), he now promises that God is able to guard and keep them, which also implies that he will. From what will God guard them? From 'stumbling'. Though a hapax legomenon, the term 'stumbling' represents a concept that is present in James 2:10, 3:2, 2 Peter 1:10, Psalms 38:16, 56:13, 66:9, 73:2, 91:12, 94, 116:8, 121:3 and 3 Maccabees 6:39. It is a metaphor for somehow being stopped (falling down) on the road of righteous living. It is another way of saying that God will preserve saints from falling into sin's domain and losing their salvation – falling short in the 'race' (cf. 2 Tim. 4:7-8). This was a timely and precious promise since the readers faced great spiritual danger in false teachers.

Yet, God not only promises merely to keep one from stumbling. There is also the assurance that he will 'present you blameless in the presence of His glory'. Here is the cultic terminology used elsewhere of believers being presented as pleasing sacrifices, without blemish, before God in the eschaton. The word 'blameless' (*amomous*) refers to a righteous life that pleases God. It is the kind of moral existence or condition for which he chose (Eph. 1:4) and saved us – in fact the purpose of Christ's salvific work is that his church would be blameless (Eph. 5:27). Certainly it is set forth as the goal of the Christian life. In 1 Thessalonians 3:13 Paul affirms that this state of blamelessness is the divine goal for saints and it will take place at the coming of Christ. In Hebrews 9:14 the term refers to the blamelessness of Christ who offered himself as a sacrifice to God without blemish, i.e. without sin. So also 1 Peter 1:19 speaks of Jesus as a Lamb without spot. Finally, saints standing before the throne with no lie in their mouth are blameless (Rev. 14:5). It seems to approach the status of a technical term for the state of being without sin, especially the state of believers who come to their final and complete end before God at the coming of Christ in the age to come.

So, once again, we see the certainty of God's preserving work in the life of the believer such that he will bring him to the point of moral perfection in the age to come. We also are reminded that the promise of moral perfection is often found in contexts also speaking of the assurance of God's preserving work. The reality of the certain goal solidifies the present ongoing work of God.

Finally, in this text we see that such a future state of perfection will be accompanied by 'great joy'. Of course, great delight, great satisfaction and contentment will be experienced in that time when we are made complete, our numb hearts are removed and we are enabled to enjoy God to the fullest extent for ever!

Matthew 5:8

It is easy to miss the glorification significance of a short statement by Jesus tucked away in the Beatitudes. It is simply this: 'Blessed are the pure in heart because they will see God.' We find in the Beatitudes an inclusio formed by the promised blessing, 'because theirs is the kingdom of heaven' (vv. 3, 10). This lets the reader know that what Jesus was doing at this point in his sermon was describing what those are like who are part of the kingdom of heaven and how they will be blessed. So, 'pure in heart' describes those who have been brought into the kingdom of heaven by God's grace. Purity, not just outward conformity to God's law, but true holiness beginning in the heart, is a prerequisite for fellowship with God (Pss. 15:1-5; 24:3-4; Heb. 12:14). The reason that Jesus connects such inward purity with seeing God is that without such divinely- accomplished purity in one's life, we would not be able to stand in the presence of a perfectly holy God! R. C. Sproul explains:

> This means that someday we will see God face-to-face. We will not see the reflected glory of a burning bush or a pillar of cloud. We will see Him as He is, as He is in His pure, divine essence.
>
> Right now it is impossible for us to see God in His pure essence. Before that can happen, we must be purified ... None of us in this world is pure in heart. It is our impurity that prevents us from seeing God. The problem is not with our eyes; it is with our hearts. Only after we are puri-

fied and totally sanctified in heaven will we have the capacity to gaze upon Him face-to-face.[32]

Revelation 21-22

We will look at one more passage which validates the certainty of future spiritual transformation before we come to what many would consider the most common text that does so. In these last two chapters of Revelation where the future eternal dwelling of believers is described, we see a number of characteristics of the new heaven and new earth, along with the 'new Jerusalem', which necessitate that sin will no longer be present with saints. Consider the following statements (all NIV) which are sufficiently clear without any commentary. 'He will wipe every tear from their eyes. There will be no more death or mourning or crying or pain, for the old order of things has passed away' (21:4). 'He who overcomes will inherit all this ... But the cowardly, the unbelieving, the vile, the murderers, the sexually immoral, those who practice magic arts, the idolaters and all liars – their place will be in the fiery lake of burning sulfur' (21:7-8). 'On no day will its gates ever be shut, for there will be no night there' (21:25). 'Nothing impure will ever enter it, nor will anyone who does what is shameful or deceitful, but only those whose names are written in the Lamb's book of life' (21:27). 'No longer will there be any curse' (22:3). There is no question that if this is what the future eternal dwelling of saints will be like, they must be completely transformed so that they are without moral failure.

Hebrews 12:22-24

The final passage which demonstrates the reality of future spiritual transformation is what many would term the *locus classicus*.[33] It reads as follows:

> But you have come to Mount Zion, even the city
> of the Living God, the heavenly Jerusalem, and
> unto innumerable angels in festal gathering, and
> to the Church of the first born ones who have

been enrolled in heaven, and unto God the judge
of all, and unto the spirits of the righteous ones
who have been made perfect, and unto Jesus, the
mediator of a new covenant, and unto the blood
of sprinkling that speaks better things than that
of Abel.

These three verses are found in the midst of a paragraph (12:18-
24) in which the author compares Mt Sinai (representing the Old
Covenant) and Mt Zion (representing the New Covenant). His
purpose is to show the superiority of the latter over the former.
This paragraph forms a key point in the argumentation running
from Hebrews 10:19 – 12:29 in which readers are called to true
worship and strong perseverance based upon Christ's superiority
as the Author and Mediator of the New Covenant.[34]

The context and the perfect *proseleluthate* ('you have come')
strongly suggest that the following places ('Mt Zion', 'The city of
the Living God', 'the heavenly Jerusalem', 'the innumerable angels
in festal gathering', and 'the Church of the first born ones who
have been enrolled in heaven') are spheres to which saints already
belong that foreshadow the future eternal abode, and they are not
speaking of the future eternal abode itself. In other words, these
saints belong to the present kingdom, the sphere of God's more
realized reign, which encompasses saints now alive and saints who
have already gone on to the age to come. Such a rendering is also
supported by the phrases 'unto God' and 'unto Jesus'. They have
already come to God and Jesus and belong to the sphere of those
who are saved.

Since the saved are part of this realm of the saints, they also
have come unto the realm of 'the spirits of the righteous ones who
have been made perfect'. This clause, as much as any other biblical
text, supports the future complete spiritual transformation of the
saint at death. Philip Edgcumbe Hughes is correct when he asserts
that 'spirits' (*pneumasi*) is being used as a 'designation of the souls
of men separated from their bodies, prior to the resurrection'. He
cites 1 Enoch 22:3, 9, 41:8, 103:3 and Revelation 6:9 as the verifi-
cation. The author says of these spirits of the righteous that they

'have been made perfect' (*teteleiomenon*). We have already seen the multiple and convincing New Testament texts which verify that the believers will be made perfect in the eschaton. The author of Hebrews makes it clear that those who have died and are in the intermediate state have already been perfected spiritually.

We have established that spiritual transformation will certainly take place for the saint upon death and that this is the first stage of glorification. We've seen that this involves complete moral perfection – we will be without sin. We also have alluded to some specifics of that moral perfection implied from 1 Thessalonians 5. However, some of the changes are so rich that we want to look at them in more detail.

SOME PARTICULARLY RICH ASPECTS OF SPIRITUAL TRANSFORMATION

In 1 Corinthians 13:12, after turning our attention to the age to come (v. 10), Paul writes, 'For we see now in a mirror with an indistinct image, but then face to face; now I know in part, but then I will know as also I am known.' Paul uses the word picture of an ancient bronze or copper mirror which reflected only a very fuzzy image of one's face to describe the knowledge that we have in this life. In all probability the two halves of this verse are parallel. This first, with the use of metaphor, drives home the partial nature of even the best enlightenment of the believer. There is much that we know, but it will always be in this life very incomplete and partial, only glimpses and fuzzy images. Yet, when we are in the presence of our Lord, we will understand things directly, more fully and with greater clarity. This does not mean that we will be omniscient (for only God can claim such an attribute), but our knowledge will be clear, have fulness and be accurate – without any distortion.[35]

Joni Eareckson Tada offers a strong illustration of how this will be such a great joy:

> The parents of the little girl paralyzed in a drunk driving accident will understand. They will see how her accident touched the lives of friends

and neighbors, sending out repercussions far and wide. They will see how God used the prayers of people halfway across the country; and how those prayers reached relatives and friends of relatives, rippling out farther than they ever dreamed. They will see how God's grace cradled their daughter, forging her little character with nobility and courage. They will see that nothing – absolutely nothing – was wasted and that every tear counted and every cry was heard ... 'You number my wanderings; put my tears into Your bottle; are they not in Your book?' (Ps. 56:8).[36]

Our knowledge of who God is, what he is like, how he worked in this life and his will for us will be perfect. The Puritan divine Thomas Boston put it this way: 'The glorified shall have a most clear and distinct understanding of divine truths, for in His light we shall see light (Ps. 36:9). The light of glory will be a complete commentary on the Bible, and untie all the hard and knotty questions in divinity.'[37]

There is no reason to believe such perfected knowledge will preclude our learning in heaven. In Ephesians 2:6-7 Paul states that God 'raised [us] up with and seated us in the heavenly places with Christ Jesus, in order that He might show in the coming ages the exceeding riches of His grace in kindness toward us in Christ Jesus.' The sense seems to be that both in this life and the life to come God will demonstrate his acts of kindness continually to his saints, those whom he has raised up and seated with Christ. This implies that throughout eternity we will continually experience new and fresh acts of God's kindness towards us – thus we will ever learn more deeply and fully how much he loves us. We will continue to learn. Jonathan Edwards explains the saint's growing knowledge this way:

If they retain by one idea for one such vast period ([a] million million of ages), their ideas shall be millions of times more in number than when they

first entered into heaven, as is evident, because by
supposition the number of such ages will be millions of times more in number; therefore, their
knowledge will increase to eternity; and if their
knowledge, their holiness; for as they increase
in the knowledge of God, and of the works of
God, the more they will see of his excellency, and
the more they see of his excellency ...the more
will they love him, and the more they love God,
the more delight and happiness will they have in
him.[38]

Again Edwards adds:

It is certain that the inhabitants of heaven do
increase in their knowledge, the angels know more
than they did before Christ's incarnation, for they
are said to know by the church, i.e. by the dealings
of God with the church, the manifold wisdom of
God: and to desire to look into the account the
gospel lives of the sufferings of Christ, and the
glory that should follow.[39]

Not only will our minds be that much sharper, but our senses
will be as well. Though in the intermediate state senses will be
exercised without the body, both then and after the resurrection
we will have a heightened ability to take in the stimuli around us.[40]
More specifically, we will see and experience God more fully. The
beatific vision is a great promise for saints. 'Blessed are the pure
in heart because they will see God' (Matt. 5:8), and 'we will see
Him as He is' (1 John 3:2). Since knowledge of God is possible
only for those who have been regenerated and initially sanctified
by the Holy Spirit (Rom. 3:9ff.; 1 Cor. 2:14; 2 Thess. 2:13; Titus
3:5), and since we will be perfected morally in heaven, we should
not be surprised that the troubles we now have with knowing,
experiencing and delighting in God will be removed at that time.
'The more perfect the sight is, the more delightful the beautiful

object. The more perfect the appetite, the sweeter the food. The more musical the ear, the more pleasant the melody. The more perfect the soul, the more joyous those joys...'[41] Again, we return to America's premier theologian for insight:

> But yet this pleasure from external perception will, in a sense, have God for its object, it will be in a sight of Christ's external glory, and it will be in a sight of Christ's external glory, and it will be so ordered in its degree and circumstances as to be wholly and absolutely subservient to a spiritual sight of that divine spiritual glory, of which this will be a semblance, an external representation, and subservient to the superior spiritual delights of the saints; as the body will in all respects be a spiritual body, and subservient to the happiness of the spirit, and there will be no tendency to, or danger of, inordancy, or predominance. This visible glory will be subservient to a sense of spiritual glory, as the music of God's praises is to the holy sense and pleasure of the mind; and more immediately so, because this that will be seen by the bodily eye will be God's glory, but that music will not be so immediately God's harmony.[42]

This also leads to the conclusion that our fellowship with the triune God will be so much sweeter and our delight in him so much sharper. Psalm 16:11 reminds us: 'fullness of joy is in Your presence; in Your right hand there are pleasures forever'. The church is spoken of as the bride of Christ (cf. Eph. 5:25ff.; Rev. 21:2), which suggests great intimacy.[43] That intimacy will, in the glorified state, be so much more satisfying and rich. Richard Baxter puts this into perspective:

> And hath the Lord such a care of our comfort here? O what will that joy be, where the soul being perfectly prepared for joy, and joy prepared

by Christ for the soul, it shall be our work, our
business, eternally to rejoice! It seems the saints'
joy shall be greater than the damned's torment;
for their torment is the torment of creatures, prepared for the devil and his angels; but our joy is
the joy of our Lord.[44]

Finally, our relationships with other saints will be so much
more holy. We know that holiness consists, in part, of love for
others (cf. 1 Thess. 3:12-13; 4:3-12). In a state of perfect holiness,
where we all are delighting in, worshipping and serving God, the
relationships with other saints will be in perfect righteousness and
result in unmatched satisfaction.

WHY THIS SPIRITUAL TRANSFORMATION IS SO SIGNIFICANT

We have given a good deal of space in this chapter to the explanation of several passages. This has been designed not only to
show that spiritual transformation is part of glorification, but also
that we might see how much this theme permeates the New Testament. However, it would be easy for this subject to remain at an
academic, impersonal level and not touch the depth of our souls.
To avoid this, I want us to exult in the ways in which this aspect of
glorification is significant.

Future significance

If we want to grasp what the complete moral transformation of
our souls will be like, we need to remind ourselves of what life
with sin is like now and then draw comparison. Let me share some
examples from my life.

This past Valentine's Day, my wife and I were on our way out
to a restaurant for the evening. This was something that we had
been anticipating for weeks. What a wonderful gift from God – to
be together, to have the resources to go out and to be in a situation in which we could leave our children. Everything about the
night was a gift to be enjoyed, one of those potential mountain

peaks of marriage. But there was one small problem – sin reared its ugly head.

I was finishing up my work on that Friday afternoon and two Mormon missionaries came to our door. I left my office downstairs to answer the door and when I saw who it was, I was immediately angered. 'This is the third time you guys have visited us in the past six months!' I let loose. 'Can't you keep track of where you've been or put us on a no-visit list?' With such comments I not only sent these young men away from the front of our home (which by the way, has a wooden 'welcome' sign with a cross underneath it) thinking within themselves that 'There must not be much of value to that man's faith!' but I also immediately felt guilty. I knew I had displeased our Lord. I knew I had sinned. Yet, rather than repent right then and remember that 'the blood of Jesus His Son cleanses us from all sin' (1 John 1:7), I went on with my work and stayed immersed in guilt. Needless to say, my joy over our anticipated evening had been tarnished considerably.

Then, an hour later, Karen and I left home. With my previous sin still working upon me, we pulled up to the intersection for the street leading to the restaurant. Two young teenage girls were in a car in front of us, stopped at the light. I couldn't quite make it into the turn lane because of their car. Seeing that they had several feet ahead of them and could creep up to let us manoeuvre from behind them so that we could turn with the green arrow, I lightly tapped the horn so they could move. They didn't. With my previous choices having coloured my heart, I blew the horn loudly now – and long. They still didn't move. In fact, they made it clear now that they were purposefully not moving. When their light turned green and the cars in front of them left, they stayed still – until the light was about to turn yellow. They then quickly took off leaving us unable to make the green turn arrow. Looking back on this, it really wasn't that big a deal. So we got to the restaurant two minutes later. It really didn't matter! Yet, I chose to make it a big deal. I chose to be angry. I chose not to turn to God's promise that he would help me deal with temptation (1 Cor. 10:13). I chose to stew in sin. My wife was now frustrated due to my anger and she responded, 'Tom, if you hadn't been so angry and blown your horn like that, they wouldn't have just sat there.' 'What!' I replied. 'Why are you taking their side?' And with these comments, our evening had taken on an altogether different direction than what we had expected.

You see, this glorious gift of life God has given us is to be enjoyed to the full. It is to be chewed and savoured and in its crisp delicious flavour we are to delight because of him. Yet, the worm of sin rears its ugly head and so often turns the wonderful red juicy fruit to a blackened hole and mush.

There is also the friend of one of our daughters whose parents had recently been divorced. Not too long ago, when I was around her, I thought back to a spring when our two families had sat together underneath a park shelter for a picnic. Outwardly they seemed to be doing fine; all were living under one roof. Yet now, mom and dad were in separate houses and this girl and her brother were bounced back and forth between the two. This teenage girl was still reeling from the way her life had been turned upside down. I don't know the specific circumstances that led to the break-up of these two professing Christians. But I do know that sin was at the very heart of the matter. Whenever the tank-like destroyer appears over the hill of one's life, it runs over whoever is in its way.

And what about the times that we walk into the place where we meet together with our other brothers and sisters in Christ to engage in corporate worship? We are there to do that for which we have been made. We are there to focus upon the very source of all beauty and joy and delight – God himself. He has given to us the privilege and ability through Christ to praise him and recount back to him his worth. And that is what we do - for a time. But then we start thinking about the tiles in the ceiling of the sanctuary that were broken and stained by the roof leak, which then gets us thinking about the work that needs to be done at our own house and the next thing we know, we are forming a mental list of things to do, ignoring the very Creator of the universe, the one who, out of his own pleasure, mercy and love, chose us from eternity past to be his child in Christ. How ungrateful! How rude! Would we do this if a high-ranking government official came to our home? Probably not. How numb and unmoved our hearts often are for the one who loves us most, the one whose presence should be prized above all others.

How self-consumed we can be, even when doing what is outwardly a good work, such as preaching, teaching, helping a neighbour or volunteering at the mission. Edward Donnelly very accurately comments, 'Is it not true that, for the believer, sin is our greatest burden, our deepest sorrow?'[45] He then adds:

> Suppose that you could wake up tomorrow morning and find no change in the world except this – no more sin. Would things be very different? Of course! The whole planet would be transformed, life in every aspect utterly altered, unrecognizable from what it had previously been. Such is the immense revolution which takes place in every Christian at the moment when our souls leave our bodies and are made perfect in holiness.[46]

Christian, think with me carefully for a moment. Can you not anticipate, even to a small degree, what it will be like someday when we can enjoy God for ever with hearts that are aflame for him, whose embers will never grow cold? Can you not imagine ever so slightly what it will be like to taste and see that the Lord is good with perfect heart and soul? What about our relationships with other believers? Imagine being in perfect harmony, kindness and love, always blessing and encouraging others, and always being blessed and encouraged by others. The pain and mistrust will be gone. There will be no barriers or shame; there will be absolute peace. This peace will not only be with God and others, but also a peace and contentment within our own souls. The fight, the wrestling match we have with sin on a daily basis, the defeats and the guilt, will all be a thing of the past. To that habitual sin with which you have made progress, but that still bites you periodically, you can bid a forever 'Goodbye'!

And this absence of sin and the perfection of the soul will always be connected in our minds with the glory of God. He has accomplished it in such a way that we will know clearly we cannot boast (Eph. 2:9); we must glory in him. He is the one to whom we will always be thankful. He is the one whom we will worship for eternity in and through all we do. All the victories, the wins, the accomplishments, the celebrations, the friendships enjoyed, the rapture of a marriage proposal accepted, anniversaries remembered, the sweet savour of sunsets, family time, lives touched, the beauty of art and music that captivates our spirits and gifts received in this age have only been small minute appetizers for the eternal main course to come! We cannot grasp fully what great delight, what unending and ever increasing joy we will have in God someday! And to know that all is to be laid at his feet will be our greatest crown and gift. 'No eye has seen, no ear has heard, and no mind has imagined what God has prepared for those who love him' (1 Cor. 2:9, NLT).

Again, Edward Donnelly helps us out when he writes:

> Never again will we break any of God's commandments. Never again will we fail our Saviour or cause pain to anyone. Never again will we have to beg forgiveness. God has predestined us 'to be conformed to the image of His Son' (Rom. 8:29) and we will be. Sinless perfection is not a fantasy, though we will never achieve it in this life. But in heaven we will be forever free from sin, unchangeably disposed towards what is good. Our prayer, offered so often and with such anguish here, will be fully answered at the last – 'Deliver us from evil'.
>
> Our perfect souls will enjoy a new intimacy of joyful communion with God. We will know for the first time what it means to 'love him with unsinning heart'. There will be no shadow of repentant grief on our souls. Between us and our Lord will be no barrier, no sin, not a cloud between us and him.[47]

Please grasp, reader, that the discussion of future complete spiritual transformation is no mere scholarly enterprise! It is a great part of the ultimate end and completion of our redemption. It is something to which we should look forward with great delight and comfort. It also is something which should bring us to worship now. And this leads to the second area in which we find great importance.

Present significance

Paul writes in 2 Corinthians 4:18, 'So we don't look at the troubles we can see right now; rather, we look forward to what we have not yet seen. For the troubles we see will soon be over, but the joys to come will last forever' (NLT). In other words, he asserts that with the revelation of future glory and spiritual transformation, he and other believers have gained an eternal perspective. Reflection upon these truths leads to a current impact upon the life of the saint.

The first way is that it brings hope. In this passage Paul has said that 'we do not lose heart'. We don't give up since we know that however hard the present difficulties of life become, they are building our faith, which is helping us persevere, and they are verifying to us that our faith in Christ is genuine and our future reward is sure. What this means, also, is that our present sufferings are put into perspective. No longer must we conclude that bad things happen to us randomly or by chance. They are part of God's present sanctifying work in us that is bringing about the good of conformity to the image of Christ (Rom. 8:28-30).

Such great assurance of God's ongoing redemptive work should also lead us to worship of him, as it did for Jude in Jude 24-25. We should give him the glory because he keeps us from stumbling and will present us blameless in his presence with great joy. The gratitude that we display to God should not just be for what he does in our metamorphosis (although it should include this). It ultimately is to rest in giving him glory because he is the one accomplishing the work. And, even more specifically, our focus is upon Christ since it is because of his work accomplished and applied and because we are in union with him and clothed with his righteousness that the present work is progressing and the ultimate work will be completed. He is our hope of glory (Col. 1:27).

Future moral perfection also brings present security. God is able to keep us from stumbling and to present us blameless before himself someday (Jude 24), to sanctify us completely (1 Thess. 5:23). In fact, we have the promise that he who is faithful will do this very thing (1 Thess. 5:24). The doctrine of glorification is one more way in which God assures us that the work he began he will complete (Phil. 1:6).

Yesterday I had lunch with a friend who was telling me about a house he recently purchased. He wants to fix it up, sell it and hopefully make a substantial profit. He said that it will 'look as good as new' when he is done with it. With that goal and promise in mind, what this means is that several deficiencies will be addressed: the gutters will be replaced, outside and inside painted, a new sliding glass patio door and shower door installed, carpeting put down on the floor, a garage door with opener put up and countless other odds and ends. In other words, the future goal determines that present problems are to be rectified.

Though not an exact parallel, nevertheless this is similar to God's dealings with us. We have seen time and again that his promise of future perfection means that he will be working in us now. This is so certain that if we don't see the sanctifying process taking place, we must examine ourselves to see if we are in the faith (2 Cor. 13:5). Yet, as we see the Spirit refining us, such is a guarantee, a down payment of our future inheritance (Eph. 1:14). The assurance of that future inheritance then also assures us that the work will continue.

Such assurance also leads to confidence that we can address present besetting sins. We can say 'yes' to God and 'no' to sin. Edward Donnelly shares the following account that illustrates this point.

> The story is told of a thief in Japan who became a Christian. He knew practically nothing about the Bible, but on the first Lord's Day after his

conversion he went to a place of worship. All week long he had been wrestling with his life-long habit of stealing. He realized that, as a new creature, he should give it up and yet he was not sure he would be able to. Thieving had been his way of life and he knew no other way to spend his time. How could he change the ingrained behaviour patterns of so many years? On the wall of the church building into which he entered were painted the Ten Commandments. The new convert had never heard of them. But, as he walked in, the first words upon which his eyes fell were, 'You shall not steal'. In his ignorance he did not realize that this was a commandment, but took it instead for a promise. His face filled with gladness and he thanked the Lord in his heart for this assurance that he would be delivered from his sin.

Was he entirely wrong? Is it not true that, in a sense, every one of God's commandments is also a promise? These laws do, of course, set out the standard at which we are to aim. But they are in addition a thrilling description of what God intends to make of us.[48]

Our future spiritual transformation also should guide us, as it did Paul, in setting out our purpose in ministry (Col. 1:28) and in how we pray for ourselves and others (1 Thess. 5:23-24). As we have discovered, God has more in store for us than merely forgiving our sins and giving us eternal life. His purpose is to transform us. This is a large part of why Jesus Christ came into the world. If that is the case, then we must shape ministry so that we are not only trying to share the gospel and see professions of faith, but also such that we are seeing transformation take place. And, as we intercede for others and bring our own requests before God, we should remember that spiritual growth and sanctification should make up a large percentage of our prayer time.

Finally, the future perfection of our souls should bring great comfort to us. The joy, peace, the lack of conflict with others (1 Thess. 5:12-24; Jude 24; Rev. 21) and all these great and glorious truths, should bring us great comfort. Lyle Arakaki, from Honolulu, Hawaii, helps us understand this comfort from his own life:

> In Hawaii, because of the time differential with the continental U.S., the NFL Monday Night [U.S.] Football game is played in mid-afternoon, so the local TV station delays its telecast till 6:30 in the evening. When my favorite team plays, I'm too excited to wait for television, so I'll listen to the game on the radio, which broadcasts it live. Then, because they're my favorite team, I'll watch the game on television, too. If I know my team has won the game, it influences how I watch it on television. If my team fumbles the ball or throws an interception, it's not a problem. I think, 'That's bad, but it's okay. In the end, we'll win!'[49]

Yes, we know that whatever takes place, in the end, we win!

As glorious as this spiritual transformation at death will be, we must acknowledge that it is incomplete. As we saw in chapters one and two, man as made in the image of God, is a spiritual and physical being (the functions of his body resembling how God works). With this being the case, man's overhaul as a God-glorifier is not complete until he is resurrected and his body also is glorified. This necessitates that we take a look at physical transformation. To that subject we turn in the next chapter.

Chapter 5

PHYSICAL TRANSFORMATION

BEING AN ART ENTHUSIAST, I enjoy going to galleries and looking at paintings. I am not only often awed by the technique, but also by the worldview portrayed. A good friend of mine who is an artist once queried whether or not his time with brush in hand was really worth it. I said that it was, most definitely. What he communicates on canvass not only births refreshed insights into life, but also enjoyment and beauty. And this is true of so many painters.

Yet, one thing I have noticed in art galleries and with my friend's works is that rarely will you find a mere canvass displayed upon a wall. The works are beautiful, but they are incomplete without a good-looking frame that matches the mood of the work. The same is true of man. We have seen in chapter four how gloriously God is transforming saints and what a work of art we will be in the age to come. Certainly our spiritual metamorphosis will radiate the ultimate Artist's glory with dazzling splendour. Yet, in that intermediate state between death and the coming of Christ, such glory, as rich, perfect, and God-honouring as it will be, is not yet finished. For in that condition man is incomplete. He awaits the all-important frame for the canvass. He awaits the resurrection of the body. This reminds us that glorification also encompasses physical transformation.

Let's begin in this chapter with why this transformation (resurrection) is important.

THE IMPORTANCE OF THE RESURRECTION FOR MAN'S COMPLETENESS

In chapters one and two we were reminded from both testaments that man has been made in God's image, which means he resembles and represents God as none of his other creatures or creation can. And part of the image is found in his body. This does not mean that God has a body. It does mean that the functions which are carried out through our body reflect God's works. Therefore, as God restores man's glory to him, as he refashions us into God-glorifiers, the process is not complete without physical transformation. Then and only then will the work of redemption be complete for then and only then will God have refashioned the entire man. Timothy George concurs when he answers the question: 'If after death we are already in the joy of God's presence, what exactly do we gain from a bodily resurrection?'

> The resurrection of the body affirms the goodness of God's original creation, and recognizes that the basic human problem is not finitude but fallenness. It also declares that God will make good and bring to perfection the human project he began in the Garden of Eden.
>
> At Jesus' second coming God will complete the restoration work he has already begun. He will redeem our bodies as well as our souls. Indeed, the

entire cosmos will be gathered up in a new unity – that is, an ultimate healing, reconciliation, and bringing together of all things in Christ (Eph. 1:10).[1]

Such an expectation of resurrection of the body is not shared by all peoples. The ancient Greeks, for example, discounted resurrection even though they believed that the immaterial part of a human was immortal and would survive after death. They did not all agree on what that immaterial part would be like, yet there did seem to be a consensus that there is no future raising of the body – nor is one needed.[2]

This idea that man will exist eternally in a disembodied state seems to have gained widespread following among much of western society. One of the ways this is seen is in the Christian community where the Scriptures are read about resurrection, yet believers often have a hard time grasping its necessity. It just seems to some as if being in the presence of the Lord with glorified soul is all that is needed. Yet, with this view, our understanding of the doctrine of man falls short. We fail to see that man is a physical and spiritual being and to be without the body is, as Paul wrote, to be 'naked' (2 Cor. 5:3) – incomplete.[3] Murray Harris correctly comments, 'Any view of the afterlife is closely related to one's view of the nature of human beings; eschatology always reflects anthropology.'[4]

There are also other biblical strands which come together to show that the body is important to the constituency of man. As such, man must be resurrected to be whole, and this future body must be perfected. To begin, God showed the importance of the body and the flesh, when the Son was incarnated (John 1:14). Certainly, this demands that there is not something inherently evil or unimportant regarding the body. The second person of the trinity was made 'in the likeness of men' (Phil. 2:7). We should not be surprised that God has future and eternal plans for our body.

Additionally, as Jesus taught the need to trust in him for spiritual sustenance, he used very physical terms. Consider: 'Whoever eats My flesh and drinks My blood has eternal life, and I will raise him up at the last day. For My flesh is food indeed, and My blood is drink indeed. He who eats My flesh and drinks My blood abides in Me, and I in him' (John 6:54-56, NKJV). Certainly, a low view of the body in which it is seen as evil or inconsequential would have precluded even such metaphorical treatment.

The resurrection is also important because, as we have seen, we are being remade into the image of the second Adam, Jesus Christ (Phil. 3:20-21; 1 Cor. 15:22; Heb. 2:5-11). And, according to 1 Timothy 2:5, Hebrews 7:24-25 and 1 John 4:2, he 'was and continue[s] to be God and man in two distinct natures, and one person, for ever.'[5] For us to be like him we must be resurrected and have a glorified body.

Finally, it is not only important to be resurrected, but to have a body that is perfectly transformed. Sin is often carried out through the body as we see in Paul's exhortations of Romans 6:12-14: 'Do not let sin continue to reign in your mortal body, with the result that you obey its lusts, and stop presenting your members as instruments of unrighteousness unto sin, but instead present ... your members as instruments of righteousness unto God.' 'The day is coming, however, when instead of being a hindrance to the spirit, the body will be the perfect vessel for the expression of my glorified mind, will, and emotions. Right now, we wear our souls on the inside. But one day we will be "clothed in righteousness" as we wear our souls on the outside, brilliant and glorious.'[6]

And, if we are to live eternally in a body without death and pain (Rev. 21:4), there is a necessity for our body to be transformed. This future physical transformation is what we might call glorification proper or the completion of glorification.

Having seen the importance of being raised and changed bodily, we will now zero in on the New Testament's teaching that we will be physically transformed.

WE WILL BE PHYSICALLY TRANSFORMED

This change will take place in the 'future bodily resurrection of believers to immortality', as we see in 1 Corinthians 15:42, 52.[7] In order to understand the future resurrection of believers, we need to compare it to the resurrections which took place in the Gospels and Acts, as well as the resurrection of Christ.

There were a number of dead ones who were raised in the Gospels and these demonstrated the divine power of Jesus.[8] One of the most well-known is Lazarus. In John 11:1-45 we see Jesus bring this brother of Mary and Martha back to life so that both the Father and Son might be glorified (11:4, 40). Also, those present could learn that Jesus is 'the resurrection and the life' (v. 25) and that he is truly sent by the Father (v. 42). Since Lazarus had already been dead fours days and was decomposing and stinking (v. 39), Jesus displayed power that went well beyond what any magic-wielding charlatan could muster. He must have the very power of God; certainly he must be who he claims. Of course, the subsequent context clarifies that even with such irrefutable evidence, many still were hardened in disbelief toward Jesus (11:45ff.).

Jesus also raised others: the deceased daughter of the synagogue ruler, Jairus, with the result that many were amazed (Mark 5:21-43) and the dead son of the widow at Nain with the end that many feared and glorified God (Luke 7:11-17). There was also a resurrection of some saints at the time Jesus was resurrected – though we are not told the purpose. A good educated guess would be that such was one of the many corroborating pieces of evidence for the resurrection of Christ. And then in Acts, showing that the followers of Jesus did many of the same works that he did (since they had his Spirit working through them), we see Tabitha (9:36ff.) and Eutychus (20:7ff) raised.

Though these were miraculous signs pointing to the identity and glory of Jesus Christ, they differed from his resurrection and the future resurrection of believers significantly. In Acts 26:23 Paul says that Christ was 'the first to rise from the dead'. To the Corinthians (1 Cor. 15:20) the apostle asserts that 'now that Christ has been raised from the dead, He is the firstfruits (*aparche*) of those who have fallen asleep'. According to 1 Corinthians 15:23 the sense is that he will be the firstfruits of believers who have died and who will be raised. Murray J. Harris explains:

In the Old Testament the firstfruits were the initial part of the annual production of grain, wine,
oil, sheared wool that was offered to God in acknowledgment of his ownership of all the produce of the field and flocks and in thanksgiving
for his generous provision (Exod. 23:16, 19; Lev.
23:10; Num. 18:8, 12; Deut. 18:4; 26:2, 10; 2
Chr. 31:5; Neh. 10:37). It seems natural for Paul
to have thought of Christ as the 'firstfruits', because the day of Christ's resurrection – Nisan 16
– was the day (viz. the second day of Passover
week) on which the first ripe sheaf of the harvest
was offered to the Lord (Lev. 23:10-11, 15) ... The
resurrection of all believers is the necessary after-
math of the resurrection of Christ since the two
are intrinsically connected, belonging as they do
to a single harvest.[9]

George Eldon Ladd provides an insightful illustration of what
Paul means by firstfruits:

Let me illustrate firstfruits by some fruit trees in
my garden ... When spring comes, the blossoms
break out and I know the trees are alive. But blossoms are not firstfruits. They are promise, for if
there were no blossoms there would certainly be
no fruit; but I have seen trees loaded with blossoms which never produced fruit. After the blossoms the leaves break out, but there is as yet no
fruit. Soon after the leaves the little hard green
fruit sets. Is this the firstfruits? One year, one tree
was loaded with small hard plums, but later there
came a wind storm which blew them all off the
tree. I had a peck of small green plums on the
ground, but I had no harvest. This is not the firstfruits.

> Firstfruits come when the fruit has begun to
> ripen. You watch the tree day by day. Then comes
> the day when that first peach is at last ripe. You
> have been waiting for that day and you pick off
> that luscious peach, the first peach of the season,
> the only one on the tree which is quite edible. All
> the rest are a little green, too hard to be eaten.
> But there is one peach. You sink your teeth into
> it and the juice titillates your taste buds, and you
> revel in the flavour of the first peach. That is the
> firstfruits. It is not the harvest, but it is the begin-
> ning of the harvest.[10]

Jesus, then, was the first to be resurrected in a way that those
in the Gospels and Acts were not. And his resurrection is the first
of the harvest of resurrections, showing that all believers (John
6:39, 44) will be raised up to this different resurrection because he
was. How was this resurrection different? Paul seems to give a hint
in 1 Corinthians 15:52: 'and the dead will be raised incorruptible
and we will be changed'. Jesus was raised bodily never to die again
and in a body that was transformed.[11] This is the kind of resurrection for which he has paved the way for saints to be raised with a
transformed body, never to die again.

This brings us to the place where we must look at the two key
passages where the New Testament teaches the reality of the future
bodily resurrection of believers.

The reality of future resurrection: 1 Corinthians 15:12-32[12]

It is apparent from this section of Paul's letter to the Corinthians
that there were some within the congregation who were teaching
that there was no such thing as bodily resurrection. Paul affirms
the resurrection of Jesus Christ in 1 Corinthians 15:1-8 where
he includes it as part of the gospel and asserts that over 500 saw
him resurrected – including the twelve and later himself. After a
parenthetical discussion of his apostleship, which also serves as a
reminder that what he is saying about the resurrection is authori-

tative and it is part of the gospel preached to them (vv. 9-11), the apostle shows the necessity for Christ's resurrection in relation to our faith (vv. 12-19).

In verse 12 Paul asks the Corinthians why some among them say, 'there is no resurrection of the dead', since true gospel preaching includes the resurrection. His point seems to be founded upon what he has argued in verses 1-11. Over 500 men have affirmed that they saw Christ resurrected. Peter, the rest of the twelve and even Paul himself saw the resurrected Christ. And Paul has preached the resurrection to them. How can they not believe apostolic authority and instead believe the false teachers who are now saying that there is no resurrection? The question implies that their willingness even to entertain the resurrection agnosticism is ridiculous.

The reason that it is ridiculous is that if there is no such thing as resurrection, the Christian faith comes tumbling down (vv. 13-19). His logic is as follows:

(1) If bodily resurrection is impossible, then Christ could not have been resurrected (v. 13).

(2) If Christ was not resurrected, then our preaching and your faith are both empty, vain and useless (v. 14).

In verses 15-19 he elaborates upon these main points. Here he says not only that the preaching would be empty, but he says that they (the apostles) would be 'found to be false witnesses because we testified according to God that He raised Christ'. The reason that our faith would be vain is stated this way: 'You are still in your sins' (v. 17). The implied reason would be that the death of Jesus would then be nothing more than the death of a criminal (at worst) or one falsely accused (at best). It would not be the death of the Saviour. After all, Jesus himself taught his disciples on at least three different occasions that he would be raised from the dead and alludes to it once more (cf. Mark 8:31-33; 9:30-32; 10:32-32; 14:28). He would be a liar and certainly not the promised suffering servant of God.[13]

Now, if Christ wasn't raised and we are still in our sins, then those who have believed in Christ and already died have perished (v. 18). After all, there would be no forgiveness, no eternal life. The conclusion is that if we only have hope in Christ in this life (implying that there is nothing to it), then 'of all men we are most to be pitied'. The implication is this: we suffer so much and go without so much in this life because of our profession of faith in Christ. We do this knowing that in the age to come, it will be worth it. Yet, if there is no hope in the age to come and we still suffer so much now, then we ought to be pitied above all men.

Implied in Paul's argument is that there is resurrection, Christ has been raised and we also will be raised – therefore, we do have legitimate hope. This he makes plain in verses 20-28. Here he affirms that Christ was resurrected and has become the firstfruits of saints who will be resurrected. He clearly affirms that Christ's resurrection makes possible the future bodily resurrection of believers and that resurrection will take place at his coming.

In verses 29-32 Paul offers two more proofs for the resurrection. Evidently, some at Corinth were being baptized on behalf of the dead, thinking that this merited some kind of favour for them (v. 29).[14] Paul in no way condones the practice. His point is simply this: the practice shows that some believe in resurrection. He is trying to show that these thoughts they are entertaining are not consistent with what they are practising. It is almost as if he is saying, 'You really know there is a resurrection. After all, look at what you are doing!'

The second argument (vv.30-32) is from his own experience. He is asserting that his life makes no sense if there is no resurrection. Consider: 'Why am I in danger every hour? I protest, brothers, by my pride in you, which I have in Christ Jesus our Lord, I die every day! What do I gain if, humanly speaking, I fought with beasts at Ephesus? If the dead are not raised, "Let us eat and drink, for tomorrow we die"' (ESV).

Though resurrection is mentioned several times in the New Testament,[15] there is one more passage that can be considered a key text.

The reality of future resurrection: 1 Thessalonians 4:13-18
It reads as follows:

> [13]Now we do not want you to be ignorant, brothers, concerning those who are asleep, that you may not grieve as the rest who do not have hope. [14]For since we believe that Jesus died and rose again, so also through Jesus, God will bring with Him those who sleep. [15]For this we say to you by a word of the Lord, that we who are alive, who are left behind at the coming of the Lord will in no way precede those who sleep. [16]Because the Lord Himself with a command, with a voice of an archangel, and with a trumpet of God, will descend from heaven, and the dead in Christ will rise first, [17]then we who are alive, who are left behind, will be caught up together with them in the clouds to meet the Lord in the air; and thus we will always be with the Lord. [18]So, comfort one another with these words.

Paul's message to the Thessalonians is straightforward. First, the certainty of future bodily resurrection is dependent upon the resurrection of Jesus Christ. Second, at the coming of Jesus Christ he will be accompanied by saints who have already died. Third, when the Lord returns, those who have already died will be resurrected. Verses 14-16 give us a picture of those who are in the intermediate state – they will accompany Christ. Their bodies will be resurrected. Fourth, those who are still alive will be caught up in the air, transformed (implied from other passages such as 1 Cor. 15:25-58 [especially verses 50-54]) without passing through death, will meet Christ and the other saints in the air, return to the earth[16] and then later go on to heaven where they will be with the Lord for ever.

The New Testament is clear that the saint will be resurrected bodily at the coming of Christ. This will be a certainty and effected by the salvific work of Christ himself.

Why our resurrection is made possible by the resurrection of Christ

We have just established that the resurrection is a future reality. We have also seen that Christ's resurrection makes possible the believers' resurrection. In fact, Jesus himself affirmed, 'A little while longer and the world will see Me no more, but you will see Me. Because I live, you will live also' (John 14:19, NKJV). Yet the question we need to take up is this: how does the resurrection of Jesus Christ bring about the resurrection of saints? In order to answer that question, we will need some biblical background on sin and death.

The Scriptures are clear that all men are sinners (Romans 3:23); in fact, there has never been a man, other than Christ, who could, in any way, claim that he was without sin (Eccles. 7:20; 1 John 1:8). This is a state that man finds himself in from conception due to the fact that his federal head, Adam, sinned – a sin that was imputed to all men – and therefore, each person is separated from God (Ps. 51:5; Rom. 5:12; Isa. 59:2).[17] Man stands guilty because he is born in sin, and also because of the actual sins that proceed from this original sin. The Scriptures are equally clear that death is the result and wage of this sin (Gen. 2:17; Rom. 5:12; 6:23). Stemming from his just nature, God created a world in which he will not in any way allow the guilty to go unpunished (Exod. 34:7; Nah. 1:3). The just deserts of sin are death. The testimony of the Scriptures is that this demise includes physical death (Gen. 2:17, separation from the body), spiritual death (Prov. 14:12; Isa. 59:2, separation from God) and the second death (Rev. 20:14-15, the permanent state of spiritual death when not rectified by the time of physical death).[18] Though we can distinguish these different aspects of death, we cannot divide them – the Scriptures have a synthetic view of death that views all three aspects as a whole.[19]

What is more is that this whole of death is a state, a realm in which man lives where he is not only perishing (1 Cor. 1:18; 2 Cor. 2:14-16), but also is at enmity with God (Rom. 5:10). It is clear from several New Testament passages that it is a state in which men exist where they have no purpose and are estranged from their original intent, estranged from God and destined for eternal perdition. Consider: 'but now has been revealed through the appearing of our Savior Christ Jesus, who has both abolished death and brought to light life and immortality through the gospel' (2 Tim. 1:10). 'Death is the last enemy which will be abolished' (1 Cor. 15:26).[20] 'Inasmuch then as the children have partaken of flesh and blood, He Himself likewise shared in the same, that through death He might destroy him who had the power of death, that is, the devil, and release those who through fear of death were all their lifetime subject to bondage' (Heb. 2:14-14, NKJV). And finally: 'And death and Hades were thrown into the lake of fire. This is the second death, the lake of fire. And whoever was not found written in the book of life was thrown into the lake of fire' (Rev. 20:14-15).

Death is the opposite of both physical life and real vibrant, abundant existence – eternal life (Deut. 30:15; John 10:10; 2 Tim. 1:10). And it seems that this death, though not synonymous with sin (after all it is the result of sin), nevertheless is closely connected – to the point that the man without Christ could be described as existing in the realm or state of sin and death. Once mankind fell by sinning against God, both he and the rest of creation were twisted and subjected to futility (cf. Gen. 3:1-19; Rom. 8:18-22). In other words, sin brings about the process of death. From the very first spark of life, every living thing is in the process of dying (2 Cor. 4:16). Because man is separated from God and the world bears the effects of this sin, every person lives underneath the tyrant of sin and death. It marks all he does, his very existence – it is our captor that keeps us under lock and key.

Once we understand this, we are ready to see how the Bible clearly teaches that Christ, in his salvific work, has defeated sin

and death (along with their lord, Satan).[21] What this means is that
when a person is united to Christ along with his death, burial
and resurrection, the victory Christ has won is applied to him. As
such he is no longer under the dominion of sin and death. This
leads not only to spiritual life and vitality, but it also ultimately
results in victory over physical death, which is part of that entire
dominion – i.e., it leads to resurrection of the believer (cf. 1 Cor.
15:54-7).

One of the key texts in which this is taught is Paul's answer to
those Roman readers whom he knew would conclude that practising sin was not a big deal, if where sin abounds, grace superabounds
(cf. 5:20). In fact, it might even be good since God's grace would
be shown in a greater way. Paul repudiates such thinking. It is in
his response that we find how Christ's salvific work results in our
future bodily resurrection. The text is Romans 6:1-10 and reads:

> [1]What therefore shall we say? Should we remain
> in the sin, in order that the grace might increase?
> [2]May it never be! We who died to the sin, how
> shall we live in it? [3]Or do you not know that as
> many of us as were baptized into Christ Jesus, we
> were baptized into His death? [4]Therefore, we were
> buried with Him through baptism unto death, in
> order that just as Christ was raised out of the dead
> ones through the glory of the Father, so also we
> might walk in newness of life. [5]For since we have
> become united in the likeness of His death, cer-
> tainly we shall also be in reference to the resurrec-
> tion. [6]Knowing this, that our old man was cruci-
> fied with [Him] in order that the body of the sin
> might be destroyed so that we might no longer
> serve the sin; [7]for the one who died has been justi-
> fied from the sin. [8]Now since we died with Christ,
> we believe that also we shall live with Him, [9]be-
> cause [we] know that Christ, since He was raised
> out of the dead ones, He shall never die again;
> death no longer is master over Him. [10]For that

which He died, He died to the sin once for all;
but that which He lives, He lives unto God.

Verse 1 reflects the question Paul knows some will raise to accuse him of libertine doctrine. Paul's answer is his characteristic response whenever he calls attention to an absurd question that he knows his opponents are raising: 'May it never be!' In other words, 'Don't even think it, it is not possible!'

The specific question is something like this: 'Shall we continue or persist in the state or power of sin in such a way that we show we are dominated by it?' Paul is not asking whether or not we can sin at all. If we could not sin at all, his exhortations here would be unnecessary. He is asking whether or not we should continue in a state such that we are chiefly characterized by sin. His answer shows that such is absurd!

Why would some suggest continuance in the dominion of sin? 'In order that the grace might increase'. In other words, so that God's undeserved well-being, forgiveness and blessing might be shown more often and to a greater extent. If all God's salvation did was forgive sins, then this logic may be solid. Yet, Paul proceeds to show that there is more to the salvific work of God.

After telling the reader in no uncertain terms how absurd such a suggestion is, the apostle explains why such thinking or behaviour would be impossible. We must find out what it means that some died to the sin. First, it must be noted that 'the sin' is definite and locative of sphere. It is the realm of sin, the same spoken of in verse one. This is clear because Paul is not speaking of a mere sin as if we cannot sin at all. Such would be out of keeping with the context (cf. 6:12-14).[22]

About all those persons who died to the realm of sin dominance and power, Paul asks the question, 'How shall we still live in it?' The living denotes continuance and persistence (see v. 1). What Paul is saying is similar to a person who has quit smoking and can no longer stand to be around smoke – especially continually. He may occasionally visit a place where a smoker lives, but how can he go back there and live permanently himself? He can't, because he is a different person. So is also the Christian.

He is a new person and cannot go back and live as he once did. Such is impossible; if he is living that way, he is either temporarily inconsistent with who he is or he has not been changed in the first place.

Beginning in verse 3 and continuing on through verse 5, Paul explains this truth that we died to the sin. He clarifies that as many as were baptized into Christ Jesus were also baptized into his death. Baptism was an initiatory rite arising out of Judaism.[23] It showed 'immersion' into or identification with a person or faith. Baptism was a commonly recognized symbol of what truly had taken place in the person's life. Those baptized in water were truly and spiritually immersed into the person of Christ. As such they are in special intimate union with Christ – he in them and they in him.

For all of those of whom this is true, they also have been immersed into his death. In other words, they have been so identified with and united to Christ's death (since they are united to him), that his death becomes theirs. In other words, all that Christ accomplished upon the cross becomes theirs.

In verse 4 Paul states a conclusion or an inference. Since we were baptized into his death, we can conclude that we were buried with him. The logic seems to be that if we were baptized into Christ's death, then we must also participate in his burial. This is significant because Christ's death led to burial which led to resurrection. When Christ was raised from the dead never to die again he was glorified. He was transformed into a person in whom there was significant difference (although there was continuity between his new and old existence). He was raised to a new life. Since we are so united with Christ, we are also united to his resurrection and the subsequent newness of life.

In verse 4 Paul reveals, by way of analogy, the purpose of identification in Christ's death. We participate in Christ's resurrection also. As such, in the same way that Christ was raised to a new life, we participate in the death, burial and resurrection so that we might live in newness of life.

In verse 5 Paul states explicitly what he has only implied in verse 4: that we have been united to Christ's resurrection also. It is because we are united to his resurrection that we walk in new-ness of life. The future tense, 'we shall also be in reference to the resurrection', is probably a real future so that Paul has in mind the future resurrection. Yet it has impacted our life now so that presently we experience the resurrection power. In verses 6-10 Paul further explains how our union with Christ in his resurrection leads to newness of life. Verse 6 begins with a present active causal participle. The flow of thought is something like this. We have participated in the power of his resurrection, for we shall be united in the likeness of his resurrection. How is this true? We know the content of vv. 6ff. 'This' refers to what follows.

Paul says we know that our 'old man was crucified with Him'. The old man is the former person, the individual we used to be before coming to and being united with Christ. This fits with the context and also Pauline theology elsewhere (Eph. 4:22-24; Col. 3:8-10). This 'old man' 'was crucified with Him'. The aorist passive lets the reader know that this act took place in the past, it is completed and it was done by God. The point is that the person we used to be, before we knew Christ, was included in Christ's death upon the cross and so the death Christ died is now the death the old man died. This old man is the person who was chiefly characterized by the power of sin or sin dominance.

The main point of verse 6, however, is not that the old man was crucified with Christ. The main point is to reveal the purpose for which we were crucified with Christ: 'in order that the body of the sin might be destroyed'. 'The body' probably refers here to the whole old person as exemplified primarily in the body. The probable reason why Paul uses this phrase is because the body is that point at which sin is usually carried out or revealed. This is obviously not always true, but it is symbolic for the person enslaved to sin – whose body is often the outlet for his sin. This also fits with the context ('old man'). In essence 'the body of the sin' is another way of referring to 'the old man'.

The purpose of the old man's union in Christ's crucifixion is that the old person dominated by sin might be destroyed. The purpose is 'so that we might no longer serve the sin'. The context lets the reader know that the former time was prior to being justified and united in Christ. Prior to union with Christ, a person is enslaved to the realm and power of sin. This does not mean that anyone is forced to sin against their will. It does mean that the sin is the totality of their boundary of desires. It is all they know. As such, practising righteousness is not an option to them.

When the old man is crucified and the sinful body is destroyed, we become a new person whose desires are radically changed (John 3; Gal. 2:20). We can live by faith in God (Rom. 1:17; Gal. 2:20) and that faith (which must necessarily be a gift from God: Eph. 2:9) produces obedience (Rom. 1:5) and love (Gal. 5:6), which is the fulfilment of God's standards (Rom. 13:8-10). Paul's point here is that one of the key purposes of our being justified and united with Christ is to be transformed from people who characteristically sin to people who love and obey God.

Verse 7 gives the grounds or reason for why the person who has been crucified with Christ no longer has to serve sin. 'For the one who died has been justified (or acquitted) from the sin.' The action is that of a judge declaring the defendant not guilty. It is the act of God's free grace whereby the sinner is forgiven of his sins and received as righteous in the eyes of God, only because of the righteousness of Christ imputed unto him and received by faith alone.[24]

How does justification make possible freedom from the dominion and practise of sin? In two ways. First, when the penalty for sin is removed, the person can be reconciled to God (Eph. 2:16; Rom. 5:1). This makes possible the inward change by which the person is transformed and sanctified that he might live a new life (2 Peter 1:3-11; Titus 2:11-12). Second, the same faith which justifies the person also sanctifies him (Rom. 1:5, 17; Gal. 2:20; 5:6).[25] So, forensic justification does in fact lead to progressive sanctification.

The emphasis in verses 8-10 shifts from dying with Christ to the subsequent living with him. Paul writes, 'Now since we died with Christ, we believe that we shall also live with Him.' The point seems to be that in some way union in Christ's death necessarily leads to union in his resurrection. This can be true only if that union with Christ means union in his entire salvific work. And that is exactly what the context has been arguing. Christ was crucified, buried and raised from the dead. So, since we are united in his entire work, we too are crucified, buried and shall be raised with Him. Yet, the point is that future resurrection life has already bled into our present life and impacted the here and now so that we can already appropriate a new kind of living. Paul's point in verse 8 is that the whole salvific work is a 'package' which we experience in total, and that includes new life.

Elsewhere, in Ephesians 2, Paul clarifies that the future resurrection truly has impacted the present. He argues that we have been made alive together with Christ (2:5) and raised up with him (2:6). United to him we are also united to his resurrection. This new life we have been given, this conquering of sin and death, is what ultimately will result in our future bodily resurrection.

Because God is restoring fallen twisted man (in full) so that he can once again be a God-glorifier, we know that the man who, in Christ, has overcome the entire realm of sin and death will ultimately have his body resurrected and glorified. It is the logical and clearly-stated goal of redemption, as we have now seen multiple times from the Scriptures. Yet, what will physical transformation be like?

WHAT PHYSICAL TRANSFORMATION WILL BE LIKE

As we discovered in chapter two, our restoration to being God-glorifiers takes place in union with the perfect man, the second Adam, Jesus Christ. This is why we also learn that our future resurrection body will be like his.

Philippians 3:20-21

In this very personal epistle, Paul exhorts the Philippians to stand strong against false teachers – who, most probably, were Judaizers (3:1 – 4:1).[26] In the last paragraph of this discussion, the apostle calls the Philippians to follow his example and note those who walk according to the end of Jesus Christ (cf. 3:12-16); he then calls their attention to the reality that not all walk this way – some walk as enemies of the cross of Christ,[27] their bellies are their gods and they set their minds on earthly things – watch out for these. Why? He tells the reason for watching out for and distinguishing between those who walk according to Christ and those who follow fleshy desires and earthly things in verses 20-21:

> For our citizenship exists in heaven, from which also we eagerly await the Lord Jesus Christ, Who will transform our lowly body that it might be in conformity with His glorious body according to the working of Him who is able also to subdue all things to Himself.

Paul says that our citizenship (*politeuma*) is in heaven. The sense is probably that of 'capital or native city, which keeps the citizens on its registers'.[28] H. Bietenhard argues for this sense based upon the second half of the verse. Paul's point seems to be that we really belong to heaven; therefore, we ought to be looking to heaven for meaning, fulfilment, joy and contentment, rather than to this world as an end in and of itself. Not only do Christians belong to heaven, but we await eagerly the coming of Christ from heaven. That is our hope and focus. Why is this so? Because of what Christ will do at that time. This brings us to verse 21.

The first half of the verse tells the reader more about Jesus Christ who is coming and thus more about why we ought to have our eyes fixed upon that glorious day as our hope. First, Paul says that Jesus Christ will transform our lowly body. Note that Jesus Christ is said here to be the one who will change our body.[29] The predictive future, active, verb, *metaschematisei*, means 'change the form of, transform'.[30] Christ will thoroughly change our outward appearance, our body. More specifically, what Christ will change is 'our lowly body'. Though the changing of a Christian will not be confined to the physical, yet at the coming of Christ and the resurrection the focus will be transformation of the physical. This seems apparent from the standpoint that the already-departed saints will be transformed in spirit prior to this time. As such, *soma* has the meaning of physical body.

The phrase *tes tapeinoseos hemon* (lit. 'of our lowliness') refers to 'humility, humble station, humiliation as a state of being'.[31] It is used only three other times in the New Testament.[32] If the term here in Philippians 3:21 has a similar meaning to its other uses, it probably connotes the lesser state of the body in that it is more temporary and not perfect as the glorified body will be. The term calls 'attention to its weakness and susceptibility to persecution, disease, sinful appetites, and death'.[33] The present body has burdensome limitations and pain.[34] The glorified body will not.

The purpose for which Jesus Christ will change the form of our body is 'that it might be in conformity with His glorious body'. In other words, the purpose of future bodily transformation will be our likeness to Christ, which, as we have seen already in our study, is the purpose also of our spiritual transformation. It is reasonable to conclude that this is one more indication that our restoration to being God-glorifiers will not be complete until we are like Christ spiritually and bodily.

What exactly does Paul mean by 'glorious body' or 'body of glory'? Gary L. Nebeker's insightful answer is worth quoting at length:

> Paul states in 1 Corinthians 11:7 that man is 'the image and glory of God'. It is significant to note that Paul associates humankind's 'glory' with 'the image of God'. It would not go too far to say that Paul regards the 'glory' of humankind and the 'image' of God in humankind as one and the same...
>
> Paul regards the future restoration of [man's] fallen moral dignity (Rom. 5:2; 8:18, 21, 30) as something that begins with union with the exalted Christ, who is the giver of eschatological life through the Holy Spirit (1 Cor. 15:45; 2 Cor. 3:17) ... The present glory is consummated at the resurrection when the physical body is 'raised in glory' and 'raised in power' (1 Cor. 15:43).

> Eschatological 'glory' in Paul, then, is a mode of moral and physical perfection that believers possess and participate in with Christ. This glory is already and not-yet ... Paul's reference to the 'glory of the Lord' (2 Cor. 3:18) includes not only the divine moral integrity, power, and honor of the exalted Christ, but also apparently, his physical brilliance and form. When referring to that which Christ will one day share with believers, doxa ['glory'] consists of the inherent moral integrity, power, and honor of a person, as well as an implied semblance of physical effulgence or brilliance.[35]

So, we learn that the future resurrected body will be like the glorious resurrected body of Christ – no longer indwelt by sin and also expressing effulgence. It is likely that the transfiguration of Jesus (Matt. 17:1-12; Mark 9:1-13) gave a glimpse of what this future glory will be like.[36]

1 John 3:1-3

This is the other main text which makes clear that our future resurrection body will be like that of Christ's.[37] The apostle writes:

> [1]See how great a love the Father has given to us, in order that we should be called children of God, and we are. Because of this the world does not know us, because it did not know Him. [2]Beloved, now we are children of God, and it has not yet appeared what we will be. We know that when He appears, we will be like Him, because we will see Him as He is. [3]And everyone who has this hope purifies himself just as He is pure.

There are three truths that John adds to what Paul has already asserted in Philippians 3:20-21. First, since we are presently children of God and the world does not know him, they do not understand who we really are. The world often concludes that our lives are worthless (at best) and downright dangerous (at worst). The implication is that when Christ returns and we are transformed to be like him, our true identity and significance will be seen by all. And this will stem from our being like him.

Second, part of the reason we will be like Christ, according to John, flows out of the beatific vision: 'because we will see Him as He is'. John Calvin is most likely on target when he comments on this verse: 'For he does not tell us that we shall be like Him because we shall enjoy the sight of Him, but proves that we shall be partakers of the divine glory because, unless our nature were spiritual and endued with a heavenly and blessed immortality, it could never come so near to God.' As we saw in Matthew 5:8, it is only the pure in heart who will see God. Such an assertion, along with 1 John 3:2, suggests that bodily transformation is also a prerequisite for the beatific vision.

Third, John writes that this future hope of Christ-like transformation should impact the saint presently – namely, to purify himself. John Piper helps explain how this is so when he writes:

> When we apprehend the spiritual beauty or sweetness of what is promised, and delight in it, not only are we freed from the insecurity of greed and fear that motivate so much sin, but we are also shaped in our values by what we cherish in the promise ... If we cherish the beauty of Christ in the gospel we will cherish behavior – even painful sacrificial behavior – that reflects that beauty.[38]

If our body will be like Christ's we know we will be without sin and there will be glorious effulgence. Yet, what else can we say from those texts which give descriptions of Christ's resurrected body? Murray Harris gives us some interesting possibilities:

> Not only was Jesus restored to life. He rose to new life in a transformed body whose capacities

seemed to outstrip immeasurably a merely physical body. He could appear and disappear at will (Luke 24:31, 36); he could 'travel' from one place to another without visible means of locomotion (Luke 24:31, Emmaus; 24:36, Jerusalem); he could pass through solid objects such as the door or walls of a room (John 20:19, 26); on occasion there was a mysterious change in his outward appearance which prevented immediate recognition of him (Luke 24:16, 31); he could ascend into the sky (Luke 24:51). Resurrection involves both bodily reanimation and bodily transformation.[39]

Harris draws attention to the fact that the post-resurrection body of Christ did seem to be different than his usual pre-resurrection existence. This is not to suggest that his glorified body was not a physical or fleshly body. It is to suggest that there was transformation; his resurrection body exceeded the pre-resurrection body.

A good friend of mine has called attention to the reality that we must be careful with this argument. After all, there were times when Jesus exceeded normal physical activity prior to the resurrection. For example, he walked on water (14:22-33), he may have been able to disappear from a crowd without anyone seeing him (Luke 4:28-30), and he was transfigured into a supernatural glorious effulgence (Matt. 17:1ff.). In light of this, we do not want to conclude that the resurrection body of Jesus is less than a true fleshly body – as if it could not be flesh and accomplish some of the post-resurrection feats recorded in the Gospels. Yet, the thrust of the New Testament record does seem to indicate that even though the future glory of Jesus did occasionally bleed into his pre-resurrection existence, nevertheless, something changed substantially after his resurrection. Though he was in a fleshly body (demonstrated by the fact that he was touched [John 20:27; 1 John 1:1] and also that he ate [Luke 24:42-43; John 21:13-15]), none the less, the resurrected body did transcend the pre-resurrection body. J. A. Schep brought light upon this issue four decades ago when he wrote:

> Moreover, his resurrection-body, though a body of flesh, apparently had qualities different from the body of his humiliation. The Spirit, who raised him from the dead, endowed him with extraordinary power (Rom. 1:4). It is not correct to say that he was now beyond space and time, which again would be a denial of his humanity. But with K. H. Rengstorf ... we may say that he was not subject to the laws of space and time or dependent on nature, but above them. This power was not something entirely new, as appears in Mark 6:48ff., where we read of Jesus walking on the sea, and in all the other accounts of miracles as well. The new element is this, that after the resurrection 'this miraculous quality completely characterizes and determines Jesus' whole life and being' (Rengstorf).[40]

We cannot say more than what we have said about the resurrection body of Christ, since the Scriptures do not do so. What we know is that his body was fleshly, there was continuity (it was his body raised), and yet it superseded His pre-resurrection body.

This, however, is not the sum of what we can say about the future resurrection body of the saint.[41] There are other New Testament texts which give us some glimpses.

1 Corinthians 15:42-45

Having taken up an apologetic for bodily resurrection in 15:1-34, Paul turns to the issue of the nature of the resurrection body (which may address some of the objections which a few in Corinth had against resurrection) in verses 35-49. In verse 35 Paul raises a question he knows some are asking: 'But someone will say, "How are the dead raised? With what body do they come?"' The first part of his answer is found in verses 36-38 where he demonstrates from the analogy of a seed how the resurrection body can come from the pre-resurrection body and how also it can be different.

In verse 39 Paul moves to the subject of the differences in flesh between man, animals, birds and fish. His point is that if there can be these differences, then there can also be differences between the mortal, perishable body of the present age and the immortal, imperishable body of the age to come.

In verses 40-41 Paul draws a comparison between different bodies (formations on earth and in the sky) and then differences between the formations in the sky (sun, moon and stars), and even between stars themselves. His point is that God has created in such a way as to allow for differences in forms of creation bodies; why could he have not also used the same pattern in allowing for different kinds of bodies, thus allowing for resurrection bodies? Another interesting item is that in verse 41 Paul introduces the term doxa ('glory') to refer to the demonstration of beauty and honour with regards to the sun, moon and stars.

All in all, Paul has demonstrated that resurrection will take place and then added to his argument from other aspects of creation. Now, in verses 42-45 Paul zeroes in on the nature of the resurrection body itself. Here is what he writes:

> [42]So also is the resurrection of the dead ones. It is sown in perishability, it is raised in imperishability; [43.]it is sown in dishonor, it is raised in glory; it is sown in weakness, it is raised in power; [44.]it is sown a fleshly body, it is raised a spiritual body. If there is a fleshly body, there is also a spiritual. [45]So also it has been written, The first man, Adam, became a living being; the last Adam a life-giving spirit.

Paul uses four pairs of contrasting clauses to get across what the resurrected body will be like for the believer. First he says that 'it is sown in perishability, it is raised in imperishability'. The present body which dies and is buried is one that is subject to decay, it is mortal. Such is the sense of 'perishability' (*phthora*).[42] The future resurrection body, however, will not be subject to decay. It will not perish or die again. It will be 'raised in imperishability' (*aphtharsia*). Its capacities and abilities will not break down. In other words, it will be eternal (2 Cor. 5:1). Our body we now have is perishing; it is dying and running down throughout life. Age begins to bring pain, as well as slow down and weaken muscles. Bones become brittle. We can no longer run, jump and work as we used to in younger days. Eventually memory begins to lag. All of these can incapacitate and take away from the enjoyment of living, not to mention diminish our zest for others. Yet, in the age to come we will be given a body that will never run down. It will no longer be subject to the realm of sin and death![43]

In the second contrast (v. 43) Paul affirms: 'it is sown in dishonor (*atimia*), it is raised in glory' (*doxa*). In context, the dishonour does not directly have to do with whether or not God is honoured. The dishonour is the state in which the body dies and is buried. Paul acknowledges what we all see in death. Often in death the weakness of the human body is exposed for others to see. The body is hurt to the point of death or it dies from the failures of old age. Either way it is shown to have great limitations. And, as a corpse placed in the ground, it is nothing but an empty shell. What can it perform or accomplish to bring any sense of honour? Nothing. There is nothing in that body to draw a sense of praise or awe. Yet, when the body is raised it is in the state of glory. If understood in light of how the term is used in verse 40, what Paul is saying is that the body itself emits beauty and strength. Nothing is wrong with it – it is perfect. As such, it brings honour and accolade to the person (and to God, as we have seen elsewhere). The focus is not upon the vindication of the believer or even a significant place in heaven. Rather, it is upon the body itself being honoured. The body will be like Christ's. It will emit a radiance of his glory; it will resound with the honour and image of God that represents and resembles him, bringing him great glory in how he is completely restored each saint.

Third, we find that 'it is sown in weakness (*astheneia*), it is raised in power (*dynamei*)'. 'Weakness' connotes physical ailments and frailty that is often associated with life and aging.[44] We can see that there is a great deal of overlap between the pairs of contrasting clauses. The weaknesses are what make the body perishable and often lead to dishonour. The present body is often full of disabilities – spinal cord injuries, failing organs, lost hearing or blurring eyesight. Even when death takes place in youth the weakness of the body is highlighted and certainly the state in which it is buried is marked by weakness. Yet, when raised it is in the state of power. Never-ending life, vitality, ability and power in the body are all descriptions of what the resurrected saint will be like. The future transformed body will be a channel for enjoyment and accomplishment without breaking down and without death!

Finally Paul says in verse 44 that 'it is sown a natural body (*soma psychikon*), it is raised a spiritual body (*soma pneumatikon*)'. There are three reasons why we must conclude that Paul is not affirming that the believer's resurrection body will be somehow non-fleshly or non-material. First, the ending upon *pneumatikon* (i.e. *ikos/ikon*) gives the term a functional or ethical meaning. As such, it is preferable to understand *pneumatikon* to mean 'animated and guided by the spirit, with the spirit as the organizing or governing principle'.[45] Paul is most likely speaking of man's spirit which is completely and perfectly revitalized and directed by the Spirit of God.[46]

The second line of evidence which leads to this conclusion comes from the immediate context. In verse 45 Paul focuses upon the contrast between the first and last Adam. The first Adam, after God breathed into him the breath of life, became a living soul (*psychen*, i.e. a living being, Gen. 2:7). In contrast, the second Adam, Christ, did not only became a living being or man; he became more – 'a life giving spirit' (*pneuma*). Just as 'soul' in this text does not signify the first Adam's constitution or state, so also 'spirit' does not signify the state of Jesus as resurrected. It has more to do with the fact that as the victor over sin and death he received the gift of the Spirit and gave this to men (cf. Eph. 4:7ff.). As such, he not only was alive as was Adam, but he also gave life – through his Spirit. This emphasis upon true spiritual life should colour how we take 'spiritual' in verse 44. The 'spiritual body' is one marked by life and the regenerating work of the Spirit of Christ upon man's spirit.

Likewise, in verse 47 we read that 'the first man was from the earth, a man of dust, the second man is from heaven'. As Paul continues the contrast between Adam and Christ, he focuses upon their main origin: earth versus heaven. Verses 48-49 demonstrate that those who are under each one's headship are like the head: 'As was the man of dust, so also are those who are of the dust, and as is the man of heaven, so also are those who are of heaven. Just as we have borne the image of the man of dust, we shall also bear the image of the man of heaven' (ESV). We see in these verses that the ultimate goal of the saint is to be like Christ, to be a man chiefly characterized by heaven – remade in his image. This thrust strongly suggests that the 'spiritual body' of verses 44 and 46 has nothing to do with the substance of the body. It has everything to do with the direction, guiding force (spirit) and origin (from heaven). It is a body that will be like Christ's, guided by the Spirit-empowered spirit in full, chiefly characterized by the heavenly and perfect in its obedience and holiness!

The third and final line of evidence that supports our understanding of *pneumatikon* in verse 44 comes from the larger context of the Scriptures. In 2 Corinthians 5:1 we read: 'For we know that if our earthly house, this tent is destroyed, we have a building from God, a house not made with hands, eternal in the heavens' (NKJV). The term *acheiropoieton* ('not made with hands') approaches something close to a technical term for that which is directly from God without human agency at all (Mark 14:58; Col. 2:11). This is not to suggest that the converse (the body made with hands) is created by man. It is to suggest, however, that the future resurrection body will be from God alone without human agency. And thus, it will be different. It will be eternal. Such a view of the future resurrection body coincides with what Paul says in 1 Corinthians 15:44ff. The spiritual body will be fashioned by God directly without the human agency, sin, pain or death that have been passed down to all people since Adam and Eve. In such a future transformed body the saint will be able perfectly to 'present [his] members to God as instruments for righteousness' (Rom. 6:13).

Before leaving 1 Corinthians 15 we need to say something about verse 50: 'Now I say this, brothers, that flesh and blood is not able to inherit the kingdom of God, nor does perishability inherit imperishability.' The first part of the verse might make it sound as if a body of flesh cannot inherit the kingdom of God. Some think this might necessitate some kind of spiritual substance that is not in any way fleshly. If this were the case, we might conclude that our above explanation of the 'spiritual body' in verse 44 is not correct. J. A. Schep, however, offers the correct understanding of 'flesh and blood':

> The expression 'flesh and blood' occurs in four other passages in the New Testament, viz. Matthew 16:17; Galatians 1:16; Ephesians 6:12; and Hebrews 2:14. In the latter two passages it is used with inversion. The words form a single conception ... a Semitic word pair.
>
> In all the passages just mentioned, it is obvious from the context that 'flesh and blood' does not denote the substance of the human body. When Jesus says to Peter after his confession (Matt. 16:17), 'Blessed are thou, Simon Bar-Jonah: for flesh and blood hath not revealed it unto thee...' Jesus cannot possibly have thought that the substance of flesh and blood give a man any revelation. Reading the expression 'flesh and blood' within the context of the other passages leads to the same conclusion: the substance of the human body is not meant.
>
> E. Schwizer shows that the expression belongs to the Rabbinic vocabulary. The Rabbis never used it for the flesh-substance or for the human body ... 'Flesh and blood' always denoted the whole man with all his functions, with particular emphasis on man's earthly condition as a frail

and perishable created, in contrast to the eternal
and almighty God.[47]

The point that Paul is making in verse 50, then, is merely that
man in his natural state cannot inherit the kingdom of God. He
must first be transformed. 'Flesh and blood' is parallel to 'perishability'. This is supported by the fact that Paul goes on in verse 51
to affirm: 'Behold I tell you a mystery: we all will not sleep, but
we all will be changed'.

Revelation 21:4

The penultimate chapter in the Scriptures tells of the future eternal dwelling of saints, the 'new heaven' and 'new earth'. That John
describes this place in the way he does (i.e. 'the holy city' and
'new Jerusalem') communicates that this is the ultimate dwelling
of God with man, the fulfilment of the covenant. From a comparison of Revelation 21:3 with a couple of Old Testament passages,
we can see that this is the ultimate fulfilment of God's covenant
with his people. Consider:[48] 'And I heard a loud voice from the
throne saying, "Behold, the dwelling place of God is with man.
He will dwell with them, and they will be his people, and God
himself will be with them as their God"' (Rev. 21:3). 'And I will
establish my covenant between me and you and your offspring after you throughout their generations for an everlasting covenant,
to be God to you and to your offspring after you' (Gen. 17:7). 'I
will make my dwelling among you, and my soul shall not abhor
you' (Lev. 26:11).[49]

Of that time in the future dwelling with God, John writes in
verse 4: 'And He will wipe away every tear from their eyes, and
death will be no more, nor will there be grief, crying, or pain because the former things passed away.' John unveils that the realm
and curse of death will be no more. As such, man's body will not
perish, decay or weaken. Likewise, there will be no sin. This means
that grief, crying and tears will be a thing of the past. John says,
'the old world and its evils are gone forever' (NLT).[50] Since all this
is true, there will also be no more pain (*ponos*). The only other

times this term is used in Revelation (16:10, 11), it refers to physical anguish and suffering. We also see the same sense in the LXX of Genesis 24:25 and Isaiah 53:4.

If the future body is pain-free, eternal and imperishable, as well as characterized by glory and power (as we saw in 1 Cor. 15 and 2 Cor. 5:1), then this necessitates that the body is perfect. It supersedes the present body as much as a lavish building supersedes a mere tent (2 Cor. 5:1). Blindness, deafness, lame legs, lost limbs and disease will all be things of the past. Every disability will be overcome in that day! And, as we see elsewhere, this does not have to do merely with arms, legs and eyes. It also has to do with the mind.

Psalm 16:11; 1 Corinthians 2:9-10; 13:12; 1 John 3:2; Revelation 22:3-4

There are a number of statements in the Scriptures that necessitate that those who are impaired mentally will also be restored by God. After all, if every saint will experience a fulness and completeness of joy as well as delight in eternal pleasures (Ps. 16:11), if the things of heaven surpass the things of this life that often boggle the best of minds (1 Cor. 2:9-10), if we will have a greater ability to know and understand (1 Cor. 13:12), if we will delight in the sight, awareness and intimacy of our Lord (1 John 3:2; Rev. 22:4) and if we will serve our God (Rev. 22:3), then there is a necessity that each saint's mind will be greatly enhanced and perfected. For the one who is united to Christ, yet challenged by a low intelligence quotient, the saint who spent the last years on this earth struggling with Alzheimer's, or whatever the mental debilitation – every person's mind will be renewed!

Does this mean that we will know all things once we are in eternity? Does this mean that we will not learn? The answer to both questions is 'No!' Even with a perfected human mind we will not know all things. To know all things would mean that we are equal with God. We will never have that capacity. Yet, we can be assured that what we do know will be true and accurate, and our capacity for knowledge and understanding will by far dwarf the greatest minds that ever lived. These future minds will not be twisted by sin, which means their ability to reason and draw unbiased conclusions in keeping with who God is and his universe will be perfect. Though perfected, we will be learning for eternity. If we will experience pleasures eternally (Ps. 16:11), as well as delight in the demonstration of God's grace riches throughout that future age (Eph. 2:7), this necessitates that we will be educated continually.

Luke 20:35

We need to look at this one last passage with regards to the nature of the future physical transformation because so many have alleged that it has reference to what the resurrection body will be like. In this paragraph, Luke 20:27-40,[51] Jesus is approached by Sadducees (who did not believe in resurrection).[52] They sought to entangle Jesus in a question he could not answer regarding this doctrine they opposed. The scenario they offered involved a married man who died, leaving behind his wife and no children. According to Old Testament laws his unmarried brother was to marry the wife and the first descendant would belong to the deceased (Deut. 25:5-10). The Sadducees suggested that this brother also dies childless and then five more brothers marry the wife in succession – also because of the death of an older brother. The question is this (Luke 20:33): 'Therefore in the resurrection whose wife will she become, for the seven had her as a wife?'

The Sadducees were showing how unthinkable they thought the doctrine of resurrection was. After all, this scenario was not completely outlandish. Perhaps it would be rare to find a situation in which seven brothers would be involved, but what about two or three? This would not be all that unusual. The use of seven brothers seems intended merely to heighten the potentially absurd conundrum.

In these situations, wondered this sect, how would it be decided in the age to come which husband would have the wife? Underlying their question was also the assumption on the part of those who did believe in resurrection in Jesus' day that the age to come would vary little from the present age. The Pharisees pictured the future life as a mere continuation of this life. According to the Rabbis 'the world to come would not differ essentially from the present, but only be more beautiful and glorious, with greater fertility, etc'.[53] As such, the thought would be that men and women who were married in this life would be married in the next.

Jesus counters with the answer that 'the sons of this age marry and are given in marriage; but those considered worthy to attain that age and the resurrection of the dead neither marry nor are given in marriage'[54] (verses 34-35). This last clause, '[they] neither marry nor are given in marriage' (*oute gamousin oute gamizontai*), the key statement for our present purpose, is found in all three of the synoptic accounts. The text goes on to say in verse 36 'for they are not able to die any more for they are angel-like (*sangeloi*)[55] and are sons of God, being sons of the resurrection'.

Some have averred that Jesus is implying that in the resurrection body we will be neither male nor female – or even more, that we will be non-corporeal beings like the angels. However, neither conclusion is demanded by what Jesus says. Luke gives insight into Jesus' meaning with the explanatory comment in verse 36.[56] The way in which we will be like angels and not marry is that we will be eternal. We will be sons of God and the resurrection who will never die again. There will be no reason for the preservation of mankind at that point since all will be eternal. What this leaves room for is that we can still be male and female in the age to come; however, we will not be engaged in marital relationships.

This does not mean that we will not recognize our spouse, nor enjoy him or her. We should note that Moses and Elijah were readily recognized by Peter on the mount of transfiguration (and this was even without resurrection bodies). See Matthew 17:3-4. This certainly makes it most probable that we will recognize others in eternity. We will recognize our spouse and, in light of all we have said regarding spiritual and physical transformation, we will love him or her and enjoy him or her with a relationship that far surpasses the delight we know now. But more, we will have that capacity for all persons. The love, unity, compassion and companionship shared from saint to saint will be far greater than even the greatest marriage relationship known now. For this reason, marriage will not be needed and yet our relational fulfilment will be far more complete and intense.

So, we find out that even though men and women (who will still be men and women for eternity) will not be married in the new heaven and earth, the New Jerusalem; nevertheless, this will in no way detract from our joy and delight. We can only conclude that we will enjoy our spouse (along with all other saints) in a much greater way – and there will be no hint of jealousy, unholiness or conflict!

We have asserted throughout this section that the future resurrection body will be the same body resurrected, yet it will also be significantly different. How can this be? Joni Eareckson Tada gives us an illustration to show how this is possible:

> Have you ever seen those nature specials on public television? The ones where they put the camera up against a glass to show a dry, old lima bean in the soil? Through time-lapse photography, you watch it shrivel, turn brown, and die. Then, miraculously, the dead shell of that little bean splits open and a tiny lima leg-like root sprouts out. The old bean is shoved aside against the dirt as the little green plant swells. The lima plant came to life because the old bean died.
>
> Not even a Ph.D. in Botany can explain how life comes out of death, even in something so simple as a seed. But one thing is for sure: it's a lima bean plant. Not a bush of roses or a bunch of bananas ... So it is with the resurrection body.[57]

Some might ask, 'How can God resurrect a body that has long since been returned to dust and its particles mixed with so many other living things?' Again Tada brings insight:

> And what about [a person's] dust and ashes scattered to the winds? How many of [their] mol-

ecules are required to be reassembled before he can be raised? Very little, I suspect. I once read that if all the DNA were collected from the five billion or so persons now inhabiting the earth, it would approximate the size of two five-grain aspirin tablets. The 'who' you are and the 'who' I am is not that big. It's actually very small (From Robert L. Sassone, THE TINIEST HUMANS [Stafford, Va.: American Life League, 1995], viii).

God will not have to use every part of your body in order to resurrect it. Anyway, you do not possess today any particle of your body that you had a few years ago. We learn in Biology 101 that human cells are being replaced every three and one-half years. The flesh and blood that make up 'you' today is not the same flesh and blood you had in your teens. Yet, somehow, the particular person that you are carries on.[58]

WHY THIS PHYSICAL TRANSFORMATION IS SO SIGNIFICANT

Again, we have waded through a lot of exegesis and theology in this chapter to lay a foundation for understanding that aspect of glorification which we have labelled physical transformation. Such study is necessary, but in some ways it is only preliminary for what we really want to do: delight in God, worship him and be changed by these truths. Let me explain.

As I write this chapter, our daughter is preparing to fly on a plane for the first time. She has been planning for weeks – making sure she can take final exams early and working out arrangements with her friend's family (with whom she is flying). What's more, there will be an hour-long trip to the airport, check-in, waiting to board, hearing the last-minute instructions from attendants and then finally – they will taxi away from the gate. The anticipation will build as the pilot positions them on the runway, then takes off quickly, picking up speed. Finally, she will feel the sensation of the plane coming off the ground and ascending into the air. For two and a half hours, from Denver to San Diego, she will delight in the sights of land and clouds below, along with what is happening on the plane. As most of us can attest, she will never forget that first flight.

With no less importance than buying tickets, mechanics going over last minute checks, attendants preparing for the flight, trips to airports, baggage check-in and seat-belt instructions, we have studied the biblical teaching on future physical transformation. What we are about to do is take off into the clouds of exultation over our certain future physical transformation. Enjoy the flight!

Future significance

Within some books, movies, television shows and commercials the future eternal dwelling of saints has been made to look about as inviting as sitting in the principal's office all day is to a young boy. Ethereal beings living among the clouds surrounded by harps smacks of boredom, lack of purpose and absence of true delight. Yet, the reality of future bodily resurrection reminds us that our eternal home is not as other-worldly as we may have thought. We will have bodies and live in a new heaven and earth. Though we might rightly assume that not all the language regarding heaven in the Scriptures is to be taken literally, none the less there are a lot of physical descriptions which sound a great deal like life now. It does lead us to believe that, though eternal life will be different than life now, there will be similarity. We will have bodies and landscape and relationships, and we will work and serve God. It is encouraging to know that we will live – and not just live, but will be fulfilled beyond comprehension.

And what is more, we will be resurrected with perfect bodies which will be flawless media for abundant life. No longer will we wrestle with sinful desires that call out to us to serve self and dishonour God. No longer will weariness and fatigue form the environment in which we choose to 'snap' at those we love.

Think of how glorious it will be for the quadriplegics to run, jump and be free of their physical prison! And what about the band director who had to quit his job due to multiple sclerosis? What delight he will have in making music in heaven! Think of the farm wife who suffered from rheumatoid arthritis for forty years before succumbing to a heart attack. What joy when she can run her straight fingers through the soil and embrace her Saviour and others whom she loves – all without pain! Can you imagine the missionary who was forced to leave the field with stenosis of the spine that robbed the use of his legs? Think of the delight he will experience in serving his Lord with unhindered ability. How about the woman who entered the fog of Alzheimer's ten years before she left this world? She was diminished from a vibrant loving deaconess to a helpless child-like resident at a nursing home who didn't even know her family. What joy to leave the fog, to have all her faculties restored and to be reunited with the sons, daughters and husband who lost her amidst such grief!

Each of us, as we age, can probably come up with our own scenario that will bring great delight. For me the physical delight will entail being able to run again, a joy that I have lost due to back problems. For you it may be something even more profound. Yet, all of us will experience the joy of the future resurrected body.

And think of how, as children, we used to delight in parents who gave us a special gift. We enjoyed the present, but it also brought us closer to the giver. The same will be true with that future change. We will enjoy and delight and revel in our new body and surroundings, and yet these will cause such intense love for our Saviour that he will be our ultimate rapture. Certainly, the greatest joy will be our ability, as complete human beings, to serve our God who has redeemed us and rescued us from the realm of sin and death. Think of how wonderful it will be to have the capacity to worship God without daydreaming or numb hearts, and to really praise him with a depth unimaginable.

What is more, we will be able to use our abilities and gifts to the fullest – with no impairment whatsoever. We will design, create, build, decorate, perform and play in such a way that we will dwarf the best architects, engineers, poets, painters and athletes that this world has produced – and all that is done will bring greatest eternal significance – glorifying God.

Think of life lived in the realm of God's glory and holiness: No war, conflict, poverty, anguish, killing, jealousy or racial division. All will worship God in perfect unity, ministering to one another without divisions over music style, needs not being met or someone being overlooked!

Never again will we be deceived. Our minds, though not omniscient, will be able to receive and process information such that we will not be led astray. We will be able to come to the right, the best, the fullest and the most helpful conclusions always. Depression will be a thing of the past. We will always remember who we are in Christ – delighting in the praise of the Father! With this will come the utmost security. Never again will we be lonely; nor will we feel overwhelmed with people – such that we are 'burned out'.

For all eternity we will experience one perfect, fulfilling, loving and God-honouring relationship after another – and never have to say 'Goodbye', yet never have these friendships grow stale. In our greatest relationship we will learn more and more about the grace and love of our God – and what he has done for us.

Word-crafters, far more capable than I, can do a better job of capturing some sense of what it will be like to be physically transformed. Yet, even at best, words fail to do justice. At some point we must merely stop and with Paul pray that 'the eyes of your understanding being enlightened; that you may know what is the hope of His calling, what are the riches of the glory of His inheritance in the saints, and what is the exceeding greatness of His power toward us who believe...' (Eph. 1:18-19, NKJV).

Present significance

It is not surprising that something as extraordinary as future bodily resurrection and physical transformation has strong impact upon life now. Peter captures this in 1 Peter 1:3-9 when he writes:

> [3]Blessed be the God and Father of our Lord Jesus Christ, the one who, according to His great mercy, caused us to be born again unto a living

hope through the resurrection of Jesus Christ from the dead, [4]unto an inheritance imperishable and undefiled and unfading, [which] has been kept in heaven for you [5]those who are guarded by the power of God through faith unto salvation ready to be revealed in the last time. [6]In this you greatly rejoice, even though now for a little while, if necessary, you have been grieved by various trials, [7]in order that the tested genuineness of your faith, more precious than gold that perishes, though tested through fire, may be found unto praise and glory and honor at the revelation of Jesus Christ. [8]Though you have not seen Him, you love [Him], though not seeing Him now, yet believing in Him, yet you greatly rejoice with joy inexpressible and glorious, [9]receiving as the outcome of your faith the salvation of your souls.

First, we find out from Peter that one of the results of God causing us to be born again is that we have a certainty about our future imperishable, undefiled, unfading and divinely-preserved inheritance that invigorates us. Our hope, focused upon Jesus Christ (Col. 1:27), is strong when we keep in mind the future that God has awaiting us. We don't have to wonder about our destination.

Second, Peter reminds us that in light of such certainty we also know that God is presently preserving us through faith for that future complete salvation. Hence, we have security.

Third, Peter reminds us of a point that Paul implied in 1 Corinthians 15:12-18 – namely that the future resurrection brings meaning and value to our present life and its suffering. The suffering helps us to become more like Christ and brings great reward to us and glory to God in the eschaton. Yet, if there is no resurrection, then those who die have perished. Yet, such is not the case.

Finally, Peter echoes Paul's words in 1 Corinthians 15:58 where the latter wrote: 'Therefore, my beloved brothers, be steadfast, immovable, always abounding in the work of the Lord, knowing that in the Lord your labor is not in vain' (ESV). The service that we render for the Lord, no matter how difficult, will not be empty or in vain in light of the resurrection.

In addition to what Peter writes in his epistle, we have three other strong implications for the present. First, if physical transformation will play such a large part in the eschaton, we are reminded that the physical is not unimportant in this life also. God has shown that he values not only the non-material, but also the material. That brings an importance to this life and our cultural mandate that Christians often forget.[59] N.T. Wright calls the resurrection a 'creation-affirming doctrine' and avers that 'it goes with the desire to change injustice in the present'.[60]

Second, we also have the assurance that the future complete victory over the realm of sin and death has bled into this life such that we are able to overcome sin now. In other words, we no longer have to operate as people who must be totally defeated by sin.

Finally, we do not have to fear death. This last enemy of ours has been defeated (1 Cor. 15:26) and its sting removed (1 Cor. 15:54-57). Adrian Dielman helps us understand this great benefit with the following true story.

> A boy and his father were driving down a country road on a beautiful spring afternoon, when a bumblebee flew in the car window. The little boy, who was allergic to bee stings, was petrified. The father quickly reached out, grabbed the bee, squeezed it in his hand, and then released it. The boy grew frantic as it buzzed by him. Once again the father reached out his hand, but this time he pointed to his palm. There stuck in his skin was the stinger of the bee. 'Do you see this?' he asked. 'You don't need to be afraid anymore. I've taken the sting for you.'
>
> We do not need to fear death anymore. Christ has died and risen again. He has taken the sting from death.[61]

Something else which arises from our physical transformation (as implied in 1 John 3:2) is that our reputation will be transformed as well. What is meant by this and what is involved? To this we turn in the next chapter.

Chapter 6

REPUTATIONAL TRANSFORMATION

In the comedy 'Shanghai Noon', Chon Wang, a nineteenth century Chinese imperial guard (played by Jackie Chan) teams up with cowboy Roy O'Bannon (Owen Wilson) to save the kidnapped Chinese princess Pei Pei. The princess has such standing in the Chinese culture that the imperial guard is not even to look upon her. Yet, once she is brought to the west, she is forced to work along side other Chinese who have come to the land of opportunity only to be forced into extending the railroad system as slaves.

None of the wearied Chinese know who is working beside them. After all, she is now wearing the clothes of a common person. Yet, in one memorable scene the young royal helps out an elderly woman who was falling under the weight of the rock she was carrying. As Princess Pei Pei gets on her knees to help the aged worker, the latter bows with her face to the ground and then reveals, 'I know who you are'. The kidnapped princess asks her not to tell anyone else her identity. It would cause too many problems.

That scene is a reminder of how the Christian lives in this world. We are citizens of another world – heaven (Phil. 3:20). Because we do not belong to the world, the world often hates us (John 15:18-19), or at the very least, does not understand who we really are (1 John 3:1-2). A Christian's humility is taken as a lack of assertiveness, our faith in God is taken as a mere crutch, our commitment to family is often out-of-step, our evangelism is socially unacceptable and our ethical convictions are seen as the forcing of morality upon others. Many will conclude that our lives are a waste. Though princes and princesses in the kingdom of God, we are taken as lowly insignificant slaves to some kind of religion at best, and dangerous to society at worst. The cover story in the February 2002 Atlantic Monthly asserted that the present concern over Islam is overblown since 'the big "problem cult" of the twenty-first century will be Christianity'.[a]

Yet, the doctrine of glorification reminds us that this is not the way it will always be. Someday it will be revealed who Christians truly are. In the future coming of Christ and subsequent judgement, the world will no longer look upon saints as the scum of the world, those to be pitied or as a threat. They will envy the church. To put it succinctly, the reputation of saints will be transformed. Let's see how this is so.

MAN HAS AN INTERNAL DESIRE FOR GLORY

We saw in chapter one that God has given man a desire to achieve and to make his life count. Were it not so, the promises that God makes to man that he will honour and reward him would have little impact. The prayer and expectation by the victorious Deborah was that the ones who love God will be 'like the sun when it comes out in its full strength' (Judges 5:31). I am convinced that this is a God-given desire that can only be fully realized when we find significance and achievement in our Lord for his glory.

This hunger makes the Christian long for justice in the world. Even though many saints are content to labour along for the glory of Christ whether recognized in this world or not, they long for the full recognition of his pleasure and for the world to see things as they really are. One of the best illustrations of this is found in Revelation 6:9-11. Consider:

> [9]When he opened the fifth seal, I saw under the altar the souls of those who had been slain for the word of God and for the witness they had borne. [10]They cried out with a loud voice, 'O Sovereign Lord, holy and true, how long before you will judge and avenge our blood on those who dwell on the earth?' [11]Then they were each given a white robe and told to rest a little longer, until the number of their fellow servants and their brothers should be complete, who were to be killed as they themselves had been (ESV).

GOD HAS PROMISED GLORY IN SALVATION HISTORY

Throughout history God has worked with his people in such a way that he has given them a foretaste of this future reputational transformation. In Psalm 20 the Old Testament congregation requests victory from God for the king as he prepares for battle. In Psalm 21 David praises God for that victory in response. Listen to some of the assertions made:[b] 'The king shall have joy in Your strength ... You have given him his heart's desire ... For You meet him with the blessings of goodness; You set a crown of pure gold upon his head ... His glory is great in Your salvation; honor and majesty You have placed upon him. For You have made him most blessed forever ... Your hand will find all Your enemies...' Here we see a common subject in the Psalter, that is, the king of Israel. He is the representative of the people and as God blesses him and gives him victory, the people also are blessed and have victory (cf.

2 Sam. 5:12; 1 Chr. 14:2). Likewise, God often promised, both in this life (especially to Israel) and in the life to come (Ps. 73:17-28), that he would show who his people really are, bless them and give them victory.

Part of this promise dealt with honouring them and removing shame. Consider promises of future restoration that God made to Judah through Isaiah: 'Do not fear, for you will not be ashamed; neither be disgraced, for you will not be put to shame; for you will forget the shame of your youth, and will not remember the reproach of your widowhood anymore' (Isa. 54:4, NKJV). In Isaiah 55:5 he puts it this way: 'Surely you shall call a nation you do not know, and nations who do not know you shall run to you. Because of the LORD your God, and the Holy One of Israel; for He has glorified you' (NKJV). Then in Isaiah 61:5-7 the prophet clarifies that shame will be removed and honour take its place:

> [5]Strangers shall stand and tend your flocks; foreigners shall be your plowmen and vinedressers; [6]but you shall be called the priests of the Lord; they shall speak of you as the ministers of our God; you shall eat the wealth of the nations, and in their glory you shall boast. [7]Instead of your shame there shall be a double portion; instead of dishonor they shall rejoice in their lot; therefore in their land they shall possess a double portion; they shall have everlasting joy (ESV).

This can be seen even more clearly as we understand that when Judah was underneath the disciplinary hand of God and the temple had been destroyed, it was the opposite of honour. They had a shameful reputation. Psalm 79:4 reads, 'We have become a reproach to our neighbors, a mocking and derision to those around us.'

Even later in Judah's history (late 600's, some hundred years after the prophesies of Isaiah), Zephaniah also warned God's people of coming destruction due to their sin. Like his predecessor, he also proclaimed the hope of restoration. This restoration would include the remnant of Judah eventually feeding their flocks upon the pastures of the Philistines (2:7), plundering and possessing Moab and Ammon (2:9), as well as God's defeat of Egypt and Assyria (2:12-15).

Part of God's covenantal promises to his people included their blessing – not the least of which was displaying to the world who they really were and how he had benefited them. Since God often dealt with more this-world concrete blessings in that era in order to teach principles that stood behind his ultimate promises for them and us (cf. Rom. 15:4; 1 Cor. 10:6; Heb. 11:13-16), we are not surprised that God often worked with Israel such that he transformed their reputation here and now. Likewise, if we understand the salvation historical shift from the Old to New Covenant era we ought not to be surprised that God does not promise the New Testament church such transformation in this life, but only in the life to come. Consider Jesus' words to his disciples recorded in Mark 10:29-31:

> Jesus said, 'Truly I say to you, there is no one who has left house or brothers or sisters or mother or father or children or fields on account of Me and on account of the gospel, who will not receive a hundredfold now and in this time – houses and brothers and sisters and mothers and children and fields, with persecutions – and in the age to come eternal life. Now many who are first will be last and the last first.'

Clearly there will be a turning upside-down of the order of things in the age to come. Those who were thought to be the losers in this life, the scum of the earth, the ones who suffered for nothing – these saints will be rewarded and honoured in the age to come. Though last here and often losing much, they will be first then and gaining all!^c

WHAT IS INVOLVED IN THE FUTURE TRANSFORMATION OF MAN'S REPUTATION

Yet, it remains to be seen: What does this aspect of future glorification entail? It will mainly involve three future blessings.

God's praise

In Romans 2 Paul is addressing primarily the Jewish readers in Rome to make sure they are convinced that neither their nationality nor their circumcision will save them. As he ends the chapter, he avers that true Jewishness and circumcision are matters of the spirit and heart, not outward or physical affairs. As he makes this point he also includes an important statement for our subject at hand (v. 29): 'But he is a Jew who is one in secret, and circumcision is of the heart in Spirit not by the letter, the praise is not from men but from God.'

Paul implicitly chides those readers who may have fallen back into the tendency to do things so that others would pay homage to and reward them. Those who have found true Judaism, those who have true circumcision and those who truly know God will be praised from God. In other words, the very Creator of the universe, the all-powerful, eternal God will openly affirm the right and good and true lives of saints. Paul intimates that this is what will be most important to believers – rather than man's recognition.

To gain the full impact of this praise from God we must understand something about judgement first. The biblical teaching seems to be that Christ's judgement of the regenerate and unregenerate (cf. Acts 10:42; 17:31; 2 Tim. 4:1; 1 Peter 4:5) will be known to all. Saints will see the justice in the judgement of the unregenerate (Ps. 58:10-11; Rev. 16:5-7; 19:1-5), but the unregenerate will also be aware of the acknowledgment of the regenerate. On this last point the Apostle John writes (1 John 3:1-2): 'See what kind of love the Father has given to us, that we should be called children of God; and so we are. The reason why the world does not know us is that it did not know him. Beloved, we are God's children now, and what we will be has not yet appeared; but we know that when he appears we will be like him, because we shall see him as he is' (ESV). The strong suggestion is that the world does not know and understand fully the significance of the saint now, but they will at the appearing of Christ. If we have understood correctly the biblical teaching upon glorification, one of the main purposes that all will be aware of this future judgement is that men and angels might see God's glory in the restoration and perfection of the saint. Such will highlight the 'riches of His glory' (Rom. 9:23).

Now that we have been reminded of this, the words of Jesus in Matthew 25:21, 23 (the strongest example of future divine praise) take on new significance. In this parable of the talents Jesus is driving home the need to be faithful stewards of that with which our Lord has entrusted us, in preparation for his coming. In the parable those servants who were faithful and industrious while their master was gone were praised by him upon his return, with these words: 'Well done good and faithful servant, you were faithful over a few things, I will put you in charge over many things; enter into the joy of your lord.' The implication by Jesus seems to be that Christians will some day hear similar words from our Saviour.

If this is true, then understand, believer, that we will have the absolute delight of hearing Jesus Christ himself acknowledge our life. For all our years we have had this great longing for who we are and what we do to count, to mean something. When we hear this public appreciation from the King of kings will we not have a satisfaction that exceeds what we can know in this life?

There is also more. We will be rewarded with great responsibility in his eternal kingdom. There will be no boredom in the life to come for any saint. It will be known for eternity that Tom Barnes, for example, is serving where he is and exercising the responsibility and authority he does because of his life in the former age. Of course, it will also be known that all this was dependent fully upon God's grace which will bring him glory for the glory upon each saint. Just think, though – we will experience honour that will not have even a hint of self-service, selfishness or unholiness. It will be fully enjoyed because of our full and rich love for our triune God. His glory will be our chief end at every moment. That God-given desire for honour that has often created in us an insatiable hunger will be always and forever fulfilled with the sweet ecstasy of knowing that it is ultimately for him and has no taint of sin. Is there anything that will exemplify any more that finally we are truly living as man was originally intended?

Please do not miss that we also see that in this praise there will be great joy. Much of our reward, honour and delight will be found in him. It will come from him as a result of his bringing everything to light and then praising us (1 Cor. 4:5).

Each one of us has had at least a handful of people through the years whose opinion of us has really mattered. Though the brief appreciation by a stranger or mere acquaintance might be gratifying, it does not measure up to the words of acceptance and praise that come from that beloved parent or cherished mentor. Truly the status in one's eyes of the person distributing the accolades heightens the value. Yet, imagine being the recipient of the praise of the very God of the universe! To receive a medal of honour from a king or a national leader would pale in comparison. To stand upon the top step at the Olympics and hear one's own national anthem played will be child's play compared to standing before God's tribunal. To be considered by the world at the top of one's field will seem as mere rubbish when one hears the words, 'Well done, good and faithful servant'!

God's reward

The remaining two treasures of reputational transformation left to discuss flow out of and, in many ways, overlap with God's praise. Paul unearths one of the remaining valuables when he shares with the Ephesians an ongoing prayer request for them: that 'the eyes of your heart, having been enlightened you might know ... what are the riches of the glory of His inheritance in the saints' (Eph. 1:18). Paul's progression of thought in his prayer is something like this: he prays that God would enable his readers, through the work of the Spirit upon their spirit, to grasp an awareness of and the significance of a true intimate knowledge of God (1:17). When this happens, then the seat of the person's intellect, will, affections and emotions will be enlightened (similar to the eyes letting in light and information for the body to respond to different situations). His desire is that as this happens, the readers will know the fantastic treasures which are part of the glorious future reward that comes from God and is found only among saints. This future reward or inheritance is that which God has promised and which will be the blessed future and eternal portion of the believer (cf. Eph. 1:14; Col. 1:12; 3:25; Matt. 19:29; Acts 20:32; Rev. 21:7).

The specific content of the inheritance involves: eternal life in the kingdom of God (Matt. 5:5; 19:29; 25:34; Mark 10:17; 1 Cor. 6:9-10; Eph. 5:5; Titus 3:7;1 Peter 1:4), the promises (Heb. 6:12, 17; James 2:5 [promise = kingdom]), blessing (1 Peter 3:9), spiritual perfection (Heb. 12:23), physical perfection (1 Cor. 15:20-58), praise and acknowledgement from God (Matt. 25:23; Rom. 2:29) and the joy of being in God's presence for eternity (Ps. 16:11; 1 Thess. 4:17-18).

How does God's reward relate to the future transformation of the saint's reputation? It is simple. Let's imagine for a moment that we are taking a tour through Washington D.C. and we come upon a large mansion with a limousine, sports car, large acreage and Olympic-size pool. We also notice a man coming out of the house with medals on the front of his jacket and there is a plaque at the gate leading up the driveway with the presidential seal on it. We ask the tour guide, 'Who lives there?' 'Oh, that is John Smith, a former secret service agent', she responds. 'He saved the president's life on numerous occasions. Upon his retirement and in recognition for his valour and faithful service, the president awarded him with this house and all you see.'

In that scenario the rewards would also serve to highlight the service and true identity of the individual. Though he worked faithfully in obscurity for years, now the world would know who he truly is and how important his labour proved to be. This is how the believer's crowns of victory and rewards will highlight his service and faithfulness. And, of course, it will be fully understood that the works rewarded were made possible by God's grace alone.

As such, the one ultimately honoured for the accomplishments will be the Giver of the future prizes – God himself.

Recognition of full identity and significance

The final blessing which is part of the future transformation of the saint's reputation has already been discovered and discussed. Yet, we do want to highlight it to make sure it is not lost in the discussion. As the saints are praised by God and rewarded for faithful service, it will be fully recognized who they are and how significant their lives on this earth were. As we saw above, the world now does not know who we really are, nor does it understand the full weight of our earthly years. Yet, in the age to come those who were last here shall be first and those who were unknown and thought to be insignificant will take centre stage. (1 John 3:2; Mark 10:31).

This recognition will not only happen in the judgement, but it will also take place when Christ comes. In Colossians 3:3-4 Paul, while he offers two reasons why Christians ought to focus their attention and trust upon all the resources we have in Christ rather than self, things or other people (3:1-2, in light of the preceding context), he affirms this truth.

The first reason for focusing our attention he offers is: 'you died' (3:3a). Each Christian can say that the old person he used to be is gone. The person who could not please God, who could not in any full way obey God, whose good works were as filthy leprous rags – that person is history. As such the new person ('since you were raised up with Christ', Col. 3:1) is able, through Christ in him, to live a new life (Gal. 2:20) which consists of a new and holy manner of living (Col. 3:12ff.). So, because each of us is a new person, we have all the resources and ability we need in order to trust in Christ's resources and to know that he is the true source of all we have, are and will be.

The second reason Paul offers is the one that pertains to our discussion at hand: 'your life has been hidden with Christ in God' (3:3b). In context 'your life' refers to the new life we have in Christ (cf. 3:1a; 3:4a ['when Christ who is our life is revealed']). The apostle asserts that this new way of existence has been and continues to be concealed with Christ in God. In other words, it is usually not outwardly evident who we truly are, how we have been changed and what is the significance of our life. Though there are outward manifestations, and yes, our changed life can and ought to be noticed by others (cf. Matt. 5:16; John 13:34-35; Gal. 5:22-23), nevertheless, a large part of the change, identity and weight remain unseen. The world is unable to see the importance of Christ and his work (1 Cor. 2:14). Even Christians cannot fully grasp the glorious nature of his undertaking in us and how this will someday be unveiled (1 Cor. 2:9).

This is also another way of saying that the resources and importance found in our new life that we have in union with Christ do not consist mainly of food, clothing, how much is in our bank account, whether or not we are affirmed by the world, who our friends are or what job we have. Instead, the core is who we are in Christ, what he has done in us, and how all this does impact us now and in the future. And all of this exists in the realm where God chiefly works his greatest works – the unseen. In no way is Paul arguing that the physical and the seen is not important or somehow is beneath God. After all, we have seen throughout this study, especially when it comes to resurrection and physical transformation, that the physical is very important to God and very much a focus of redemptive history. Paul is merely distinguishing between the two realms and teaching that meaning is given to seen and unseen starting with what is taking place in us regarding the work of Christ. So, don't trust in or seek after other things in and of themselves. Instead, make your primary focus the work and resources of Christ.

Once Paul has made this argument in verse 3, he senses the need not to leave the reader hanging with this truth of our new life being hidden with Christ in God. He knows that it will not always be this way. Therefore, in verse 4 he affirms: 'When Christ who is our life is revealed, at that time you also will be revealed with Him in glory.' Paul affirms that when Christ, who is the source of our true and vital existence, is shown openly at his coming, at that same time, we also will be shown openly with him in the state of glory. In other words, at Christ's appearing we as saints shall be openly acknowledged. Though our full true existence is not evident, it will be at that time.

Contrary to Paul arguing that somehow our present life is not significant, what he is writing actually gives it more significance. To the pastor who is faithfully labouring in a ministry in which he is not appreciated now (in fact, some may think it is a waste), the apostle says that someday it will be clear how the fruit produced by the Spirit in his life was influential for eternal matters. To the mom who, seemingly all alone, works day in and day out to love, nurture and train her children in spite of a husband who no longer cares about her or their sons and daughters, the promise is that someday she and others will see how her life was the effect of Christ's work in her and for his glory. And to the middle-aged man who wonders if all his efforts in his congregation, at home and the office (as unspectacular as they may be) are really all that important, Paul assures him that one day his prayers, faithfulness to his wife and love for those children down the street he picked up for church will all serve as a neon advertisement for God's glorious grace.

THE ULTIMATE GOAL OF MAN'S FUTURE REPUTATIONAL TRANSFORMATION

This brings us to the goal of our future reputational transformation. We don't have to assume what this goal is or make some kind of educated guess, for God tells us clearly what it is. As the prophet Isaiah describes a coming eternal day of restoration and reward for the people of God, he records the Lord's words (60:19-21, NASB):

> [19]No longer will you have the sun for light by day,
> nor for brightness will the moon give you light;
> but you will have the LORD for an everlasting
> light, and your God for your glory. [20]Your sun will
> no longer set, nor will your moon wane; for you
> will have the LORD for an everlasting light, and

the days of your mourning will be over. [21]Then all
your people will be righteous; they will possess
the land forever, the branch of My planting, the
work of My hands, that I may be glorified.

Even a casual reading of this text shows that its focus is the
age to come (compare vv. 19-20 with Revelation 21:4; 22:5). At
that time, our covenant God, who will eternally be in an intimate
relationship with us, will be our 'glory' (*tiph'arah*). In other words,
he will be to us as a beautiful garment or crown that displays
our greatness, rank, honour and who we really are.[d] Our glory in
the new heaven and earth will be from God's very presence with
and work in us. Isaiah goes on to say of that time, literally, 'and
your people, all of them, will be righteous'. The wording suggests
that all saints will be perfectly righteous in position and practice.
Such suggests the spiritual perfection of which we discovered in
the fourth chapter. The clause, 'They will possess the land forever',
is a way of showing that the Old Testament land promise has its
ultimate fulfilment in the eternal New Jerusalem, the new heaven
and earth. These perfected saints who will have eternal life in that
land will be the branch of God's planting, the work of his hands.
In other words, it will be clear that they exist and are perfect, all
because of what God has done.

Now, why will all of this be as it is? The final clause in verse 21
reveals this: 'that I may be glorified' (*t'hitpa'er*). This verbal form
of the noun we saw in verse 19 means 'get glory to oneself, be
glorified', or 'to show the beauty of'.[e] Saints will be perfected, recognized, and highlighted so that God himself might be glorified.
God desires that all might see just how great, powerful, magnificent and gracious he truly is. Nothing will do this any more than
his transformed, redeemed saints in their full eternal reward.

Truly, we will not only obtain God's prizes, but we will be his
prizes. We will not only receive his crowns of victory, but we will
also be his crowns of victory. Oh, reader, I cannot do justice to the
joy and delight we shall find in this our last and eternal purpose.
With nothing held back, no sin, pain, inability, numbness of heart
and mind or misery to divert our task, we will fully and richly

carry out the purpose for which we were initially created. With fulfilment beyond our wildest dreams we will be the instruments of God. We shall significantly serve the King of kings and the Lord of lords, knowing all the time that nothing could be more lasting or more important.

Yet, even more than this, we will revel in displaying the beauty of our great Lover. From the time that my wife, Karen, and I met, I have delighted in her beauty, companionship and everything about her. I have treasured her as a glorious gift from God. Nothing has brought me greater joy than to meet someone for the first time and to introduce her as my wife. I love to acknowledge her positive traits. I love to please her. I am hopelessly in love with her. No other explanation needs to be given as to why I enjoy honouring her – I love her. Now, take that kind of love, that kind of delight in another, and multiply it a hundredfold, a thousand-fold – then and only then will we begin to grasp what our delight and joy in God will be like. Nothing will excite us more than to lift up, cherish and honour, the Lover of all lovers!

Christian, I hope the image of this coming day causes your heart to flutter and to skip a beat. I pray that it moves you to joy and tears, and washes over you like a refreshing shower after a hard, dirty and sweaty day of labour. Such is our future inheritance!

Yet, believe it or not, there is more. Yes, we will be spiritually and physically perfected. Yes, our reputation will be transformed such that we can reflect back to our Lover of all lover's honour and glory. But, we must understand that all of this will ultimately and for eternity take place in a transformed environment – the New Jerusalem, the new heaven and earth. Such becomes the last focus of our future glorification in the final chapter.

Ye saints, who here in patience your cross and suff'rings bore, shall live and reign forever, when sorrow is no more: around the throne of glory the Lamb ye shall behold, in triumph cast before him your diadems of gold.

-Laurentius Laurenti, 'Rejoice, All Ye Believers', Trinity Hymnal, 320

Chapter 7

ENVIRONMENTAL TRANSFORMATION

RECENTLY OUR CHURCH SENT OUT A POSTCARD to homes in our town that featured a picture of a toddler in a highchair who had dumped a bowl of spaghetti on his head. The pasta and sauce were dripping down his face and onto the tray. He was crying. The image reminded me of similar scenarios when our three children were that age and not only ate their food, but also wore it. When it came time for clean up, the messy tray would have to be taken away before little hands, arms, and faces were washed. The reason? Because if you did not, then the freshly washed appendages would be right back into the food. Not only must the child, clothes and bib be washed, but the surroundings also had to be changed, if the job was to be complete.

So it is with God's work of glorifying the believer. It would do little good to perfect the soul, body and reputation, only to throw the cleansed child of God back into a morally soiled setting. If glorification is to be complete, the environment also must be transformed. This is why the doctrine of glorification also encompasses the metamorphosis of the heavens and earth. Others agree. 'Part of the glorification of man will be the provision of a perfect environment in which to dwell.'[1] 'The doctrine of glorification is no small or narrow subject. It encompasses not only the final and complete transformation of believers, but also of the cosmos.'[2]

This future transformed environment is often referred to as heaven. The passage which teaches us about it with the greatest detail is Revelation 21-22. We will employ these last two chapters of the Bible to describe what God has awaiting the glorified church.

THE SETTING: REVELATION 21:1-4

One summer I received a call from one of our neighbours who was upset because her bed-ridden mother was terrified at the imminency of her own death. The neighbour asked if I would go by the nursing home and help comfort the aged woman. I assured her that I would be happy to go. After talking about what it means to know Jesus Christ as Saviour and to have the full assurance that our destiny is set through trusting him alone for eternal life, I sat holding the hand of this dying precious soul and it hit me that one of the things she needed to focus on is what God has awaiting those who belong to him. She needed to know that her diabetes-pounded, failing body would one day be replaced with one lacking any pain or illness.

Yet, she also needed to be reminded of what the destination is like for those who are in Christ. After all, it is hard to look forward to a trip when we know little, if anything, about the destination – or if we know something, yet the destination is not pleasant. Think about the difference between the woman sitting on a bus making her way to the state penitentiary and the woman who, after departing from a plane, is now sitting on a bus that is taking her to a weekend getaway at a ski resort in the mountains of Colorado!

Jesus Christ comforted his disciples during the Last Supper with the reality that he was going to prepare a place for them – a place that would enable them to be with him again some day (John 14:1-3). Yet, if this place is to inspire comfort and strength, we must know something about it.

The Apostle John gives us such knowledge. His opening words in Revelation 21, 'And I saw a new heaven and a new earth' (v. 1) let us know that what we have in Revelation 21-22 is a vision that he received of the future state.[3]

We need to be clear about what John is affirming, for we are often rather fuzzy about what the future eternal state will be. The popular thought is that somehow we will be ushered into an altogether other place or 'world' called heaven – the same heaven without change that is now in existence and the abode of those saints who have already died.[4] Yet, notice that John saw a 'new heaven and a new earth' (emphasis added).[5] In some way the future heaven will be 'new' and it will be coupled with 'a new earth'. It seems most probable that heaven and earth will become one in light of the later context in which this future abode is all referred to as 'the holy city, New Jerusalem' (21:2, 10). In other words, it will all be the special place of God's more realized presence.[6] Before we consider what John means by 'new', we need to be clear about both 'heaven' and 'earth'.

The terms 'heaven' and 'earth' are often used together to refer to all of God's creation (e.g. Gen. 1:1; Exod. 20:4; 1 Kings 8:27; Jer. 32:17; 51:48) in that, generally speaking, 'heaven' and 'earth' were viewed as the two main parts of the entire creation (cf. 2 Sam. 18:9).

The word 'heaven' could be used to refer to that which was above the earth or above man. More specifically, it had three references: the atmospheric space or sky immediately above us (Gen. 27:39; Deut. 11:17; 33:13; Hag. 1:10), the stellar heavens consisting of the sun, moon and stars, i.e. outer space or the rest of the universe (Gen. 1:14; Pss. 19:1; 33:6) and the heaven of heavens, the abode of God (Isa. 63:15; 2 Cor. 12:2).[7]

It is the third use of 'heaven' that most interests us because this seems to be the sphere which the seer deals with in these chapters. Heaven is not only the present abode of perfected disembodied saints who have already died (Heb. 12:23), but it is also the special dwelling of God (cf. Matt. 6:9). Yet, what do we mean by this latter assertion? John MacArthur is helpful:

> Someone inevitably asks, If God is omnipresent, how can Scripture say heaven is His habitation? ... 1 Kings 8:27. It is certainly true to say that 'the heaven and heaven of heavens' cannot contain God. He is omnipresent. There is no realm to which His presence does not reach ... Ps. 139:8.
>
> So to say that God dwells in heaven is not to say that He is contained there. But it is uniquely His home, His center of operations, His command post. It is the place where His throne resides. And it is where the most perfect worship of Him occurs. It is in that sense that we say heaven is His dwelling-place.[8]

Though John uses the term 'heaven' (*ouranos*) in Revelation to refer to the skies or universe above (cf. 6:13; 11:6; 12:1, 3, 4; 15:1), the vast majority of his uses refer to the heaven of heavens or God's special dwelling (cf. 3:12; 4:1, 2; 8:1; 10:1, 4, 8; 11:12, et al). When John uses 'heaven' and 'earth' together he has a tendency to refer primarily to the abode of God, angels and departed saints, along with the abode of man in this life (cf. 5:3, 13).

So, what John saw was a new creation from the ground that we stand upon (the earth) to the skies, outer space and even the dwelling of God which we commonly refer to as heaven. And, his main focus most likely was the transformation of the present existence of man (earth) and the special dwelling of God and departed saints (heaven of heavens).

The reality that John saw a new heaven and a new earth was necessitated by the fact that 'the first heaven and the first earth had passed away'.[9] This raises a question: Will God totally destroy the earth and heavens as we now know them before creating *ex nihilo* a new heaven and earth? Or will he drastically renovate the present heaven and earth?

There is nothing in this clause which necessitates that the present heaven and earth will be completely destroyed and that God will remake heaven and earth from scratch. In fact, in Revelation 21:4 John writes, 'The first things passed away' and refers to death, sorrow, crying and pain. His point is that man is transformed physically and spiritually and placed in a transformed environment. As such these things no longer will exist. There is renewal and redemption, not destruction and recreation. So, God will remake this world, rather than destroy it and make an altogether other one.[10]

Those texts which are often interpreted to say that the world will be totally destroyed (and thus necessitate an altogether different world) do not require such an understanding (see 2 Peter 3:10ff.; Isa. 34:4; 64:1-4; Matt. 24:29f.; Rev. 6:14; 20:11). Revelation 20:11 is one of those texts: 'And I saw a great white throne and the one who sat upon it, from whose face the earth and the heavens fled and there was no place found for them.' Regarding 20:11 Ladd writes:

> This statement undoubtedly involves poetic imagery; in the face of the glory and grandeur of the presence of God, the natural universe flees away. But it is more than poetry; it is the expression of an important theological truth. This statement takes us back to the first anticipation of the end at the opening of the sixth seal (6:12ff.). This describes a great cosmic convulsion when the sun became black, the moon became like blood, the stars fell, the sky vanished, and the mountains were shaken ... This announcement of the end is now fulfilled in the statement of our passage.
>
> Behind such statements is a profound theology. Earth was created to be the dwelling place of a man, and man as a creature of God stands

in solidarity with the rest of creation. Therefore, the created world is pictured as sharing the results of man's sin, finding itself in bondage to decay, groaning and travailing until now (Rom. 8:19-22). The old order is a fallen order, laboring under the curse of man's rebellion. Therefore, before the new redeemed order can be inaugurated, God's judgment must fall upon the old order; but this judgment is not one of destruction but the prelude to re-creation. This motif of the judgment of nature and the new creation runs throughout the Old Testament prophets and is pictured with great variety of detail, but always with the same basic motif ... Isa. 11:6-9 ... 65:17 ... 65:6.[11]

Returning to Revelation 21:1, we are served well by considering the words of R. C. Sproul:

Interpreters are divided ... Some view the passing away of the original creation as an act of divine judgment on a fallen world. The old order is destroyed, annihilated by God's fury. Then the old is replaced by a new act of creation. Out of nothing God brings forth the new order.

A second view of the matter, and the one that I favor, is that the new order involves not a new creation out of nothing, but rather renovation of the old order. Its newness is marked by the work of God's redemption. The Scripture often speaks of the entire creation awaiting the final act of redemption. To destroy something completely and to replace it with something utterly new is not an act of redemption. To redeem something is to save that which is in imminent danger of being lost. The renovation may be radical. It may in-

volve a violent conflagration of purging, but the
purifying act ultimately redeems rather than an-
nihilates.[12]

I think the clearest evidence that the heaven and earth will be
restored and not first annihilated and then created anew comes
from Romans 8:19-22. In these four verses Paul uses the creation's
patient waiting for its renewal as an example for the Christian of
how he ought to wait for his future glory. The language in these
four verses strongly favours the understanding that God shall renovate the present world without completely destroying it.

Paul writes that 'the creation itself will be set free from the
slavery which results from corruption unto the freedom which results from the glory which belongs to the children of God' (Rom.
8:21). This is the same creation that is groaning together (v. 22)
and waiting eagerly for the complete revealing of the sons of God
in the future (v. 20) since the creation's renewal will be at that
time. Paul's main point in the personification of the creation is
that the creation awaits transformation. We must follow its example of patient waiting and expectation. This language would
hardly make sense if the creation was to be destroyed and replaced
with an altogether different one.

So, what John sees in verse 1 is that in the future God will make
all of creation (heaven and earth) the special dwelling for himself
and saints and that this will be a renewed, redeemed place.

The vision emphasizes the importance of both the heavenly
and earthly aspects of the future dwelling when it is affirmed,
'there is no longer any sea'. The fact that the sea or ocean is commented upon at all reminds the reader of the continuity with the
present earthly existence. There will be land and water – the things
of this world – as opposed to some ethereal eternal dwelling in the
clouds.[13] The heavenly aspect is also driven home in the truth
that there will be no sea, for the ocean in the mind of the ancient
person represented danger and chaos.[14] In the book of Revelation
it is out of the sea that the beast had arisen (13:1, 6-7). Osborne

calls attention to the link between the sea and 'Death and Hades' in the judgement of Revelation 20:11-15 and then lists five uses of the concept in Revelation:

> The origin of evil (12:18; 13:1); (2) the nations that persecute the saints (12:18; 13:1; 17:1-6); (3) the place of the dead (20:13); (4) the location of the world's idolatrous trade activity (18:10-19); and (5) a body of water, part of this world (5:13; 7:1-4; 8:8-9; 10:2, 5-6, 8; 14:7; 16:3) ... All five are related to this, but it is likely that the first two predominate. The sea as a symbol of evil would best explain why it is added here.[15]

This eternal state for the saint will be a place where there is no danger, no chaos and nothing to fear. As we will see later on, it will be a place of perfect security.

After John envisioned a new heaven and earth, he also saw in verse 2 a New Jerusalem coming down out of the heaven from God.[16] Jerusalem, from the days of King David, has been the place where God dwelt in a more realized fashion among his people. It is known as 'the holy city' because of the temple and God's special presence – it is set apart as his special dwelling (Isa. 52:1).

Evidently, what John saw was not heaven and earth becoming one without distinction. Though the context suggests that heaven and earth have both become the special dwelling of God, he implies that, in a sense, heaven was still something that can be distinguished from the earth, for he saw the new Jerusalem coming down from heaven. Yet, the overall sense seems to be that all becomes the dwelling of God and his saints – what we popularly call heaven. So he sees the new heaven and earth put in place, and then he sees a new city, the dwelling of God, emerging out of the new heaven coming down to the new earth. George Eldon Ladd adds:

> The New Testament conceives of a heavenly Jerusalem as the dwelling place of God, the true

homeland of the saints, and the dwelling place of 'the spirits of just men made perfect' (Heb. 12:22; see Gal. 4:26; Phil. 3:20). While this heavenly Jerusalem is represented as the dwelling place of the departed saints, heaven is not their ultimate destiny, but only the temporary abode of the saints between death and the resurrection (Rev. 6:9-11; 2 Cor. 5:8; Phil. 1:25). In the consummation after the resurrection (20:4), the heavenly Jerusalem will descend from heaven and take up its permanent location in the new earth.[17]

The mixing of images most likely is portraying that the true tabernacle, heaven or special dwelling of God will take its place upon earth and then encompass all of man's existence. This is also supported elsewhere in the New Testament. The author of Hebrews writes in Hebrews 13:14 that 'we seek the one [i.e. the city] to come'. This city is synonymous here with the homeland or eternal rest which God's people seek (cf. 4:1ff.; 11:14).

The fact that it has been adorned like a bride for her husband brings to mind its beauty. It also alludes to the fact that it is the dwelling of Christ's bride (cf. 19:6-10). This bride consists of the Old and New covenant people of God (cf. 21:12-14). Again Ladd's comments are helpful:

> One wonders if John means to identify the heavenly Jerusalem with God's redeemed people, even as the church is likened to the temple of God in the New Testament (1 Cor. 3:16; Eph. 2:21). If so, the details of the description of the holy city are altogether symbolic terms in describing the redeemed church. In any case, it is at this point that the marriage supper of the Lamb takes place, as the next verse shows.[18]

Verse 3 leaves little doubt what the vision is communicating. God will be with his people in the fullest sense. Jerusalem had always been the physical representation of the fact that God dwelt with his people. The temple was the type of the reality in heaven (cf. Heb. 8:5; 9:1-11). Yet now, affirms the seer, God's perfect dwelling and covenantal presence will be with man for ever. Note what John writes: 'And I heard a loud voice from the throne saying, "Behold the dwelling of God is with men, and He will dwell with them, and they will be His peoples, and God Himself will be with them."' Let's look more closely at this glorious verse.

John heard a voice at this point and it was speaking from the throne. A throne has not been introduced previously in this vision. However, 'the throne' must refer back to Revelation 20:11 and the 'great white throne'. From God's throne the apostle hears a voice. The voice, which most probably comes from God (cf. v. 5), explains the new heaven and earth, along with the New Jerusalem. God has made his dwelling with man; man will belong to him and he will be with them. This is rich with covenantal terminology. (See Lev. 26:11-12; Jer. 31:33; Ezek. 37:27; Hag. 1:12; Zech. 8:8; Zech. 2:19; 8:3). God's presence with man and man's belonging to God is a great part of what God has promised through the ages. God's covenant with man will, forever more, be complete and fulfilled.[19] The text clarifies that God is fulfilling his covenant in its entirety. This is the culmination of all God's promises and of salvation history.

This future dwelling of God with man represents the final progression in the salvation historical drama. God first dwelt with his people through the tabernacle and later through the temple. Then, with the coming of Christ, he dwelt with them through Christ (John 1:14) and later on in the indwelling of the Spirit among the church, his temple (Eph. 2:22). Yet this presence of God among his people has been caught only by faith (2 Cor. 5:17). Yet, 'in the consummation, all this is changed; faith will be changed to sight, and "they shall see his face" (22:4)'.[20]

The New Jerusalem will be, in a sense, all temple, tabernacle and church. The entire place will be the special realized, immediate presence of God.[21] This is foreshadowed in the promises made in Isaiah 4:5-6. Consider the words of the prophet as he speaks about the restoration of Zion: 'Then the Lord will create over the whole site of Mount Zion and over her assemblies a cloud by day, and smoke and the shining of a flaming fire by night; for over all the glory there will be a canopy. There will be a booth for shade by day from the heat, and for a refuge and a shelter from the storm and rain' (Isa. 4:5-6, ESV).

Ezekiel 48:35 also is helpful as it foreshadows what the New Jerusalem will mainly be – the presence of God with man: 'The circumference of the city shall be 18,000 cubits. And the name of the city from that time on shall be, The Lord is there' (ESV).[22]

Since God will be present with his people in the fullest sense we should not be surprised that existence for the saint will be completely transformed. Verse 4 drives home the magnificent and comforting benefits of such a changed environment: 'And He will wipe away every tear from their eyes, and death will be no more, nor grief, nor crying, nor will there be pain any more; because the first things have passed away.' Concerning this promise, Osborne writes:

> There is a major contrast between [*kainos* (new)] and [*protos* (first)] ... with [the former] emphasiz-ing more qualitative newness than temporal new-ness ... There will be a whole new reality, a new kind of existence in which all the negatives of the 'first' (Gen. [3]) world will be removed, all the discoloration by sin will be gone.[23]

All of these great blessings were promises made in the Old Testament – to God's covenantal people regarding future restora-tion (See Isa. 25:8; 35:10; 65:19. See also 1 Cor. 15:26, 54-55). Specifically, John reveals that there will be no tears which rep-resent sadness – there will be no sadness because there will be no sin, nothing to separate us from God. There will be no more separation from God or from self (death). Pain will be gone. The reason is that 'the first things have passed away'. The first things most probably refer to the first order of things – the ways of the world as we know them now, the effects of the fall.

Since we now know that God will transform man physically and spiritually and will transform his reputation and environment, we will not be surprised to find out that there is nothing left to cause pain, tears or death.

So, all of existence becomes the realized dwelling of God and the glorious abode of the saint. As such, God will dwell with man as he hasn't since before the fall. Pain and death will be removed.

THE SIGNIFICANCE: REVELATION 21:5-8

After introducing the new heaven and the new earth, God clarifies to John just how significant this future transformation is. He does this in three ways.

First, God reminds John what this future is all about. 'Behold, I am making all things new.' This is not simply the heavenly abode of the glorified church of all times. It is the culmination of God's redemptive work. Not only will he have redeemed a large portion of mankind, but he will have redeemed creation. This will show with a final exclamation point that God's intention from the very beginning of history was not to allow sin and evil to have the final say. His purpose was not merely to throw away his creation due to sin. It was to reclaim it. At this point all will know that the cosmos has been saved from the claws of sin, death and evil.

Similarly, making all things new will finally fulfil a decree God gave to man. In the beginning God commanded man, 'Be fruitful and multiply; fill the earth and subdue it; have dominion over the fish of the sea, over the birds of the air, and over every living thing that moves on the earth' (Gen. 1:28, NKJV). This cultural mandate, as it is commonly labelled, called man to stewardship of the entire earth, to oversee it and keep it orderly. Sin has marred man's work in this area. With the new earth, however, the cultural mandate will finally be realized in full.

Second, the significance of this transformation is emphasized by the exhortation at the end of verse 5. The king of the universe ('the one sitting upon the throne') commands the apostle: 'Write, because these words are faithful and true.' In other words, what God is revealing to John regarding the future consummation can be trusted to come to pass. God who always keeps his word, who always speaks the truth and who is sovereign and able to bring about his will such that the events he purposes can be spoken of as existing even before they are created (cf. Rev. 4:11), can be counted upon to bring about this future heaven and earth. As such they are to be inscripturated that generations to come can read of what the future will be.

The certainty of this future environmental transformation is further driven home in verse 6: 'And He said to me, "These things have been done! I am the Alpha and the Omega, the beginning, and the end."' God who is the beginning and end of all things (just like Alpha and Omega are the start and finish of the Greek alphabet), i.e. he started all things and will bring them to his desired finish, can say to John that these things are as sure as if they had already taken place. Should we doubt the certainty of this ultimate stage of glorification? Absolutely not! It will be the finale of God's salvation history.

Finally, the significance of what John is seeing is unveiled in the implied eternally distinguishing character of the new heaven and earth. If, as we have seen, tears, death, sorrow, crying, pain and yes, even sin, will be absent from therein (v. 4), the unregenerate, unjustified, unsanctified and unglorified must also be absent. As such, the reader is confronted with the truths that believers will be lavishly blessed and rewarded (vv. 6-7), and yet unbelievers will be eternally punished and locked out of the glorious gates (v. 8).

Notice the rich nature of the believer's promised rewards in verses 6-7. 'I will give to the one who thirsts from the spring of the water of life without cost' (NASB). We need to notice from the outset that it is only the one who thirsts who receives this great gift. Thirsting has been a picture of intense desire for God from the Old Testament era (e.g. Pss. 42:1; 63:1). The only one who desires God is the one in whose heart God is working – in other words, the elect (cf. Acts 16:14; Rom. 3:11; 1 Cor. 1:18; 2:14). So, to those whom God has elected, justified, sanctified and given a desire for him, he will soothe, nourish, fill and delight their soul – he will give them to drink of the waters of eternal life. John is fond of using the picture of a spring of water to refer to the true abundant life that Christ brings (cf. John 4:14) which is administered by the work of the Spirit (John 7:37-39).

Saints have been exhorted to delight in God (Ps. 37:4) and to taste and see that he is good (Ps. 34:8). The eternal reward will be to dive into the depths of the ocean of God's presence and being and to drink of him without end. The one who is the source of all good, love, kindness, mercy, holiness, beauty and even all satisfaction – this one shall give of himself to all saints.

The art gallery for the art enthusiast, the stadium filled with the victorious favourite team for the sports fan, the placement of a newborn child into a mother's hands seconds after birth, the first sight of the uncovered beauty of a man's wife on the wedding night, the award handed out by the boss for a job well done and the joy of being curled up with a favourite book by the side of a lake with coffee in hand, are all only tastes of the glorious delight we have in God and will have for eternity. They pale in comparison!

This future reward will be the climax of God's covenantal promises. 'The one who conquers' in the Johannine corpus is the person who perseveres by God's grace. He overcomes and is victorious through the work of Christ. (cf. 1 John. 2:13, 14; 4:4; 5:4, 5; Rev. 2:7, 11, 17, 26, et. al.) John says of all these that 'they will inherit these things'. As sons and daughters of God, they will, without fail or exception, find the most glorious of estates awaiting them. The new heaven and new earth will be theirs (cf. Matt. 5:3, 5, 10) – along with all that is in them. Jonathan Edwards gives a helpful commentary on this promise when he writes:

> The believer shall possess all things in heaven. What do we mean by this? I mean that God, three in one, all that he is, and all that he has, and all that he does, all that he has made or done, the whole universe, bodies and spirits, light, heaven, angels, men, and devils, sun, moon, stars, land, and sea, fish, and fowls, all the silver and gold, all beings and perfections, as well as mere man, are as much the Christian's as the money in his pocket,

the clothes he wears, or the house he dwells in, or the [food] he eats; [yes], more properly his, more advantageously, more his than if he commanded all these things mentioned to be just in all respects as he pleased, at any time, by virtue of the union with Christ; because Christ, who certainly doth here possess all things, is entirely his, so that he possesses it all ... All the universe is his, only he has not the trouble of managing it; but Christ, to whom it is no trouble to manage it, manages it for him a thousand times as much to his advantage as he could himself, if he had the managing of all the atoms in the universe. Every thing is managed by Christ so as to be most to the advantage of the Christian. Every particle of air, or every ray of the sun; so that he in the other world, when he comes to see it, shall sit and enjoy all this vast inheritance with surprising, amazing joy.[24]

The greatest reward (in fact it is the source of all the others) will be that each resident of the holy eternal city will be his child and to each person he will be their God. This implies the closest and most intimate of relationships between God and man and the culmination of God's covenantal promises.

What a contrast there is with those who never receive Christ as Saviour and continue through life and into eternity to be chiefly characterized by their sin (v. 8). Their part (the counterpart to the gift and inheritance of the saint) will be in the burning lake that is the second death.

This explanatory paragraph in the midst of John's vision of the future heavenly existence ought to remind every reader and hearer that if there is a heaven to be received and a hell to be shunned, then there is also a choice to be made. Will I rest upon my own wisdom for direction in this life and answers to the life hereafter? Or, will I turn my trust from myself to Jesus Christ (the only way to God, as John wrote elsewhere [John 14:6]) and receive and rest upon him alone for salvation and eternal life? 'Will we be "overcomers" or "cowards"...? That will determine whether we are part of the New Jerusalem.'[25]

This is the most important question you will ever face, ask and answer. It is at the foundation of this book, as well as at the heart of the entire Bible. Man has been created as a God-glorifier, one who will resemble and represent God such that he reflects the full weight of who God is. The man or woman who refuses this purpose refuses God and all God has awaiting those who are his. As you ponder what the new heaven and earth will be, do not leave this at a mere academic level. I plead with you; take to heart the significance of this vision and whether or not it will be your everlasting home!

THE SPECIFICS: REVELATION 21:9 – 22:5

In Revelation 21:9, John records that an angel came to him and told him to come because he would show to the apostle more about this bride, the Lamb's wife and the New Jerusalem, the future abode of God's people. This verse sets the stage thematically for this next section running through Revelation 22:5. Here John records the more specific details regarding the New Jerusalem, which will be the heart of the new heaven and earth, and he sets forth the specifics of what that future transformed environment will be like.

In verse 10 we see the angel carrying John away by means of the Spirit (not physically – this is a vision – see Rev. 4:2; 17:3). He ends up on a high mountain where he can look down upon the city. Most probably, we are to gain the idea of John standing upon the mountain, the vision encompassing the whole city and then zooming in on particulars. The fact that the text again speaks of Jerusalem coming down out of heaven (see v. 10; cf. 21:2) shows that the first eight verses showed John generally what would take place with the new heaven and earth. Now, the vision will focus in on the particulars. Read on and allow these great and glorious traits to wash over your soul with hope and comfort!

God's visible glory: Revelation 21:11, 18-21

The first detail John records is that God's glory will be present visibly in the New Jerusalem. He writes, 'having the glory of God; its radiance was like a precious stone, as a stone of crystal-clear jasper'. The city is illuminated like a sparkling jewel by the glory of God. It is dazzling. This should not surprise us for we have already seen that sometimes God reveals his glory with the radiance of brilliant light.[26] Later on John gives further description of the particulars that also dazzle us with the beauty and brilliance of God's glory. Revelation 21:18-21 reads:

> The wall was built of jasper, while the city was pure gold, clear as glass. The foundations of the wall of the city were adorned with every kind of jewel. The first was jasper, the second sapphire, the third agate, the fourth emerald, the fifth onyx, the sixth carnelian, the seventh chrysolite, the eighth beryl, the ninth topaz, the tenth chrysoprase, the eleventh jacinth, the twelfth amethyst. And the twelve gates were twelve pearls, each of the gates made of a single pearl, and the street of the city was pure gold, transparent as glass[27] (ESV).

What we have subtilely introduced is none other than an aspect of the beatific vision of God which saints so anticipate (Matt. 5:8; 1 John 3:2). God has created us to love and delight in the beautiful. In heaven we shall see the one who is the headwaters of splendour and comeliness. And we shall not only see him, but that future dwelling will have the mark of his glory all over it. We are told now that 'The heavens are telling of the glory of God; and their expanse is declaring the work of His hands' (Ps. 19:1, NASB). God's creation makes evident his own weightiness, power, wisdom and yes, a great deal about his divine attributes (Rom. 1:20). Yet, in the new heaven and earth, God's visible glory will be manifest in and on all things.[28]

No doubt words fail us at this point in unearthing just exactly what that radiance will be like. John is employing analogies from life which convey a sense of the greatness. We want to avoid two extremes as we deal with these descriptions. On the one hand we want to refrain from dogmatically concluding that heaven will be literally what John says that it is. Keep in mind that here John says 'its radiance was like a precious stone' (emphasis added). It probably will far exceed his pen. On the other hand we must also keep ourselves from concluding that there will not be any connection with John's descriptions. God may very well construct heaven with some (if not a great deal of) oneness with these descriptions found in the Apocalypse.[29]

One other observation we should make about this glorious radiance is that it reminds us that the end of all existence, of all history, of every believer and of all that God is doing revolves around his glory. The rich weightiness of God, displaying and delighting in that glory, will be the eternal joy of the saint. 'Heaven itself is an infinite, eternal expression of the divine glory. We might say that the essence of heaven is God's glory manifest in its midst.'[30]

The dwelling of all God's people in their diversity: Revelation 21:12-14, 24-26

Years ago there was a Coca-Cola commercial which featured people from different parts of the world standing out on a hill, holding their soft-drinks and singing, 'I'd like to teach the world to sing in perfect harmony...' The impression left upon the viewer was unmistakable. This particular product could bring diverse peoples together. Even though this was a marketing tool, it did express a longing that is present among many, namely, that people can get along and live in peace.

When we move from the commercial to the front page of a newspaper we see that the reality is altogether different. It almost seems as if no one can get along. There are countries fighting against each other, tribal groups vying for superiority, racial unrest, a continuous string of court battles in which people clash over broken contracts and custody of children and an endless litany of employer-employee tensions. It often seems as if the only peace we can find is with those who are very similar to us: fellow blue collar workers or fellow white collar peers, those who like to frequent the same sports bar or belong to the same club. The instances of people coming together in spite of diversity are few and far between. When people of similar place in life get along we might say that is to be expected, it is not that special of a phenomenon. Yet, when people put aside their differences and come together, that is very rare and impresses us with the sense that something very special has taken place – something we would like to see more often.

Yet, what we find out about heaven is that the ordinary, run of the mill, daily experience is that peoples from the most diverse backgrounds and cultures will truly live in perfect harmony. Transcending language, racial, historical, cultural, generational, political and tribal barriers, we will live in the true melting pot where we will delight in the differences and find joy in the ability of Jesus Christ to work in each person perfect love.

This is first seen in John's description of the twelve gates and twelve foundations of the city in Revelation 21:12-14. The great and high wall around the city will have three gates on each of the sides – east, north, south and west. With an angel at each gate, they will also have written upon them the names of the twelve tribes of Israel. The imagery seems clear. This glorious celestial city will be the dwelling place of those from among Israel who truly placed their faith in God – those for whom Christ paid the penalty for their sins and purchased a place in heaven. Written on the twelve foundations of the wall (which were visible to John) were the names of the twelve apostles. Again, in dealing with foundations of the wall, which lets in or keeps out, the imagery has to do with the make-up of the city. Who will be in it? It will be the New Testament church. So, we have the Old Testament church and the New Testament church, Jews and Gentiles, the covenant people of the old and new eras. This will be the eternal dwelling of God's people of all times and places!

It is no small thing to see Jews and Gentiles brought together as citizens of heaven. H. Porter captures the mood of Jews and

Gentiles in the New Testament era when he writes:

> But as we approach the Christian era the attitude
> of the Jews toward the Gentiles changes, until we
> find, in the NT times, the most extreme aversion,
> scorn and hatred. They were regarded as unclean,
> with whom it was unlawful to have any friendly
> intercourse. They were the enemies of God and
> His people, to whom the knowledge of God was
> denied unless they became proselytes, and even
> then they could not, as in ancient times, be ad-
> mitted to full fellowship. Jews were forbidden
> to counsel them, and if they asked about Divine
> things they were to be cursed. All children born
> of mixed marriages were bastards. That is what
> caused the Jews to be so hated by Greeks and
> Romans, as we have abundant evidence in the
> writings of Cicero, Seneca and Tacitus.[31]

Such diversity is emphasized even more in verses 24-26. Here it is revealed that people from all nations (cf. 5:9) will be in heaven and walk by its light. At this point, all people (other than those separated from God's presence) will live in the light of God's glory. In fact, the kings of the earth who are redeemed and know God will bring all their glory (the weight of their influence and honour here upon the earth) into it (cf. also Isaiah 60). In other words, it is implied that this glory will be subsumed underneath God's. It also is most probably intended that part of the richness of heaven will be its diversity – people from all nations and walks of life will be there. We also have an indication that though it is hard often for the rich to see their need for God (Matt. 19:23-24), nonetheless, the wealthy will be in heaven (This is a fulfilment of what David saw would take place: cf. Ps. 22:29.).

Ladd avers that the language is not suggesting a literal presence of the unregenerate outside the New Jerusalem (some argue this and that therefore it is the millennium). Human language is employed to do 'no more than the statements of the prophets:

"and many peoples shall come and say: Come let us go up to the mountain of the Lord, to the house of Jacob'" (Isa. 2:3).[32] Mounce agrees and adds that John employs the language of the prophets to communicate the presence of the redeemed from every tribe, tongue, nation and people.[33]

Unlike our present experience in which diversity often leads to unrest, violence, death and heartache, there will be none of this in the heavenly Jerusalem. 'Its gates shall not be shut at all by day (there shall be no night there)' (21:25). There will be access for all, coming and going of all and yet absolute security and safety (Cf. also Isa. 60:11).

The full weight and renown of the nations will be brought into heaven and no doubt will honour God. Why? Because heaven will be the place where all dwell together in unity. Because of the spiritual, physical, reputational and environmental transformation each saint will delight in the love that Christ has not only for him, but also for other saints. Likewise, he will delight in the rewards of others, even if they are of greater status than his own – such will be the holiness of heaven.[34]

This aspect of the new heaven and earth deals with the full restoration of the social aspect of the *imago dei*. God told Adam in Genesis 2:18 it was not good for him to be alone, so God created an equally prominent helper – woman. This, coupled with the truth that man was created in the image of the triune God (Gen. 1:26), demonstrates that man is a social being. It is in relationship, i.e. in family and in the church, that man most fully shows his ability to resemble and represent God and to display God's redeeming grace (cf. John 13:35). What we see, then, is that the glorification of believers deals not only with the perfection of individual saints. It deals with the glorification of the church collectively as well.

The dwelling of God: Revelation 21:15-16, 22-23

Not only will heaven's citizens enjoy full and perfect communion with each other, but this unbroken fellowship will also take place between them and their Creator. Such is implied in these two verses: 'And the one speaking with me had a measuring rod of gold to measure the city and its gates and wall. The city is laid out as a square; and its length the same as its width. And he measured the city with his rod, 12,000 stadia. Its length and width and height are equal.'

The same angel who was explaining the New Jerusalem to John also had a gold measuring rod in his hand. The gold probably has no significance other than to show that it fits with everything else in the city – it is such a magnificent place that even something as insignificant as the measuring rod is gold. The fact that the city is a cube reminds us of the Holy of Holies in the temple (1 Kings 6:20).[35] The Holy of Holies was a very sacred place that only the high priest could enter once a year with great preparation (Lev. 16). It was the very heart of the realized presence of God in the tabernacle and temple – his throne room. Yet, the New Jerusalem will be all Holy of Holies. Saints of all ages will live for eternity, in the words of the Old Testament, not just near the temple and not only within the Holy Place. Man will live in the very Holy of Holies. Never will it have been clearer that there is no longer any barrier between God and man at all.

This language would have been shocking to readers of John's day. The entire book of Revelation is largely dependent upon imagery and teaching from the Old Testament, so we know John's readers must have been well familiar with the sacred Scriptures. They would have been familiar with the untouchable nature of the Holy of Holies. It was a place that very few ever got to enter and see. Yet, now, John is shown that the future eternal dwelling place of man is in a mammoth Holy of Holies. This depicts an intimacy with the Godhead that has been unheard of prior to this. Yes, the Son, the eternal Word, came and tabernacled with man (John 1:14), but in eternity future man shall live in the rich full presence of the Godhead!

John drives home this great truth even further in verses 22-23. 'And I saw no temple in it, for its temple is the Lord God the Almighty and the Lamb. And the city has no need of sun or moon to shine on it, for the glory of God gives it light, and its lamp is the Lamb.'

Why ought this to thrill our hearts? To begin with, it is a strong picture of the culmination of the reconciliation and peace we have with God (cf. Rom. 5:1; Eph. 2:16-18; 2 Cor. 5:18-19). What we have understood by faith during this life, namely that God has united us to himself in Christ and brought us into his continual presence (1 Cor. 1:9; 2 Cor. 6:16; Heb. 13:5), at that time we will know by sight. For eternity we will delight in the reality that God has removed all enmity between us and him. Never before will our forgiveness and Christ's atonement on our behalf be so evident.

What is more, we will live in the presence of the one who is love (1 John 4:8), beautiful (Ps. 27:4), holy (Lev. 19:2), eternally merciful (Ps. 136), good (Ps. 52:1), always truthful (2 Sam. 7:28; Ps. 93:5), all powerful (Luke 1:37), just (Deut. 10:17) and wise (Ps. 104). The one who is the source of all that is good and righteous will envelope us within his glorious presence – always in the realized strong arm of our Heavenly Father. This, more than anything else, will transform us and our environment! Oh, what it will be like to be rid of hatred, bitterness, evil, pain, temptation, isolation, fear and lies, and to live only in the one who is pure and righteous!

Security: Revelation 21:17

In the Bible the concept of peace refers to the lack of conflict and the presence of wholeness between man and God (Num. 6:26; Isa. 9:7; Ezek. 37:26; Rom. 5:1), between man and man (Eph. 2:15) or within one's own self (John 14:1ff.).[36] We have just seen that heaven is the consummation of perfect peace between man and man and between God and man. Now, we see that heaven will include the absence of any conflict and presence of internal wholeness in that there will be complete safety. This is revealed in the angel's measurement of the wall which John saw surrounding the city. 'He also measured its wall, 144 cubits by human measurement, which is also an angel's measurement' (Rev. 21:17).

A cubit is about eighteen inches (forty-six centimetres), so the wall around the city is 216 feet (sixty-six metres) thick.[37] That this is figurative language is suggested by verse 25 where we are told the gates are never closed. Why have such thick walls with gates always open, unless what is being communicated is safety and security, along with total access to God's people?[38]

In this security we find the ultimate fulfilment of a promise that has run throughout the Scriptures: rest. In the Old Testament God gave a specific land to his people so that they may have rest which includes safety from enemies, ability to worship and a situation in which they could obey him fully (Deut. 12:10; 28:7; Lev. 26:5-8; Ps. 105:44-45). This was a rest that the Old Testament people, in large part, did not enter due to their sin (Ps. 95:11; Heb. 3:11; 4:3). Yet, rest still remains for those who have truly trusted in him (Heb. 4:1-3).[39]

With the inheritance of the new heaven and earth in which we will be in the full rich presence of God where all is temple and the Holy of Holies, we will be absolutely safe. We will not have to fear physical or spiritual enemies. We will not have to fear physical or spiritual harm. We will not have to fear trials, hardships or deprivation of any kind. We will not have to fear war, terrorist attacks, drive-by shootings, rapes, incest or convenience store hold-ups. It is a place where thieves do not break in and steal our treasures (Matt. 6:20). We will live in a security that man has never known. Each day and moment will bring ever new and fresh joys and fulfilments in the work and service we will engage in before God. Each day and moment will be filled with accomplishments and relationships that will thrill the soul. But fear, disappoint and pain will be things of the past. No one and nothing will be present to thwart our projects, joy or peace.

The United States learned September 11, 2001 just how insecure it truly is as a nation. Prior to that day, terrorist attacks and threats from outside enemies had mostly been 'over there'. And, we would go about our business of work, raising families, going to athletic events and attending concerts, thinking nothing of it. Yet, in one day, in fact, in less than an hour that all changed. A whole nation was reminded that this earth is often a cruel place where life can be snuffed out in an instant and security dashed to pieces. For scores of people their family was devastated from loss, the economy was weakened and travel and employment were made much more difficult. None of this will be present in the age to come. There will be no such surprises to wreak havoc.

If we can think back to when we were children and felt absolutely secure in the presence of our parents (after all, nothing could happen to us, so we thought), we can gain a small taste of the security we will have in the New Jerusalem and how it will be a gift beyond measure.

There is something that we must clarify at this point since the concept of rest could imply a common misunderstanding. The picture of heaven as a place in which people do nothing but sit on clouds and play harps has been propagated so often that it has become difficult for people to conclude that heaven will be anything but boring. Since God created us to accomplish and to create, it grates against our very being that we would not be involved in some purpose. As we get older the idea of rest does seem nice. But ask anyone in retirement who has little purpose and they will tell you that inactivity loses its appeal after a couple of months at the most.

The Bible reveals that heaven will be a place of activity, service and work – all of which will be enjoyable, fulfilling and lacking of any circumstances that would bring frustration.[40] (See Matt. 25:21, 23; Rev. 2:27; 4:9-11; 7:15) Again, this should not surprise us. We have seen repeatedly that God has created us as God-glorifiers. The very concept implies that we are made with a purpose and goal in mind, with things to do. And, now that we have seen in Revelation 21 that there is a great deal of continuity between the present earth and the new heaven and earth, we should not be surprised that there will be work and most probably play as part of our eternal existence. The implication seems to be that we will work, serve and accomplish with greater joy than we now play, and day in and day out this very involvement will refresh and bring rest!

Consider how a saint of a different era described this rest:

> They will have an eternal rest, with an uninterrupted joy; for heaven is not a resting place,

where men may sleep out an eternity; there they rest not day or night, but their work is their rest, and continual recreation. Toil and weariness have no place there. They rest there in God who is the center of their souls.[41]

Joni Eareckson Tada adds:

The closer we draw to the Lord Jesus and the more we set our hearts and minds on heavenly glories above, the better prepared we shall be for heaven's perfection. Fellowship won't mean sitting at the feet of Jesus and fighting back boredom while everyone else is enraptured. No. Fellowship will be the best of what earthly friendship merely hinted at.

I would like to tell [those who think heaven will be boring], 'Hey, don't forget, Christ knows better than you what it means to be human.' He sailed on the seas, hiked mountains, and slept under the stars by rushing brooks. He realizes what gets your heart pumping. Remember, He made you. You won't stop being human. Rather, you'll enjoy the full richness of all that your humanity was designed to be.

In heaven there will be no failure in service. No disappointment in doing. We will never struggle with failing to do the task God puts before us, as in a failed marriage or mission. We will never fall short of meeting our responsibilities.

And boy will we do! [Doers] will be on cloud nine, but only for a short time, because they will be busier than they ever were on earth. No idling away eternity strolling streets of gold. No passing time while plucking harps by the glassy sea. We will have jobs to do ... For me, this will be heaven. I love serving God.[42]

Absence of evil: Revelation 21:27

Chapter 21 ends with these words concerning the heart of the new heaven and new earth, i.e. the New Jerusalem: 'And nothing unclean will ever enter it, nor anyone who does what is detestable or false, but only those who are written in the Lamb's book of life.' Here it is stated explicitly to John and his readers what has been only implicit to this point. In the future dwelling of God and his saints there will be absolutely no sin, no hint of evil whatsoever. Of course, this is necessitated by what has already been said. If there will be no tears, death, sorrow, crying or pain (21:4), this means that sin must be absent. Additionally, if these glorified individuals will be immersed in the ocean of the glorious more realized presence of God for ever (21:15-16, 22-23), it stands to reason that they will be completely separated from sin (cf. Isa. 59:2; Hab. 1:13).

Why is this so important? Simply for this reason: all the pain we suffer in this life is either directly or indirectly the result of sin. Alcoholism, drug addiction, victimization by theft, divorce, abandonment, relationship conflict, being lied to, being taken advantage of by an employer, rape and sexual harassment (and we could go on and on) are all the direct result of sin. Even what we often term natural disasters (tornado, fire, hurricane and flood) and health problems (cancer, diabetes, etc.) arise from the fact that we live in a fallen, sinful world (cf. Rom. 8:20-22).

The new heaven and new earth would not be heaven if it were infected with sin as is this present world. We said at the beginning of this chapter that if we are perfected in spirit, body and reputation, yet then placed in a world filled with sin, the former transformations would be tainted – just like cleaning up a baby and leaving her in a dirty high chair. The cleaning would be useless.

Reader, I invite you to worship God for this future perfectly holy destination. Delight in what it will be like to be surrounded by absolute goodness and righteousness where there will be no evil intent or practice, and where everyone will have as their chief ends to love and glorify God, as well as to love each other![43] If you have received Jesus Christ as your Saviour this will be your glorious reward. 'Comfort one another with these words'!

Eternal life: Revelation 22:1-2

As John's vision of the new heaven and new earth comes to a close, he focuses in with greater intensity upon the very presence of God, namely his throne, as well as the life of his saints in that presence. He makes it clear that all who are in the New Jerusalem will experience consummated eternal life. This is communicated through two figures: a river of life and a tree of life. Let's look at each.

First, John writes, 'Then he showed me the river of the water of life, bright as crystal, flowing from the throne of God and of the Lamb' (22:1). The same angel who has been showing John the details of the New Jerusalem from Revelation 21:9 points out in the vision a river. It is a river whose brightness displays the nature of heaven in which God's glory and radiance is upon all things. It also contains the waters of life. George Eldon Ladd writes of this figure: 'This is a symbolic way of describing the reign of eternal life in the age to come. The symbolism of a river of life is a common one in biblical thought.' See Psalm 46:4, John 4:10, 14, Ezekiel 47:1-12 and Zechariah 14:8. He adds, 'The fact that the river flows from the throne of God and of the Lamb means simply that God is the source of all life.'[44] In the hot arid climate of Palestine this great picture of the age to come would hold very rich, comforting and invigorating meaning.[45] To be in the New Jerusalem means that one will have access to the refreshing cooling waters of the Father's and Son's spiritual strength and sustenance which flow from the throne, from the one who reigns over all.

Next we read: 'In the middle of its street; also, on either side of the river, the tree of life with its twelve kinds of fruit, yielding its fruit each month. The leaves of the tree were for the healing of the nations' (22:2). There is not only a river flowing from God's throne which gives life, but also trees on either side which give life. It is most probable that the point is not that we must drink from the river or eat from the trees to have eternal life. Both are figures to impress John and his readers with the reality that the lavish, lush and abundant life God promises (which the Son came to accomplish and apply [John 10:10]) is possessed by the saint in full in heaven. Both pictures have their origin in the Old Testament.[46] Ezekiel 47:1-12 speaks of such a river and trees on either side when describing the future restored Jerusalem (which had reference ultimately to the age to come). It is made clear in that passage that these figures represent life. Ladd is also helpful at this point when he comments:

> This is another traditional feature in Jewish apocalyptic going back to the Genesis narrative. God planted in Eden the tree of life (Gen. 2:9); but after man sinned, God excluded him from access to the tree (Gen. 3:22). Jewish thought looked forward to access to the tree of life by whose fruit men would attain to eternal life (Enoch 25:2ff.; IV Ezra 7:53; 8:52; II Enoch 8:3). Jesus brought to men this eternal life in the midst of history through his incarnation, death, and resurrection (John 3:36; 6:54; 20:31); and the present reference to the tree of life means the consummation of what Jesus accomplished in his earthly mission.[47]

Most likely the trees bear fruit monthly and provide healing because of the water flowing from the throne. Ezekiel 47:12 clarifies this: 'And on the banks, on both sides of the river, there will grow all kinds of trees for food. Their leaves will not wither, nor their fruit fail, but they will bear fresh fruit every month, because the water for them flows from the sanctuary. Their fruit will be for food, and their leaves for healing' (ESV).

We must remember when reading these descriptions that not every detail should be assigned extravagant meaning. That the trees are for healing is not to suggest that men there will be sick (compare with 21:4 which shows that healing is not needed). The point is that contrary to this age, the age to come will be a place of

perfect, rich and abundant life. Strength, vitality, energy and purpose, which will never diminish, will mark the saint at that time.

We must not miss that in this part of the vision a main focus
is that our true and eternal life flows from God himself. The water
proceeds from God's throne and the fruit trees are a result of that
water. We have eternal life because of our connection into God
himself. Such a vital union is the source of our spiritual life from
the beginning (cf. Eph. 2:16-18); however, it is made even more
evident in the new heaven and new earth. Though God is present
everywhere, he is not present everywhere in the same way. His
presence in the New Jerusalem will consist of its fullest expression.
Heaven will be heaven because we are with God.

Why is this eternal life significant? First, because it shows that
we will be truly living in heaven. We will not be merely existing,
but thinking, 'I wish there were more to this.' We will be fulfilled
and invigorated in all that we do. Additionally, we will know that
our strength and energy will never diminish. Such fatigue is often
a great source of pain and frustration in this life. Yet, what we have
then – our health and welfare – will last for all eternity! And in
no way will the saint tire of this glorious eternal existence. It will
be a continual progress in joy and blessedness. Jonathan Edwards
agrees:

> And how happy is that love in which there is an
> eternal progress in all those things wherein new
> beauties are continually discovered, and more
> and more loveliness, and in which we shall for
> ever increase in beauty ourselves; where we shall
> be more capable of finding out and giving, and
> shall receive more and more endearing expres-
> sions of love for ever ... [The saints'] having of
> perfect happiness does not exclude all increase,
> nor does it exclude all hope, for we do not know
> but they will increase in happiness forever ... If
> nothing be too much to be given to man, and
> to be done for man in the means of procuring
> his happiness, nothing will be too much to be

given him as the end, no degree of happiness is too great for him to enjoy.[48]

The eternal delight of heaven can be understood, in part, by reflecting upon the Christmas season. For the average person December holds a special mystery. When we see the beauty of lights, experience the joy of familiar carols, anticipate time off of work, look forward to the presence of family and friends and are reminded of very noble and righteous purposes for mankind, we are lifted up, invigorated and warmed to our depths; we find great security in the traditions. We can't wait until the day. Weeks of preparation build up to it and then it comes. Even adults, if the truth be known, bound out of bed – even if it is only because they find it so much fun to see their children jump for joy with their gifts.

Yet, the downside of Christmas is that about midday you are reminded that it is almost over. It will be another 365 days until we experience this again. The calendar teases us with only a yearly taste. For the healthiest of persons there is almost always a let down after Christmas and especially after New Year's day when the holiday season is completed and now it is back to the daily grind of regular schedules and work. In some ways, if Christmas lasted all year, we would lose the special feel, anticipation and intense delight. Yet, isn't that what we want deep down? So, we face a dilemma. We'd love to have that ecstasy all year long and yet in this life something that is constant tends to lose its lustre.

Yet heaven is different. Though its joy and blessedness can be compared to the lesser version of what we have leading up to Christmas, it will never lose its intensity, even though it is eternally constant. To the contrary, it will grow. Can you imagine the joy of Christmas all year long and it not only will not diminish in its intensity and fulfilment, it will actually grow? Of course, we can't fully imagine it. But we can catch just a taste of it and know that it will surpass all we know here!

Again, Edwards brings clarity:

If the saints knew there would be an end to their happiness, though at never so great a distance, yet it would be a great damp to their joy. The greater the happiness is, so much the more uncomfortable would the thoughts of an end be, and so much the more joyful will it be to think that there will be no end. The saints will surely know that there will be no more danger of their happiness coming to an end, than there will be that the being of God will come to an end. As God is eternal, so their happiness is eternal; as long as the fountain lasts, they need not fear but they shall be supplied.[49]

Covenant blessing: Revelation 22:3-5

Heaven, in every way, will be the complete fulfilment of all that God has promised his people throughout history. These promises have been part of his covenant and include: the existence of a great number of covenant people (cf. Gen. 13:14-16; 15:5, 16; 17:8), blessing (cf. Gen. 12:2, 3; 26:3), land and rest (Gen. 12:5-7; 15:18; Deut. 12:8-32), God as their God, providing for, protecting and being with them (Gen. 17:7; Exod. 29:45; Josh. 1:9) and kings (those who reign) being part of God's people (Gen. 17:6). As we have seen in this description of the New Jerusalem so far, God has truly blessed his people and has given them not only land, but the entire heaven and earth. He has given rest and security and is present with them, protecting and providing for them. People from all nations are part of the people of God, and even kings from the nations are part of the assembly of saints.

What we see in verses 3-5 is the climax of covenant blessings. First, 'every curse will not be there any longer'. Curse is the opposite of covenant blessing (Lev. 26; Deut. 28; Josh. 23) as well as the result of man's sinfulness (Gen. 3:17; Deut. 27:26; Gal. 3:10). Yet, there will be no curse in heaven because those there will be united to Christ and perfectly holy. The weight of sin under which we now live will be lifted.

What is more, the vision emphasizes again the presence of God with his people (which stands at the centre of the blessings of heaven) in the rest of verse 3 and in verse 4: 'And the throne of God and of the Lamb will be in it, and His servants will serve Him.[50] And they will see His face, and His name will be upon their foreheads.' God will be present and the inhabitants of the holy city will belong to him.

Notice that these covenant people will serve him. The verb utilized in verse 3 is *latreuo* which often connotes service within the cultic context and can be synonymous with worship.[51] This service or work will be part of our worship of God (which seems to make up a great deal of heaven's activities: Rev. 4-5; 14:1-5). From the beginning of God's formalizing of his covenant with his people they were meant to serve him (Exod. 19:5-6; 1 Peter 2:9). Now, for eternity, this will be the lot of saints. Passivity will not be the lot of heaven. We will serve God. We will work and be engaged in accomplishment that will no longer be infected with sin and failure. After all, this eternal reward into which we enter is described elsewhere as our 'joy' (Matt. 25:21-23). As the Westminster Shorter Catechism says in its well-known first answer, part of the chief end of man is to enjoy God for ever.

What is more, the radiance of God's presence will light all things, and there will be no night. These glorified believers will reign for ever and ever. The sons of Adam, created to be billboards for God's glory and given a prominent place for that reason, will be completely restored. As a result they will reign for ever and ever – prominently displayed as God's trophies who display individually and collectively the full weight of who he is.

Summary

When we bring together all the teaching of Revelation 21:1 – 22:5, we have a breathtaking portrait of heaven, the future dwelling of saints. It will be a real place that consists of the renovated heaven and earth where everything has been reclaimed and made new. The entire existence for believers will be the Holy of Holies, that is, the unmitigated, full and realized presence of God where we will swim in the ocean of the radiance of his glory! What is more, pain, death and all that is evil will be history. We will have absolute security and rest in our work and play. Though we will cohabit with people from every tribe, tongue, nation and people, we will live in perfect harmony, delighting in the love for each other that Christ works in us and revelling in the rewards of others, as well as our own.

All of this rich existence can be described as true, rich and abundant life. It will never end or diminish in any way. We will be blessed of God as his people and we will delight in seeing him, the source of all beauty and goodness. We will be given prominent places of service as billboards for his greatness. Our initial purpose will be realized in full and for eternity.

All of this is certain. For the saint, this can be 'taken to the bank'. It will happen. It will be our full inheritance!

Christian, never lose sight of our future destination and reward. It should not only comfort us, but also excite us, build our hope, lead us to holiness and build a Christ-like community now. It also should bring renewed energy to the work we are now doing in this present age – in light of the fact that we will live on this earth in the age to come, albeit after it is transformed.

> As citizens of God's kingdom, we may not just write off the present earth as a total loss, or rejoice in its deterioration. We must indeed be working for a better world now. Our efforts to bring the kingdom of Christ into fuller manifestation are of eternal significance. Our Christian life today, our struggles against sin – both individual and institutional – our mission work, our attempt to develop and promote a distinctively Christian culture, have value not only for this world but even for the world to come.[52]

Remember, though we have been able to set forth an outline of what it will be like, 'Eye has not seen, nor ear heard, nor have entered into the heart of man the things which God has prepared for those who love Him' (1 Cor. 2:9, NKJV). May the words of this chapter whet our appetite for the fulness of our future transformed environment and the ultimate glorification of the church!

CONCLUSION

I HOPE THIS JOURNEY through one of the most neglected, yet richest of biblical doctrines has been as helpful and enjoyable for you as it has been for me! Since we have covered a good deal of ground, it might be hard for us to grasp fully why this is so delightful and beneficial. Therefore, we will close with a summary of what we have learned throughout this study and then highlight some key practical discoveries which arise from glorification teaching.

Summary

God created mankind with glory, full and rich weightiness and significance that consisted of being made in his image. Man's original identity was one in which he was intended to represent and reflect God in a way that none of the other creation was. The very purpose for his existence was to bring other men and the angelic world to worship God, to glorify God in response to his glorification of man.

With the fall of mankind into sin his original identity and purpose were twisted. Man's history has been one of only wanting to honour himself and reflect his own glory, not God's. The history of redemption has consisted of God's planning for, accomplishing and working out his restoration of man to his full identity and purpose of God glorification.

Man's restoration takes place in and through Jesus Christ alone who is uniquely qualified as the perfect and second Adam. He is the only begotten Son of God who reflects the glory of God to and through man as no one else can. Once united to Christ, man, through the salvific work of Christ, is continually transformed into his image.

This transformation begins with spiritual change. Within the area of thought life, behaviour and how he relates to God, man becomes more like Christ and thus is able to serve as a billboard for the greatness of God. This change progresses through life and becomes complete at the time of death.

Yet it doesn't stop here. At the return of Christ, God's perfected saints will be resurrected, thus being changed physically. This physical change will enable man to resemble Christ in his glorified body. This transformation is necessary since man is whole only as both soul and body. This shows the importance of the physical; it also increases God's glory – his redemption of man includes the whole person.

Once man is glorified fully, his reputation also will be transformed. The entire world will see who each believer is, who the church is in community and how significant they are as billboards for God's glory. Their true identity may be hidden now; in fact, they may even be scorned. Yet, at the time of their glorification they will be the very trophies of God whom he will praise and glorify so that, in turn, he will be glorified. Our desire for significance and purpose will be fulfilled throughout all of eternity as we dive into the highest of all purposes – God himself.

God also will transform man's environment. The curse of sin extended to the rest of creation and, as such, it must be transformed in order for the restoration to be complete. It is also necessary for the realization of God's covenantal promises and as an accompaniment to man's other aspects of transformation. Glorified man cannot live in a fallen world.

Finally, we must see that glorification not only deals with the perfection of each individual, but also with the perfection of the church collectively. It is only as men are in perfect community with one another in the new heaven and earth that the image of God and the glory of God through his redeeming grace will shine forth with the greatest intensity.

SOME KEY DISCOVERIES

We have highlighted throughout the book the significance of this doctrine. However, there are some discoveries that have not been focused upon as they ought. The first is that in this study we have seen an aspect of the essence of man's identity which is often overlooked. Typically, we will say that man is made in God's image. Yet, what we miss is that man was created to be a God-glorifier. As a gun is designed to launch a bullet, a bow was made to shoot arrows and a hammer was fashioned to drive nails, so man was crafted for the very purpose of glorifying God.

This leads us to the next discovery. Man's identity reveals his purpose. His beginning uncovers his end. Perhaps more than any other doctrine, the teaching of man's glorification shows the full and rich way that the Bible teaches man's chief end. It seems to this writer that often Christians will spout off the well-known answer to the Westminster Shorter Catechism's first question: 'Man's chief end is to glorify God and to enjoy Him forever.' Yet, when it comes to anthropology, we are not able to make the connection. We go from a God-centred Theology Proper and purpose in life to a very man-centred exposition of what the Bible teaches about man. We build man's self-esteem through anthropology and talk about his worth. Yet, at the heart of the Bible's teaching about man is his purpose of glorifying God – something highlighted in this doctrine. To look at this another way, if something as earthy and horizontal as man even leads us to the purpose of glorifying God, it shows us just how much this chief end permeates the Bible.

Perhaps of lesser significance, yet equally true, is the discovery of why this work of God in man is called glorification. We stated in the introduction that this was a question which was carried into this study, and we have found the answer. It is an answer inherent in the overview of glorification which we offered above.

Glorification also shows just how interconnected the different doctrines of the Scriptures are. It reminds us regarding Theology Proper that the chief end of man is to glorify God. Concerning Christology we have learned that the means whereby man glorifies God and is restored to a God-glorifier is through Jesus Christ. And as we have seen, in the area of anthropology we have discovered an important aspect of man's identity: he is a God-glorifier and until he realizes this, he does not understand why he is on earth, nor will he find the purpose and fulfilment for which he so longs. Soteriology cannot be fully understood unless we understand that the history of redemption is, in part, the restoration of man to a God-glorifier and that in his salvation and sanctification he is being glorified and being led toward complete glorification.

In the area of ecclesiology we have gained a new perspective on the church. Man from the beginning has been a social being. God has placed him in marriage and the family, as well as in the church, because it is in such relationships that he displays most fully his likeness to the social triune God. Also, nothing displays the greatness of God any more than to take diverse men and women and to bring them into perfect unity for eternity. Given this end for the body of Christ, we should realize that some of this perfect community should seep into the church presently. In ever-increasing measure, the church should be living out what Christ has wrought in us!

And finally, our eschatology is informed by man's ultimate end. The world and all of history are moving in one direction – the glorification of the church purchased with our Saviour's blood.

The final key discovery has to do with the practical application that arises from this teaching. We have focused upon a number of application points. However, some deserve a concluding remark:

1. Our future glorification causes our present sufferings to look very small in light of what awaits us (Rom. 8:18ff.). In fact, our present sufferings are put in a brand new light as we see that they help us fulfil our purpose of glorifying God (2 Cor. 4:7, 17, 1 Peter 1:7).

2. It shows us that our labours for Christ are not in vain (1 Cor. 15:58).

3. It encourages us toward faithfulness and Christ-like living now (1 John 3:1-3).

Similarly, it defines what sanctification looks like for us: becoming like Christ (2 Cor. 3:18).

4. It shows us that seeking to glorify God in every aspect of our life, in the very nuts and bolts of each day, ought to be the fruit of our redemption and our goal (1 Cor. 10:31; Phil. 1:9-11). This brings simplicity to life that helps us focus and find fuel for obedience. Whether a person mocks me because of my faith, takes advantage of me or whether I experience a breakdown out on the highway late at night in the rain, what my Lord asks of me is that, out of love for him and interest in his glory, I respond by his grace in the way that honours him. As such, as I lose myself and my own selfish desires in him, and I find true life purpose.

5. It provides motivation for contentment and drive in life – we know that our purpose and calling, by command and design, is that we 'proclaim the excellencies of Him who called me out of darkness into His marvelous light' (1 Peter 2:9). As a result, what joy we find in glorifying

God in evangelism, missions and compassion ministries (John 14:12-14; 16:24; Matt. 5:16; James 1:27).

6. It puts our marriage and parenting in a whole new light. Fighting for patience, love, nurturing and time spent with our family is a large part of our service as billboards for his glory (Mal. 2:15; Eph. 5:32).

7. It places our involvement with other believers in new perspective. Arising out of Christ's work in us, restoring us to our representation and reflection the triune God, we must pray, work towards and fight for Christ-like unity and love among the body of Christ (Phil. 2:1-11).

8. Its certainty also encourages us that he who began a good work in us will complete that work (Phil. 1:6; Rom. 8:29-30).

9. It gives shape to the good that is the goal of God's orchestration of all world events on behalf of his church: it is to conform us to the image of Christ (Rom. 8:28-30).
It demonstrates the importance of the physical world (Rom. 8:19-25).

10. It shows us that though great joy and fulfilment can be found in our Saviour in this life, nevertheless, death is even better; it is gain. Christians of all people are most blessed! Not only do we no longer have to fear death, but we realize it is the door to our future glory and presence with our beloved Saviour! (Phil. 1:21-23).

With this in mind, may our prayer be:

Finish, then, thy new creation; pure and spotless let us be: Let us see thy great salvation perfectly restored in thee; Changed from glory into glory, till in heaven we take our place, Till we cast our crowns before thee, lost in wonder, love, and praise.

-From Charles Wesley [1747], 'Love Divine, All Loves Excelling'

NOTES

INTRODUCTION

1. Douglas J. Moo, *The Epistle to the Romans*, Eerdmans, 1996, p.531.
2. Millard Erickson, *Christian Theology*, Baker, 1994, repr., p.997.
3. John Murray, *Redemption Accomplished and Applied*, Eerdmans, 1984, repr., p.174.
4. Erickson, *Christian Theology*, p.997.

CHAPTER I

1. Tom Schreiner, 'Romans', Moises Silva, ed., *Baker Exegetical Commentary on the New Testament*, Baker Book House, 1998, p.187, in speaking of the view many have of Romans 3:23 that it refers to the glory Adam lost when he fell into sin, writes, 'In Apoc. Mos. 21:6 Adam blames Eve, "you have deprived me of the glory of God". Third Baruch 4:16 says Adam "was stripped of the glory of God" and became "distant from the glory of God" because of his sin

(cf. Gen. Rab. 12:6 on 2:4). The glory refers to what Adam possessed upon his creation and lost upon his fall.'

2. S. Aalen, 'Glory, Honour', Colin Brown, ed., *The New International Dictionary of New Testament Theology*, Zondervan, 1982, vol. 2, p.45, writes, 'In Qumran it was expected that the elect would "inherit the glory of Adam..."'

3. The natural sense of the MT (coupled with the unlikelihood that David is speaking of pagan gods) suggests that the first alternative is the correct one, even though the LXX and Hebrews 2:7 favour the rendering 'heavenly beings' (or angels: angelous).

4. Willem VanGemeren, 'Psalms', Frank E. Gaibelein, gen ed., *The Expositor's Bible Commentary*, Zondervan, 1991, vol. 5, p.113 writes, '"Glory" and "[majesty]" are attributes of God's kingship (29:1; 104:1) extended to man's royal status.'

5. In Psalm 30:12, for example, David uses the term *kabod* ('glory') to refer to himself. More specifically the reference is to his inner man (soul or heart) which is the place of his full weightiness and the primary source of his being able to display the weightiness of God through praise and righteous living (see also Gen. 49:6; Pss. 7:6; 16:9; 57:9; 108:2). Man's glory is so much tied to God's glory that a synonym for 'me' or 'soul' or 'heart' is 'glory'.

6. When not designated as a particular version, all Scripture citations are the author's own translation.

7. Stanley J. Grenz, *The Social God and the Relational Self: A Trinitarian Theology of the Imago Dei*, Westminster John Knox Press, 2001, p.184 refers to Psalm 8 as 'The best commentary on Genesis 1:26-28 available'.

8. James R. Tony, 'Keeping up the Image', Moody, Nov./Dec.,1998, pp.34-36.

9. The following, unless otherwise noted, is taken from Millard Erickson, *Christian Theology*, Baker, 1994, repr., pp. 495-517.

10. Grenz, *The Social*, p.142, refers to it as the 'structural' approach and defines it this way: 'The divine image refers to 'something within the substantial form of human nature, some faculty or capacity man possesses ... Because the *imago dei* is a quality or capability within human nature, proponents theorize, it remains present whether or not a person acknowledges God. It constitutes a person as human, and therefore it cannot be lost.'

11. *The Westminster Shorter Catechism*, No.10; Wayne Grudem, *Bible Doctrine* (Zondervan, 1999), pp.191-192; Louis Berkhof, *Systematic Theology* (Eerdmans, 1996, repr.), p.204; J. I. Packer, *Knowing Man*, Cornerstone, 1979, p.21; John M. Frame, 'Men and Women in the Image of God', John Piper, Wayne Grudem, eds, *Rediscovering Biblical Manhood and Womanhood*, Crossway, 1991, p.226.

12. Berkhof, *Systematic*, pp.204-205; Tony, 'Keeping up the Image', p.34; *The Westminster Shorter Catechism*, No.10.

13. This would include the early church fathers and the reformers (as Berkhof, *Systematic*, pp.202-203, asserts), *The Westminster Shorter Catechism*, No.10; Louis

Berkhof, *Systematic*, pp.204-205; Packer, *Knowing Man*, pp.21-32; Frame, 'Men and Women', pp.225-226; and Tony, 'Keeping up the Image', p.34.

14. Erickson, *Christian Theology*, pp.502-508.

15. Erickson, *Christian Theology*, pp.508-510.

16. John M. Frame, 'Men and Women', p.227; *The Reformation Study Bible*, p.8; Craig Smith, unpublished ordination thesis presented to the Rocky Mountain District of the Evangelical Free Church of America, pp.14-15; and Willem VanGemeren, *The Progress of Redemption*, Baker, 2000, repr., p.63.

17. Grudem, *Bible Doctrine*, p.192; Packer, *Knowing Man*, pp.21-32; Tony, 'Keeping up the Image', pp.34-36.

18. Frame, 'Men and Women', p.226; Packer, *Knowing Man*, pp.21-32; Tony, 'Keeping up the Image', pp.34-36.

19. Berkhof, *Systematic*, pp.204-205; Packer, *Knowing Man*, pp.21-32.

20. Packer, *Knowing Man*, pp.21-32.

21. Packer, *Knowing Man*, pp.21-32.

22. Though I do not agree with the theological methodology or all of the theological tenets of Stanley Grenz, nevertheless he does do a good job of highlighting that man in God's image is a social being who reflects the social God, i.e. the Trinity. See Stanley Grenz, *The Social God and the Relational Self*.

23. Grudem, *Systematic Theology*, p.444, after affirming that fallen man is still in God's image, adds, 'However, since man has sinned, he is certainly not as fully like God as he was before. His moral purity has been lost and his sinful character certainly does not reflect God's holiness.'

24. See also VanGemeren, *The Progress*, p.63.

25. Grudem, *Bible Doctrine*, p.189. One should note that they are not communicating two different ideas, but are synonymous and both are used for emphasis.

26. Unpublished ordination thesis, pp.14-15. Grenz, *The Social*, p.166, adds that most see Calvin as the one who truly set forth the Reformed view of the *imago dei* and that it emphasizes representation. 'At the heart of Calvin's teaching ... is his [use] of a metaphor ... namely, the idea that the divine image is similar to a mirror. The idea that the divine image is like a mirror is linked with another theological theme ... namely, the assertion that God's creative intention is that the glory of the Maker shine through what is made, so that the creation becomes "the sphere of divine glory."'

27. Grudem, *Systematic*, pp.442-443, agrees.

28. John N. Oswalt, 'Kabod', *Theological Word Book of the Old Testament*, Moody, 1980, vol. 1, p.42.

29. Bernard Ramm, *Them He Glorified*, Eerdmans, 1963, p.9.

30. Erickson, *Christian Theology*, p.997, agrees when he writes that glory refers to 'the greatness of [H]is entire nature'.

31. John N. Oswalt, 'Kabod', TWOT, p.1, 42, agrees.

32. Ibid, p.42.

33. John Piper, *Desiring God: Meditations of a Christian Hedonist*, Multnomah, 1986, p.31.

34. Ramm, *Them He Glorified*, p.10.

35. John N. Oswalt, 'Kabod', TWOT, p.1, 42.

36. In addition to the statement in Psalm 8:5 which identifies glory with the *imago dei*.

37. Os Guinness, 'America's Last Men and Their Magnificent Talking Cure', JBC, 15, 2, 1997: p,31.

38. For a more thorough defence of the centrality of the glorification of God by man in the Old Testament see John Piper, *Let the Nations Be Glad*, Baker, 1993, pp.17-22. See also Grudem, *Systematic*, p.440.

39. J.I. Packer, Thomas Howard, *Christianity: The True Humanism*, Word, 1985, p.41. Tony, 'Keeping up the Image', p.36, agrees when he writes, 'the image of God is revealed most completely in [Christ]'. Thomas R. Schreiner, *Paul: Apostle of God's Glory in Christ*, InterVarsity Press, 2001, p.156, adds, 'Only through Jesus Christ, the one and only image of God, can human beings attain what God intended in making Adam according to his image.'

40. Grudem, *Systematic*, pp.441-442, agrees: 'This understanding of the doctrine of the creation of man has very practical results. When we realize that God created us to glorify him, and when we start to act in ways that fulfill that purpose, then we begin to experience an intensity of joy in the Lord that we have never before known. When we add to that the realization that God himself is rejoicing in our fellowship with him, our joy becomes "inexpressible and filled with heavenly glory" (1 Peter 1:8, author's expanded paraphrase).'

41. Brevard S. Childs, *The Book of Exodus*, The Westminster Press, 1976, repr., pp.591-593, argues that this older tradition, i.e. the account of Moses and the tent of meeting, functions in this context to highlight his intercessory function, to show that the people had a greater respect for Moses who had more piety toward God than they did, and finally it shows that God had not abandoned them fully.

42. Walter Kaiser, *Exodus in the Expositor's Bible Commentary*, Zondervan, 1990, p.483.

43. Leonard J. Coppes, 'Nuach', TWOT, p.2, 562.

44. The term *paneh* literally means 'face'. However one of its connotations is 'presence', because to see one's face is to be in one's presence. Here in this text it denotes to be in Yahweh's presence as a privilege, to have access to him (Brown-Drivers-Briggs, p.816) such that he can help. In Exodus 25:8 we read, 'Let them construct a sanctuary for Me, that I may dwell among them' (NASB). This was at the heart of the purpose of the sanctuary. The sacrificial system which was built around it was to make possible for the perfectly holy God to dwell in the midst of the Israelites in a more realized way and in a way to bless. Because of their gross sin of the golden calf and

because of their obstinacy, God had threatened that he would not dwell in their midst (33:3).

45. Certainly the *waw* can be used to introduce result or logical flow and what tips the reader off to that function is the presence of the enclitic particle ('*echo*'), which in interrogatives has both a logical and temporal connotation: 'If something happens, then at that time what...?' (BDB, p.66). Such is the case here: 'If Yahweh's blessing realized presence does not go with Israel as a whole continually, then how...' The interrogative (*ma*), with the articulator inseparable preposition (*b'*) makes the question somewhat specific: 'By means of what evidence, events, by means of what phenomena will it be known...?' Moses wanted there to be concrete evidence that they had found favour in the eyes of Yahweh. If one looks forward to the book of Joshua and Rahab's words (2:10-11) it becomes apparent that Yahweh's subsequent presence with them and his working in their midst and their behalf became well known among many of the peoples and was seen as evidence of his favour upon them (cf. also Josh. 5:1; 10:1-2). In our present study this point is important because it is one more confirmation that man is to be about glorifying God.

46. First Moses, as the leader, wanted it to be known that he had found favour in the eyes of Yahweh, as people saw Yahweh's blessing upon him. Certainly, to find favour (*chen*) in the eyes of Yahweh means that the Lord has looked upon one favourably. Often, it is based upon the person(s)'s righteous behaviour and as such Yahweh rewards them with blessing. However, sometimes, as here, it is clearly not deserved. None the less, Yahweh still looks favourably upon people out of his undeserved favour. (cf. Edwin Yamauchi, '*chen*', TWOT, p.1, 303; and BDB, p.336.) Yet, Moses not only wanted others to see that he personally had found favour with Yahweh, but also the people. Such realization was crucial to Israel, the covenant people, glorifying God in the midst of other peoples, an integral part of the covenant (cf. Gen. 12:1-3; Exod. 19:5-6; and exemplified: Josh. 2:10-11). This blessing leading to glorification was absolutely dependent upon Yahweh's continued presence with them (such gives a clear idea of the significance of his presence).

47. BDB, p.811.

48. Victor P. Hamilton, 'Palach', TWOT, p.2, 724

49. John Piper, *The Justification of God: An Exegetical and Theological Study of Romans 9:1-23*, Baker, 1996, repr., p.80, argues, 'the request to see God's glory should be understood in this context as a desire to have God confirm his astonishing willingness to show his favor to a stiff-necked, idolatrous people (33:16ff.)'. In other words, Moses wanted to see God's glory, to understand somewhat his nature, so that he would know if God is a God of mercy and would forgive. Here is how Yahweh answers Moses (33:19-34:7): (a) 'And He said, "I Myself will make all My goodness [Probably all that is right, beautiful, praiseworthy – God's attributes] pass [Hiphil] before you [to be

seen]".' (b) 'I will proclaim the name [Here: reputation. It is encompassing God's goodness.] of the Lᴏʀᴅ before you.' With letters a and b it becomes very obvious that God wants to show Moses his attributes (at least in part) to fuel his faith and assure him of God's mercy and forgiveness. He begins doing that with the next statement. (c) 'I will be gracious to whom I will be gracious [Probably exercise saving and sanctifying grace], and I will have compassion on whom I will have compassion.' Piper, *Justification*, p.82, writes of this statement, 'Brevard Childs (*Exodus*, 596), J. P. Hyatt (*Exodus*, 317) and S.R. Driver (*Exodus*, 362), among others, have pointed out that to understand the intention of Exodus 33:19 c-d one must recognize that it is an example of the Hebrew formula called idem per idem. Other examples of the idiom are Exodus 4:13 ("I pray, Lord, send now by the hand you will send"); Exodus 16:23 ("Bake what you will bake, boil what you will boil"); 1 Samuel 23:13 ("They went about where they went about")... By leaving the action unspecified the force of this idiom is to preserve the freedom of the subject to perform the action in whatever way he pleases. By simply repeating the action without adding any stipulations the idem per idem formula makes clear that the way the action is executed is determined by the will of the subject within the limits of prevailing circumstances. Therefore when God [makes this statement], he is stressing that there are no stipulations outside his own counsel or will which determine the disposal of his mercy and grace.' Additionally, Piper, Justification, pp.82-83, demonstrates that *chesed* (covenant loyal lovingkindness) is behind *racham* (have mercy) and that God's willingness to be true to the covenant 'is owing solely to the sovereignty of God'. (d) God tells Moses that he cannot see God's face and live so he will put him in a cleft of the rock and will cover him with his hand and pass by and then remove his hand and let Moses see his back. In other words, Moses can see God only very partially due to his intense glory upon which man cannot fully look (Exodus 33:20-23). (e) God instructs Moses to go back up on the mountain and receive the ten words again as a renewal of the covenant (34:1-4). (f) The Lᴏʀᴅ descended in the cloud and stood with him and proclaimed his name (This is the fulfilment of 33:19b). What did he proclaim? 'The Lᴏʀᴅ, the Lᴏʀᴅ God, merciful and gracious, longsuffering, and abounding in covenant loyal love and truth, keeping covenant loyal love for thousands, forgiving iniquity and transgression and sin, by no means clearing the guilty, visiting the iniquity of the fathers upon the children's children to the third and fourth generation' (34:5-7).

So, in a context in which God reveals his character to Moses to fuel Moses' faith and assure him of Yahweh's mercy and forgiveness for the continuance of the journey through the wilderness and to the Promised Land, God assures Moses that he will go with him, that he will be sovereignly gracious, that he is merciful, gracious, patient, good, truthful, forgiving, faithful to the covenant and just. Clearly the quote is designed to bolster Moses' faith by showing that God will be sovereignly gracious upon those whom he has chosen, along with the context that shows he will be abundantly gracious and forgiving and will go with his people. All of this grace goes hand in hand with God's justice (34:6-7). God assures the man of God then that he will be gracious to them because they have been chosen by him, yet he will be in no way unjust in dealing with man. No one who lives a life of sinfulness will be let go and no one who knows him will fall out of his mercy. Even though God sovereignly chooses, each man will still receive his just deserts or will receive better — God's undeserved favour. Additionally, this section shows that God's glory and his name consist largely of his willingness to show mercy, but to do it by his own free and sovereign choice. As such, God is not being unjust or inconsistent with his own character and what is just and righteous, because these are defined by God's glory. Hence, God decrees what will take place and these decrees are consistent both with a biblical sense of right and also God's glory. As such, the quote does show that God is not unjust.

50. Kaiser, EBC, p.2, 484: *"horay* ('my back') is used of the 'back' of the tabernacle (26:12), the 'backs' of the twelve bronze oxen holding the molten sea in the temple courtyard (1 Kings 7:25) and of the 'backs' of men worshipping in the temple in Ezekiel's day (Ezek. 8:16). But since God is Spirit and has no form, and since no one can see him and live (v. 20), the word ... could just as well and more accurately be rendered 'the after-effects' of his radiant glory, which had just passed by'.

51. R.C. Sproul, *The Holiness of God*, Tyndale, 1998, revised, p.22.

52. 'The normal translation of the Hebrew noun and verb as "judge" and "to judge" can be misleading to modern readers, since the judges of Israel were military and political leaders rather than officials presiding over courts of law. Deborah is the only judge who is mentioned as having a judicial function in the usual sense (4:4, 5). The last judge, Samuel, was a priest and prophet.' *The Reformation Study Bible*, p.332.

53. Daniel I. Block, *Judges, Ruth, in The New American Commentary*, Broadman and Holman, 1999, vol. 6, p.243, writes of this verse, 'The conclusion is cast in the form of a double petition to God, reflecting a consciousness of the covenant blessings and curses as spelled out in Leviticus 26 and Deuteronomy 28.'

54. BDB, p.485.

55. BDB, p.1; R. Laird Harris, TWOT, pp.1, 3; Deut. 4:26; 8:19, 20; 11:17; 30:18; 23:16.

56. Block, *Judges, Ruth*, p.244, says of *ahab*: 'It denotes, fundamentally, "covenant commitment".' He calls attention to Exodus 20:5-6 (those who love me and keep my commandments) as the background.

57. Block, *Judges, Ruth*, pp.244-245.

58. It seems to me that God's covenantal blessings form a backdrop for the

biblical teaching on glorification. Glorification is, in part, the eschatological fulfilment of the covenantal blessings. Such is supported by the statement in 1 Samuel 2:30: 'But now the LORD says: "Far be it from Me; for those who honor Me I will honor, and those who despise Me shall be lightly esteemed."' See also Leviticus 26, Deuteronomy 28 and Joshua 23. VanGemeren, The Progress, p.26, adds, 'The history of redemption unfolds a progression in the outworking of God's plan of redemption that will unfold completely in the restoration of all things. All blessings, promises, covenants, and kingdom expressions are reflections or shadows of the great salvation in Jesus Christ that is to come at the end of the age.'

59. BDB, p.150.

60. With regards to *tiph'eret* ('beauty') Victor P. Hamilton, TWOT, pp.2, 713-14, argues that the meaning is 'beauty', 'glory' or 'pride'. The meaning can be seen best from the basic connotation of the related verb (*pa'ar*): 'to clothe with beauty'. With this in mind, along with the context of Lamentations, it is best to interpret this phrase such that God has humbled Israel in taking away the beauty of her physical appearance as a city, as well as her admired reputation of being a blessed people of Yahweh. Her reputation has been destroyed. This is also supported by uses of *tiph'eret* elsewhere in the Old Testament: Deuteronomy 26:19; Judges 4:9 (the attention and acclaim [praise] one would receive for acts of valour and courage); 1 Chronicles 22:5 and 2 Chronicles 3:6 (refers to the reputation for beauty of Solomon's temple that helped display God's glory); Esther 1:4 (a king's wealth and resultant reputation). We should also note with the use of this word group that the idea of beauty can also often be part of glory and glorification.

61. Stemming from this covenantal promise, the psalmists often ask that God would not let them be ashamed and conversely that he would bring shame upon their enemies – both centring upon the term bosh ('shame'): Pss. 6:10; 22:5; 25:2, 20; 31:1, 17; 35:4, 26; 40:14; 44:7; 53:5, et al.

62. Ramm, *Them He Glorified*, pp.55-56.

63. Ramm, *Them He Glorified*, p.56. Throughout the history of the church, this future vindication has also been recognized in creeds. For example, the Belgic Confession (1618), Article 37 on the final judgement, reads, 'In contrast, the faithful and elect will be crowned with glory and honor. The Son of God will "confess their names" before God his Father and the holy and elect angels; all tears will be "wiped from their eyes"; and their cause – at present condemned as heretical and evil by many judges and civil officers – will be acknowledged as the "cause of the Son of God". And as a gracious reward the Lord will make them possess a glory such as the heart of man could never imagine. So we look forward to that great day with longing in order to enjoy fully the promises of God in Christ Jesus, our Lord.'

64. John Calvin, *Institutes of the Christian Religion*, Henry Beveridge, trans., Eerdmans, 1981, Book 1, ch. 15, sec. 6, p.167, seems to have this in mind when

he writes, 'For whence have men such a thirst for glory but from a sense of shame? And whence this sense of shame, but from a respect for what is honourable? Of this, the first principle and source is a consciousness that they were born to cultivate righteousness...'

65. One of the richest, yet most overlooked, ways that these blessings are developed is in Psalm 21 where David affirms his joy in the LORD's victory wrought through and in behalf of him as king. In verses 2 through 6 he recounts several blessings which God bestows upon him as king. They include: God has answered his prayers and met his needs (2); gives him good blessings (3a); set a gold crown upon him recognizing his God-given place of rule (3b); granted a long life (4); bestowed glory, honour, and majesty as a result of God's gracious dealings and salvation (5); and rewarded him with great gladness in the presence of God (6). All of these are the results the Davidic Covenant (cf. 2 Samuel 7:12-16) which is a more narrow and focused restatement of the Abrahamic covenant (cf. 1 Chr. 17:13-14, 21-22; Jer. 33:19-22). David's dynasty is exalted and blessed not only for the benefit of David, but also for the benefit of the people (2 Sam. 5:12; 1 Chr. 14:2). In other words, the people are blessed in the king, their representative. His blessings and glory and honour become theirs. As such, Psalm 21 becomes a type of the relation of the saint in union with the King, Jesus Christ, in the New Testament. In the King we will find the great, glorious, and honouring blessings spoken of in Psalm 21.

66. VanGemeren, *The Progress*, p.447, adds, 'The message of radical transformation came progressively into focus through the ministry of Moses, Samuel, Elijah, and the prophets. Toward the end of the Old Testament canon it was clear that only God's Messiah could bring deliverance, vindication, and a permanent era of peace.'

67. See John N. Oswalt, 'Judgment and Hope: The Full-Orbed Gospel', *Trinity Journal*, 17, 2 (Fall 1996): pp.191-202.

68. F. Delitzsch, *Isaiah, in Commentary on the Old Testament in Ten Volumes*, C. F. Keil and F. Delitzsch, Eerdmans, 1986, repr. vol. 7, 2nd part, p.174: 'The idea of "the servant of Jehovah" assumed, to speak figuratively, the form of a pyramid. The base was Israel as a whole; the central section was that Israel, which was not merely Israel according to the flesh, but according to the spirit also; the apex is the person of the Mediator of salvation springing out of Israel. And the last of the three is regarded (1) as the centre of the circle of the promised kingdom – the second David; (2) the centre of the circle of the people of salvation – the second Israel; (3) the centre of the circle of the human race – the second Adam.'

69. Wayne Grudem, *Systematic*, pp.830-831, agrees and adds as proof the reality that Jews in the time of Jesus expected resurrection (John 11:24). Also, Hebrews 11:10-16 affirms that Old Testament saints expected resurrection.

70. J. A. Schep, *The Nature of the Resurrection Body*, Eerdmans, 1964, p.12.

71. J. A. Shep, *The Nature*, p.23.

72. Murray J. Harris, From Grave to Glory, Academie/Zondervan, 1990, p.66; Schep, The Nature, pp.41ff.; Elmer B. Smick, *Job*, in *Expositor's Bible Commentary*, p.4, 943, all agree. Moreover, this is an affirmation of the future hope of beatific vision. See below.

73. The term I have translated 'my mouth' (*k'bodiy*) can mean 'great', 'liver', 'glory' or 'glorious', depending upon the vowel pointing. Some versions (NKJV, NASB) have taken it as 'glory'. However, Harris (TWOT) takes it as a figurative use of 'liver' based upon the context (Note the figurative use of 'liver' in verse 7b and here in 9 the use of 'heart' and 'flesh') and also upon the Septuagint which has 'tongue'. It seems that the LXX translators were probably seeking to render 'liver'. In light of this, the NIV ('tongue') and the NLT ('mouth') seem to be the best renderings. VanGemeren, *Psalms*, EBC, p.5, renders it as 'inner being' (p.159), which may be even closer to the meaning yet.

74. VanGemeren, Psalms, p.160, argues that it is a designation for God's servant.

75. VanGemeren, Psalms, p.158.

76. VanGemeren, Psalms, p.159.

77. This is 'the name used traditionally for the vision of God as he is, which will be the joy of the redeemed in heaven'. Alan Richardson, ed., *A Dictionary of Christian Theology*, The Westminster Press, 1969, p.30.

78. See 1 Chronicles 6:22. These were descendants of Kohath, a son of Levi. They served in the temple as musicians.

79. TWOT, pp.2, 716.

80. BDB, p.391.

81. 'Asaph (Pss. 50, 73-83) was one of David's choirmasters and a descendant of Gershon, son of Levi (cf. 1 Chr. 6:39; 15:17; 2 Chr. 5:12). The collection is also known as the Asaphite Psalms.' VanGemeren, *Psalms*, pp.34-35.

82. See BDB, p.420 and Isaiah 44:26.

83. This is the only occurrence in the Asaphite Psalms. In Psalm 1 the counsel of the wicked is offset against the law of the LORD. In Psalm 20:4 it refers to the purpose of a person, the results of their self deliberation. In Psalm 33:11 the term, used with Yahweh, refers to his purposes and his will (see also Prov. 19:21). This meaning is also supported by how the verb nachah is often used in Hebrew poetry. It refers to guidance in the way of righteousness.

84. Moody, 94, 11 (July/August, 1994): p.4.

85. Gary V. Smith, *The Prophets as Preachers*, Broadman and Holman, 1994, p.119. For additional introductory comments see my previous treatment above.

86. D. Brent Sandy and Martin G. Abegg, Jr., 'Apocalyptic', in D. Brent Sandy and Ronald L. Giese, Jr., eds, *Cracking Old Testament Codes*, Broadman and Holman, 1995, p.185.

87. This may very well be a case of what Craig L. Blomberg terms 'double fulfilment'. He explains, 'in a number of texts from the latter prophets ... especial-

ly in Isaiah, the results of an ordinary grammatico-historical exegesis of the OT text point clearly to a referent within the time frame of the OT books. Yet those same passages, especially when read within the context of their immediately surrounding paragraphs or chapters, disclose a further dimension of meaning never approximated by any OT-age event'.

'It seems plausible, therefore, to affirm that the prophetic author consciously looked both for a relatively immediate referent and for a more longer-term eschatological fulfillment.' See Craig L. Blomberg, 'Interpreting Old Testament Prophetic Literature in Matthew: Double Fulfillment', *Trinity Journal*, 23, 1 (Spring, 2002): p.19.

88. These two themes are not in opposition to one another. God is at the same time merciful and just. As such, he will give his people hope, but will also judge sin and discipline wayward children. Likewise, if Judah was to be the people of God out of whom the Messiah would come, punishment was necessary. God's refining of them was actually an indication that he had not given up on this purpose. Hence, the very presence of such hard times was to be part of their hope (cf. Prov. 3:11-12). See John N. Oswalt, 'Judgment and Hope: The Full-Orbed Gospel', *Trinity Journal*, 17, 2 (Fall 1996): pp.191-202.

89. Neil O. Skjoldal, 'The Function of Isaiah 24-27', *Journal of the Evangelical Theological Society*,, 36, 2 (June 1993): p.169.

90. Schep, *The Nature*, p.51 (cf. 2 Sam. 15:30; Jer. 14:3ff.; Esth. 6:12).

91. Schep, *The Nature*, p.51, writes, 'Instead of rendering the verb bala' [in the past tense]..., it seems better to employ the future, as do many modern versions and commentators. The Hebrew perfect tense is sometimes used to denote future actions.'

92. Schep, *The Nature*, pp.52-53.

93. Such fits with the emphases of this entire section. Skjoldal, 'The Function of Isaiah 24-27', p.172, writes in regard to the function of these chapters: 'The ungodly people of the world, especially the apostate nation of Israel, were put on notice that God is still in complete control over man and the elements. For the godly – that is, those who trusted God and were waiting on him – God provides great encouragement. He has promised that he will conquer all his enemies, including death, and that the sinful nation, after its conversion, will eventually prosper and become the center of universal worship. The "new world order" has been introduced: God is king. He must punish sinners and bless the faithful.'

94. See Geoffrey W. Grogan, *Isaiah*, in *The Expositor's Bible Commentary*, Zondervan, 1986, vol. 6, p.163 for a succinct and helpful overview of Isaiah 26.

95. This is why the NLT renders the clause, 'Those who belong to God will live'. Calvin, in his commentary on Isaiah agrees.

96. BDB, p.615.

97. Schep, *The Nature*, p.55.

98. It can also be said that the context seems to demand that death has taken place, rather than some form of humiliation alone. The term *'aphar* ("dust") is often used in Isaiah to refer to a state of humiliation (cf. 25:12; 26:5; 29:4; 41:2; 47:1; and 52:2), however the connotation seems to be more than that here, although humiliation can be part of death and returning to the dust as it is part of the curse and fall of man, along with the curse upon Satan (cf. Gen. 3:15, 19; Isa. 65:25).

99. Isaiah uses the verb ranan ('sing/shout for joy') in texts in which people (12:6; 24:14; 35:6; 65:14) or the heavens (44:23; 49:13) are exulting with great joy for the merciful and redemptive works of Yahweh. In Isaiah 49:13 the verb is used synonymously with the verb giyl, which denotes rejoicing, going around or about and being excited (BDB, p.162). This is not some mundane or anemic happiness. No, it is the great excitement and delight that reaches deep within the heart because great good (see 65:14: 'out of the joy [mitub: lit. "from the good"] of their hearts' – NIV) has happened. In fact, Isaiah, in looking forward to the time that God would come to save his people (probably a reference to the coming Messiah, Immanuel), says that 'the mute tongues shout for joy' (35:6, NIV). Singing for joy is that which the mute would do when their speech is restored. This is the excitement, the sheer exuberance, which the resurrected will have someday according to the prophet Isaiah. Though the reader is not given the specifics of why, certainly some of the reason is clear: there will be life after death and great delight in the presence of God (cf. Ps. 16:9-11). We will find out that the NT fills in the holes and explains the reasons.

100. Concerning the clause we did not address, 'for your dew is like the dew of herbs' (or 'dew of light'), Schep, The Nature, pp.55-56, comments, 'The Lord, who by means of the dew and light in nature causes the earth to bring forth plants and fruits, will raise his righteous dead from the dust of the earth in which they "dwell", quickening them by the life-giving dew from the realm of light in which God dwells.'

101. BDB, p.952.

102. Schep, *The Nature*, pp.55-56.

103. Das Buch Jesaia, Vandenhoeck und Ruprecvht, 1922. Cited in Geoffrey W. Grogan, *Isaiah*, in *The Expositor's Bible Commentary*, Regency Reference House, 1986, vol. 6, p.7.

104. Grogan, Isaiah, p.18.

105. See Willis J. Beecher, 'The Servant', in *Classical Evangelical Essays in Old Testament Interpretation*, Walter C. Kaiser, Jr., ed., Baker, 1985, repr., pp.187-202.

106. Grogan, *Isaiah*, p.303.

107. Lit. 'seed'. The sense is as the ESV, NASB, and NIV translate it: 'his offspring'. The offspring is probably those who follow him and partake of his sacrificial death. Calvin, *Commentaries* (in loc.), writes, 'Isaiah means that the death of Christ not only can be no hindrance to his having a seed, but

will be the cause of his having offspring; that is, because, by quickening the dead, he will procure a people for himself, whom he will afterwards multiply more and more; and there is no absurdity in giving the appellation of Christ's seed to all believers, who are also brethren, because they are descended from Christ.'

108. It is not clear if God or the Servant is the subject. But the main point is clear enough. Though the Servant will die, none the less he will have more days, he will see his offspring. Hence, there is only one conclusion that one can draw, there is life after death, i.e. resurrection, in store for the suffering Servant. Note what Calvin, *Commentaries* (in loc.) says of this clause: 'Christ shall not be hindered by his death from prolonging his days, that is, from living eternally. Some persons, when departing from life, leave children, but children who shall survive them, and who shall live so as to obtain a name only when their fathers are dead. But Christ shall enjoy the society of his children; for he shall not die like other men, but shall obtain eternal life in himself and his children. Thus Isaiah declares that in the head and the members there shall be immortal life.'

109. The main thought seems to be that the suffering Servant will see that which results from the suffering (i.e. the vicarious atoning suffering and death) of his whole person.

110. The satisfaction will come from his seeing the salvific results, i.e. the justification of sinners, the spiritual offspring.

111. These final two clauses seem to picture the post-mortem, yet, living again, suffering Servant as triumphant over enemies – as if he is returning victorious from battle. He has defeated sin and death.

112. Consider the following:

Isaiah 52:13b is fulfilled in Jesus in Philippians 2:9.

Isaiah 52:14 is fulfilled in Jesus in John 19:3.

Isaiah 52:15c is fulfilled in Jesus according to Romans 15:21 and Ephesians 3:5, 9.

John 12:38 applies the words of Isaiah 53:1 (which may have initially referred to the message proclaimed by the believing remnant [cf. Isaiah 52:7]) to Jesus. Romans 10:16 applies it to Christians proclaiming the good news.

John 8:17 applies Isaiah 53:4a to Jesus in regard to diseases. Hebrews 9:28 and 1 Peter 2:24 apply it to Jesus and death.

Romans 4:25, 1 Corinthians 15:3 and 1 Peter 2:24-25 apply Isaiah 53:5 to Jesus with regards to his vicarious atonement.

Isaiah 53:7a,b is fulfilled in Matthew 26:63, 27:12-14, Mark 14:61, 15:5, Luke 23:9 and John 19:9 with regards to Jesus.

Acts 8:32-35 makes it clear that Isaiah 53:7-8 is talking about Jesus and his vicarious atonement.

Isaiah 53:8a was fulfilled in Jesus as recorded in Matthew 27:11-26 and Luke

23:1-25.

Isaiah 53:9a,b and 53:12d were fulfilled in Jesus according to Matthew 27:38, 57-60, Mark 15:27, Luke 22:37 and Luke 23:33.

1 Peter 2:22-23 applies Isaiah 53:9d to Jesus and his suffering.

Isaiah 53:10c is fulfilled in Jesus as recorded in John 1:29 and 2 Corinthians 5:21.

Isaiah 53:10d is fulfilled in Jesus as recorded in Acts 2:24 and 1 Corinthians 15:4.

Isaiah 53:11b is fulfilled in Jesus as recorded in Acts 13:38-39 and Romans 5:15-18.

Isaiah 53:12f is fulfilled in Jesus as recorded in Luke 23:34.

113. Cf. Schep, *The Nature*, p.57.

114. Willem A. VanGemeren, *Interpreting the Prophetic Word*, Zondervan, 1990, p.342, cited in George M. Schwab, Sr., 'The Book of Daniel and the Godly Counselor', JBC, 14, 2 (Winter 1996): p.33.

115. Richard D. Patterson, 'Holding On to Daniel's Court Tales', JETS, 36, 4 (December 1993), pp.445-454, argues that the first six chapters resemble a number of ancient works which tell of foreigners in court who undergo great tests of faith and triumph.

116. F. F. Bruce, *New Testament History*, Doubleday and Company, 1980, repr., pp.3-4.

117. These texts out of the Gospels reveal that the destruction of the temple in Jerusalem in A.D. 70 also became a type of the end-times activity of the Antichrist. Schep, The Nature, p.59, agrees that the text does refer to Antiochus IV, but does also look beyond to eschatological events.

118. C. F. Keil, *Daniel*, pp.9, 481, agrees that 'the partitive interpretation of min [i.e. "from", prefixed to "those sleeping"] is the only simple and natural one'.

119. One other possibility may be that Daniel's focus was only upon the dead of Israel at that point and not of the other nations. This accounts for the partitive nature of the text. See Schep, *The Nature*, pp.60-61. Another would be C. F. Keil, Daniel, pp.9, 481-482, who argues that the 'many' has only in view those who will die during that great and future tribulation. Gleason Archer, *Daniel*, in *The Expositor's Bible Commentary*, Zondervan, 1985, vol. 7, p.153, argues that the 'many' refers only to believers and that the rest of the verse then takes up the resurrection of all people – 'some to everlasting life, others to shame and everlasting contempt'. However, the text does not seem to allow for this interpretation. The 'some' and 'others' are most likely taken as delineating further the 'many'.

120. J. Schupphaus, 'yashen', *TDOT*, pp.6, 441.

121. Ibid.

122. See also Calvin, *Commentaries*, in loc.

123. The verb is used elsewhere to refer to an awakening from death: 2 Kings

4:31, Job 14:12, Jeremiah 51:39, 57, Isaiah 26:19.

124. Calvin, *Commentaries*, in loc.

125. Alan A. Macrae, TWOT, pp.2, 672.

126. BDB, p.358.

127. BDB, p.201.

128. Cf. S. H. Travis, 'Immortality and Eternal Life', under 'Eschatology' in Sinclair Ferguson, David F. Wright, eds., *New Dictionary of Theology*, IVP, 1986, p.230.

129. For this understanding of 'life' in the Old Testament, see our discussion of Psalm 16:11 earlier.

130. Charles Colson, Nancey Pearcey, *How Now Shall We Live?*, Tyndale, 1999, p.135.

131. BDB, p.968.

132. Louis Goldberg, 'Sakal', TWOT, pp.2, 877.

133. See Leon J. Wood, TWOT, pp.1, 237, for both homonyms.

134. Schep, *The Nature*, p.60, agrees and adds, 'In this connection Daniel 7:27 is also significant because it announces that the Messianic Kingdom will be established on earth. This implies that the risen saints will live there, though the glorification of their bodies ... suggests a far-reaching change in life's conditions on earth...'

135. C. F. Keil, *Daniel*, p.484; Gleason Archer, *Daniel*, p.152.

136. One last Old Testament passage we can cite that implies resurrection is one we did not cover – Proverbs 23:13-14 (ESV): 'Do not withhold discipline from a child; if you strike him with a rod, he will not die. If you strike him with the rod, you will save his soul from Sheol.'

137. Murray J. Harris, *From Grave to Glory: Resurrection in the New Testament*, Academie, Zondervan, 1990, pp.69-79.

138. S. Aalen, 'Glory, Honor', *Dictionary of New Testament Theology*, pp.2, 45; Gerhard Kittel, 'doxa', *Theological Dictionary of the New Testament*, pp.2, 246.

139. S. Aalen, 'Glory, Honor', DNTT, pp.2, 44; Gerhard Kittel, 'doxa', TDNT, pp.2, 246.

Chapter 2

1. It is called the Septuagint (Latin for seventy) because tradition suggests the original Greek translation was done by either seventy or seventy-two Hebrew elders in Alexandria. There are, however, later recensions. Richard N. Soulen, *Handbook of Biblical Criticism*, 2nd ed., John Knox, 1981, p.176.

2. Moises Silva, *Biblical Words and Their Meaning*, Academie/Zondervan, 1983, p.66.

3. Bernard Ramm, *Them He Glorified*, Eerdmans, 1963, p.24.

4. Millard Erickson, *Christian Theology*, Baker, 1994, repr., one volume ed., p.997.

5. R. C. Sproul and Robert Wolgemuth, *What's in the Bible*, W Group, Thomas Nelson, 2000, p.286, write, 'The glory of God is His worthiness, His holiness

... His "God-ness.'"

6. Thomas R. Schreiner, *Paul, Apostle of God's Glory in Christ*, InterVarsity Press, 2001, pp.28-29 comments on Paul's view towards sin this way: 'The origin of all sin is failure to serve and worship God.' Later on he adds (pp.102-103): 'Sin is first and foremost a rejection of the supremacy of God and his lordship over our lives ... It is a refusal to honor and praise God.'

7. More specifically, D. A. Carson, *The Farewell Discourse and Final Prayer of Jesus*, Baker, 1980, p.137, writes, 'In the New Testament, the Spirit is the down payment of eternal life, the foretaste of the eternal, unshielded presence of Deity, the one who incorporates us into the body of Christ, the one who regenerates us and indwells us: how could these blessings possibly come to us until the basis for them was established? And that basis is the triumph of Christ, his return to the Father via the cross and the grave.'

8. Jonathan Edwards, *A History of the Work of Redemption*, in *The Works Of Jonathan Edwards*, Banner of Truth, 1995, repr., vol. 1, p.535, agrees: 'God's design was perfectly to restore all the ruins of the fall, so far as concerns the elect part of the world, by his Son; and therefore we read of the restitution of all things...[and] to perfect and complete the glory of all of the elect by Christ.' Consider also the comments of Willem VanGemeren, *The Progress of Redemption*, Baker, 2000, repr., pp.26-27: 'Jesus Christ is the theological center of all history ... The center of the Bible is the incarnate and glorified Christ, by whom all things will be renewed.' Schreiner, *Paul, Apostle*, p.33, puts it this way: 'The completion of salvation history does not occur apart from Jesus Christ.'

9. These phrases come from Leon Morris, *The Gospel According to John*, in *The New International Commentary on the New Testament*, F.F. Bruce, ed., Eerdmans, 1984, repr., pp.122-123, who wrote, 'John's thought is his own. He uses a term which would be full of meaning to men whatever their background. But whatever their background they would not find John's thought identical with their own. His idea of the Logos is essentially new.

'We may sum up this part of the discussion in the words of William Temple. The Logos, he says, "alike for Jew and Gentile represents the ruling fact of the universe, and represents that fact as the self-expression of God. The Jew will remember that by the Word of the Lord were the heavens made; the Greek will think of the rational principle of which all natural laws are particular expressions. Both will agree that this Logos is the starting-point of all things."'

10. A point affirmed by John Calvin, *Institutes of the Christian Religion*, Henry Beveridge, translator, Eerdmans, 1981, repr., Book 1, ch. 13, sections 27-29.

11. Of course, John does not deal with the one way in which Jesus Christ did not become like us – 'like us in all respects apart from sin' wrote the Fathers at Chalcedon. That was beyond the purpose of his Prologue. He wanted at this point to make it clear that Jesus was fully human. Again quoting Chalcedon:

'...complete in manhood ... truly man, consisting also of a reasonable soul and body ... of one substance with us as regards his manhood...' Elsewhere Paul makes the distinction between Jesus Christ and every other human when he wrote of His incarnation: 'coming in the likeness [homoiomati] of men' (Phil. 2:7 [cf. also Rom. 8:3]). Based upon the fact that the apostle makes it clear in the Philippians 2 context that Jesus was fully man and that he uses the term homoiomati uniformally in his epistles as denoting a similarity that retains at least some slight difference (Rom. 1:23; 6:5; 5:14 [this occurrence is less clear, but does not necessitate one to one correspondence]; 8:3), we conclude that Paul's point in Philippians 2:7 is that Jesus was and is fully man. Yet he seemed to want to make some slight distinction between Jesus and the rest of mankind and most likely it was that Jesus Christ was not conceived and born with a sin nature, nor did he ever sin (cf. 2 Cor. 5:21; Heb. 4:15; 7:26; 1 Peter 2:22; 1 John 3:5). See Alva J. McClain, 'The Doctrine of the Kenosis', *The Masters Seminary Journal*, 9, 1 (Spring 1998): 85-96; Marvin R. Vincent, *The Epistles to the Philippians and to Philemon*, in *International Critical Commentary*, Samuel R. Driver, Alfred Plummer, Charles A Briggs, eds, T & T Clark, 1976, repr., p.59; *The Reformation Study Bible*, 1877; and Homer A Kent, Jr. *Philippians*, vol. 11 in the *Expositor's Bible Commentary*, Zondervan, 1978, pp.437-438.

12. K.-H. Bartels, 'One', DNTT, 2, Colin Brown, ed., Zondervan, 1982, repr., p.725. See also the following versions: ESV, RSV, NIV, NLT, NCV.

13. H. E. W. Turner, 'Generation', in *A Dictionary of Christian Theology*, Alan Richardson, ed., Westminster, 1969, p.132: 'The term, Generation ... has been increasingly used from the time of Origen to express the relation of the Son to the Father. Its scriptural basis lies in the correlation between the Father and the Son in the Gospels (particularly the Fourth Gospel). Origen interpreted the Generation of the Son as an eternally continuous act, though Cyril of Jerusalem ... preferred to interpret it as a single event before time ... The Cappadocian Fathers employed the term as the differentiating particularity of the Son.' Louis Berkhof, *Systematic Theology*, Eerdmans, p.94, adds, 'It is that eternal and necessary act of the first person in the Trinity, whereby He, within the divine Being, is the ground of a second personal subsistence like His own, and puts the second person in possession of the whole divine essence, without any division, alienation, or change.'

14. F. Buchsel, 'monogenes', TDNT, 4, Gerhard Kittel, ed., Eerdmans, 1993, repr., pp.737-741.

15. It seems most probable that it is derived from gennao ('born' or 'beget'). Ibid. However, contra Bartels, DNTT, 725.

16. In fact the LXX uses *agapetos* ('beloved') in some places to render the word that is also rendered as monogenes, which is yachiyd. We must not conclude that the two Greek terms are synonymous. However, their field of meaning does overlap – in most cases the monogenes is greatly loved due to his or

her unique status.

17. The LXX in Genesis 22:2 and 16 has *agapetos* for *yachiyd* and nothing in verse 12.

18. Timothy George, *Is the Father of Jesus the God of Muhammad?*, Zondervan, 2002, p.63.

19. Louis Berkhof, *Systematic Theology*, Eerdmans, pp.93-94, does a masterful job of showing that the son status of the Word (Jesus Christ) is a necessary act of God because this is the only way the Son is of the same essence with the Father. Following from this it is also eternal. As such, this is the main sense of the doctrine of eternal generation. For all eternity the Word, the second person of the Trinity, has been in relationship with the Father such that he is Son.

20. John Piper, *The Pleasures of God: Meditations on God's Delight in Being God*, Multnomah, 1991, p.29. The eternal generation of the Son has been affirmed throughout the history of the church. One very good and clear example is the London Baptist Confession of 1689, ch. 2, par. 3: 'In this divine and infinite Being there are three subsistences, the Father, the Word or Son, and Holy Spirit, of one substance, power, and eternity, each having the whole divine essence, yet the essence undivided: the Father is of none, neither begotten nor proceeding; the Son is eternally begotten of the Father; the Holy Spirit proceeding from the Father and the Son; all infinite, without beginning, therefore but one God, who is not to be divided in nature and being, but distinguished by several peculiar relative properties and personal relations; which doctrine of the Trinity is the foundation of all our communion with God, and comfortable dependence on him.'

21. The Heidelberg Catechism, question 33, asks, 'Why is Christ called the "only begotten Son" of God, since we are also the children of God?' The answer: 'Because Christ alone is the eternal and natural Son of God; but we are children adopted of God, by grace, for his sake.'

22. It was C. S. Lewis who very astutely made the point in *Beyond Personality*, Macmillan Co, 1948, p.5 that the begotten status of Jesus implies deity. He wrote, 'When you beget, you beget something of the same kind as yourself. A man begets human babies, a beaver begets little beavers, and a bird begets eggs which turn into little birds. But when you make, you make something of a different kind from yourself. A bird makes a nest, a beaver builds a dam, and man makes a wireless set – or he may make something more like himself than a wireless set, say a statue. If he's clever enough a carver he makes a statue which is very much like a man indeed. But, of course, it's not a real man; it only looks like one. It can't breathe or think. It's not alive.' Cited in Piper, Pleasures, p.37.

23. A. C. Thiselton, 'exegeomai', DNTT, 1, 575.

24. See Schreiner, Romans; Moo, Romans, in loc.

25. Thomas R. Schreiner, 'Head Coverings, Prophecies, and the Trinity', in *Re-*

covering Biblical Manhood and Womanhood, John Piper and Wayne Grudem, ed's., Crossway, 1991, pp.124-139, agrees.

26. Schreiner, 'Head Coverings', p.132, agrees when he writes: 'I understand the major burden of 11:3-6, then, to be as follows: Women can pray and prophesy in public, but they must do so with a demeanor and attitude that supports male headship because in that culture wearing a head covering communicated a submissive demeanor and feminine adornment.'

27. See Wayne Grudem, 'Does kefalh mean "Source" or "Authority Over" in Greek Literature? A Survey of 2,336 Examples', TrinJ, 6, 1 (Spring 1985): 38-59; and Wayne Grudem, 'The Meaning of kefalh ("Head"): A Response to Recent Studies', TrinJ, 11, 1 (Spring 1990): 3-72.

28. In this text Paul argues for distinction in roles (vv. 3-10), yet, in verses 11-12 he makes it clear that women are not somehow inferior to men (See Schreiner, 'Head Coverings', pp.136-137). In Genesis 2:18 we read, 'And Yahweh God said, "It is not good for man to be alone; I will make for him his equally prominent helper [`ezer k`negeddo]."' Woman has a different role (helper), yet she is in no way man's inferior (equally prominent). Regarding abilities, Scriptural examples prove that women are not necessarily inferior to men in abilities. One needs only think of Rahab, Deborah, Jael, Abigail, Huldah the prophetess and Priscilla to remember that women can be very capable leaders, militarists, teachers and counsellors. And, can we not easily point to men in the Scriptures who failed in all these areas (We need look no further than Saul, Solomon and so many other kings of Israel and Judah.)? So, the issue is not about worth or ability. It is about divinely-ordained roles.

29. Cf. Westminster Shorter Catechism, No.6.

30. This can also be seen in the immediate context. When Paul writes that 'the head of every man is Christ, the head of woman is man, and the head of Christ is God' (v. 3), he does not intend to imply that since God the Father is the authority over Christ the Son, therefore, he is not the authority over males or females. Nor does he intend to imply that because Christ is the authority over every male and the male over the woman that Christ is not also the authority over the woman. Christ is Lord over every woman (whether it is realized [cf. 1 Cor. 12:3] or not [cf. Phil. 2:10-11]). The point is to establish a descending order of authority and roles, yet as each level is descended, the levels above are also authorities and not just the immediately ascending one. It is most likely that Paul is following the same kind of logic in this verse. This would leave woman as the image and glory of God as well, but not in the exact same way as man.

31. That 'glory' is being used here to refer to honouring another is seen from the relationship of 'dishonour' (v. 14) and 'glory' (v. 15). See Schreiner, 'Head Coverings', p.133.

32. How do males show God's image and glory in a way that women do not? Calvin, 1 Corinthians, in loc., is probably leaning in the right direction

when he writes, 'The glory of God is seen in the higher standing which the man has, as it is reflected in every superior authority.' In other words, man, in his leadership and authority, represents God in a way that women do not. Calvin, *Institutes*, Book 1, ch. 15, sec. 4, writes, 'As to that passage of St. Paul (1 Cor. 11:7), in which the man alone, to the express exclusion of the woman, is called the image and glory of God, it is evident, from the context, that it merely refers to civil order.'

33. For proof that there was division consider Romans 2:1-29; 12:3, 9-21; 13:8-10; 14:1-23; 15:7-13.

34. For a good overview of the purpose of Romans and the historical background as stated, see the many fine articles in Karl P. Donfried, ed., *The Romans Debate*, Hendrickson, 1991, revised.

35. The Romans 8:19 passage is especially important in establishing this key aspect of glorification. Found in this very context of glorification discussion, we see that Paul refers to the event of glorification as 'the revealing of the sons of God' (ten apokalupsin ton huion tou theou). It will be a time when God unveils the true identity, character, and special place in his eyes the saints have.

36. D.A. Carson, *Matthew*, in *Expositor's Bible Commentary*, Frank E. Gaebelein, gen. ed., Zondervan, 1984, vol. 8, p.426, rightly argues that those passages speaking about the twelve judging Israel mean that Christ will include them in the judgement upon Israel for the wide scale rejection of the Messiah. On the 1 Corinthians 6:2 passage, F. W. Grosheide, *The First Epistle to the Corinthians*, in *The New International Commentary on the New Testament*, Ned B. Stonehouse, gen. ed., Eerdmans, 1964, p.134, n. 2, suggests that the inclusion in judgement for the church as a whole has to do with the fact that believers will be present (and we might add in the place of prominence) when Christ judges the world. Of course, for Paul's argument in 1 Corinthians 6:2 to work, the idea at least has to include the fact that believers will have the God-given wisdom to agree with Christ's judgement. If that is present in the believers, in seed form, then why can they not settle their own disputes? The point for the present study is that believers will be given a tremendous place of prominence in the age to come.

37. See also William Hendriksen, *Exposition of Paul's Epistle to the Romans*, Baker, 1980, vol. 1, p.264; and Douglas J. Moo, *The Epistle To The Romans*, Eerdmans, 1996, p.511.

38. Schreiner, *Romans*, p.477.

39. BAGD, p.602.

40. Murray, *Romans*, p.300.

41. Moo, *Romans*, p.511, agrees when he writes of these sufferings that they 'are not only those "trials" that are endured directly because of confession of Christ – for instance, persecution – but encompass the whole gamut of suffering, including things like illness, bereavement, hunger, financial reverses,

and death itself.'

42. If you are not familiar with baseball, Barry Bonds has been as much of a phenomenon in this sport as Lance Armstrong has been in cycling's Tour de France.

43. Schreiner, *Romans*, p.478, writes, 'Do the words eis hemas ("in us") ... mean that the glory is revealed "to us" or "for us"? Neither English phrase captures precisely the meaning of the text, for the idea is that the glory apprehends us and is bestowed upon us.' Murray, *Romans*, p.301, adds, 'That is to say, it is to reach unto us, to be bestowed upon us, so that we become the actual partakers; it is not a glory of which we are to be mere spectators.' Hendricksen, *Romans*, p.265, agrees: 'Significant is also the fact that the apostle ... [says] the "glory that is to be revealed in us". In other words, this glory will, as it were, come to us, enter us, and then, having filled us and enveloped us, will be revealed in us. We ourselves will be part of that glory: the redeemed will see it in each other. The angels will behold it in us, and will be filled with thanksgiving and praise to God.'

44. Sproul, Wolgemuth, *What's in the Bible*, p.308. Robert H. Mounce, Romans, in *The New American Commentary*, Broadman and Holman, 1995, vol. 27, p.184, adds, '...the glory of the coming age will be qualitatively distinct from the trials of the present. If we allow the difficulties of life to absorb our attention, they will effectively blot out the glory that awaits us. Our focus needs to be on things above (Col. 3:2)...'

45. Mounce, *Romans*, p.184: 'The personification of nature would not sound strange to those who were at home with rivers that "clap their hands" and mountains that "sing together for joy" (Ps. 98:8; cf. Isa. 55:2).'

46. Mounce, *Romans*, pp.187-188: 'The good of which Paul spoke is not necessarily what we think is best, but as the following verse implies, the good is conformity to the likeness of God's total plan for changing us from what we are by nature to what he intends us to be.'

47. It seems that *sunergeo* ('works together') is always used to speak of two components or beings operating in conjunction with one another to carry out the same task or goal. See Mark 16:20 (though textually questionable); 1 Corinthians 16:16; 2 Corinthians 6:1; James 2:22. In light of this, what Paul seems to be saying here in Romans 8:28 is that God sovereignly designs all events in such a way that all the events in the life of a believer (in the life of the church universal) are orchestrated together such that they work hand in hand, in conjunction with one another, to bring about good for the saint. God is the great Conductor of the symphony of history, bringing together all the parts for the beautiful music of the sanctification and glorification of the church!

For example, two years ago my wife's aunt lost her husband. That in and of itself does not bring about good unless certain other things are working with it. For Aunt Mary, these other things were probably teaching and reading on the providence and goodness of God, the work of the Holy Spirit, the emotional and prayer support of saints, the work of God's Spirit in her and no doubt countless other events and circumstances that were all working together. Even in the tragedy of losing her husband, Aunt Mary was being sanctified and certainly taken forward towards glorification. Cf. also Murray, *Romans*, p.314.

What this means is that believers have at least two strong answers to the question, 'Why do the things that happen in the world take place?' Ultimately they happen for the glory of God. Penultimately, they are divinely orchestrated to sanctify and glorify the church.

Moo, *Romans*, p.529, disagrees with this understanding of sunergeo and suggests that in many places this verb loses its 'with' connotation and means simply 'help', or 'assist someone to obtain something'. However, since he is unable to provide any New Testament examples, his take upon the verb seems less likely than what is argued above.

48. Grudem, *Bible Doctrine*, p.286, offers the following translation for this clause in Romans 8:29: 'those whom he long ago thought of in a saving relationship to himself'. S. M. Baugh, 'The Meaning of Foreknowledge', *The Grace of God the Bondage of the Will*, Thomas R. Schreiner, Bruce A. Ware, eds., vol. 1, p.188, shows that God's foreknowledge is addressed five times in the New Testament: Acts 2:23; Romans 8:29; 11:2; 1 Peter 1:2, 20. Three of these passages have to do with the salvation of man (Rom. 8:29; 11:2; 1 Peter 1:2) and two of them with Christ himself, God's foreknowledge of him as Saviour and his death (Acts 2:23; 1 Peter 1:20). In all five instances, as Baugh asserts, the connotation is not that God looked ahead in history and saw that something was going to happen and then he responded and made something good out of it. Rather, it is that he determined beforehand to bring about certain situations or a certain intimate relationship with one. In the texts concerning Christ, the Father determined beforehand that the Son would be an atoning sacrifice. In 1 Peter 1:2 Peter writes that saints are elected according to God's foreknowledge. He chooses them based upon whatever foreknowledge is. Based upon the Old Testament background of 'know' (it deals with intimate relationship often and not just a detached knowledge) and the logical problems with it being a non-active mere awareness (e.g. How can the outcome be assured?), what Peter is saying is that God determined that he would enter into an intimate close covenant relationship with these and therefore choose them. In 192ff. Baugh argues from Old Testament passages such as Amos 3:2 and Daniel 11:32 that to know carried with it the idea of commitment within covenant. We see examples of similar uses in the New Testament (e.g. Matt. 7:23; John 10:14; Gal. 4:8-9). Baugh also brings to light that the classic Arminian understanding of this passage (that God had previous awareness of our faith and therefore predestined us) is clearly reading one's theology into the text. Paul does not say 'he foreknew

our faith', but instead 'those whom He foreknew' – he foreknew us.

49. P. Jacobs, H. Krienke, DNTT, 1, 695-696, writes of this verb, 'The compound prohorizo (formed from pro, in front, before and horizo, to ordain...) is only used from the fourth century onwards ... and means to preordain. It is not found in the LXX. The NT uses prohorizo, preordain, six times to speak exclusively of God's decrees.' Those six uses include the following. In Acts 4:28, after Peter and John had been released from prison and the custody of Jewish leaders, they recounted what the chief priests and elders had said. In response, the disciples all lifted their voices to God in praise for his sovereignly-designed plan working in their lives, which is like the plan he worked in the life of Christ. In speaking of this they say, '...whatever Your hand and Your purpose determined before to be done'. This is somewhat parallel to Acts 2:23 which reads, 'this one [Jesus] by the ordained will and foreknowledge of God...' The second use is here in Romans 8:29-30. It is also used in 1 Corinthians 2:7. This speaks of God's predestination of the gospel, before time, for the glory of the elect: 'but we speak God's wisdom in a mystery, the hidden wisdom which God predestined before the ages to our glory'. Fourthly, in Ephesians 1:5 we read that we are predestined unto adoption as sons to the Father through Jesus Christ and according to the good pleasure of the Father's will. Finally in Ephesians 1:11 Paul says that we receive an inheritance because we have been predestined. This is according to the purpose of the one who works all things according to the counsel of his will. In conclusion, everything points to this verb meaning that God determined beforehand to effect in us the rest of the clause: 'to be conformed to the image of His Son...'

50. The reader needs to note an implication that we have found throughout the Scriptures beginning in Genesis – namely that the *imago dei* not only has an individual, but also a social element. Man, in relation with one another in the redeemed and glorified Church, will be the goal of the redemptive work of God. In this community, as each resembles Christ and as the church collectively reflects the triune God in relationship, Jesus Christ will receive great praise and adulation in that his redemptive work has made this all possible.

51. Schreiner, *Romans*, p.500.

52. Piper, *Desiring God*, p.111. We must also note that as each 'brother' is like Christ, in relation to every other brother, this is the point at which the social aspect of the *imago dei* will be reclaimed in full. Man, not only individually, but in Christ-like community, will fully reflect the glorious complete work of redemption – which has its precursors now in the present age as the Church is matured and lives out the unity (albeit imperfectly) for which Christ prayed (John 17:20-23). The answer to this prayer will be realized fully in the age to come.

53. There are no better short definitions for these verbs than what the Westmin-

ster Shorter Catechism offers in answers 31 and 33 respectively: 'Effectual calling is the work of God's Spirit, whereby, convincing us of our sin and misery, enlightening our minds in the knowledge of Christ, and renewing our wills, he doth persuade and enable us to embrace Jesus Christ, freely offered to us in the gospel.' 'Justification is an act of God's free grace, wherein he pardoneth all our sins, and accepteth us as righteous in his sight, only for the righteousness of Christ imputed to us, and received by faith alone.'

54. H. E. Dana, Julius R. Mantey, *A Manual Grammar of the Greek New Testament*, Macmillan, 1955, p.192.

55. Cf. also Hendricksen, *Romans*, p.285; and Moo, *Romans*, p.536, who both agree as to the implication of certainty in how this last clause is worded.

56. John Piper, *The Purifying Power of Living by Faith in Future Grace*, Multnomah, 1995, p.124.

57. R. C. Sproul, 'Works or Faith?' *TableTalk*, 15, 5 (May 1991): 6, writes, 'Our justification is always unto good works. Though no merit ever proceeds from our works, either those done before our conversion or those done afterwards, nevertheless good works are a necessary fruit of the faith. '"Necessary fruit?" Yes, necessary. Good works are not necessary for us to earn our justification. They are never the ground basis of our justification. They are necessary in another more restricted sense. They are necessary corollaries to true faith. If a person claims to have faith yet brings no fruit of obedience whatsoever, it is proof positive that the claim to faith is a false claim. True faith inevitably and necessarily bears fruit. The absence of fruit indicates the absence of faith.'

58. Grant R. Osborne, *The Hermeneutical Spiral*, InterVarsity, 1991, p.106.

59. 13 December 1998 sermon on Romans 2:6-10 preached at Bethlehem Baptist Church, Minneapolis, Minnesota.

60. 13 December 1998 sermon on Romans 2:6-10 preached at Bethlehem Baptist Church, Minneapolis, Minnesota.

61. Murray, *Romans*, p.89, comments on why this phrase is included: 'We must remember that he began his address to the Jew in v. 17, by an allusion to the name on which he prided himself ... Jew, and that he has just described in this verse the Jew that is worthy to be so-called. What, then, can be more natural, or more like St. Paul's style, than a renewed reference to the meaning of the name Jew? When Leah bore her fourth son she said, "Now will I praise the Lord: therefore she called his name Judah" (Gen. 24:35). When Jacob [was dying] this was the beginning of his blessing upon Judah: "Judah, thou art he whom thy brethren shall praise" (Gen. 49:8). St. Paul, in like manner, alluding to the meaning of the name, says of the true Jew that his praise is not from men, but from God.' pp. 89-90: 'He is striking again at what lies in the background of his thought throughout this chapter and which forms the basis of his indictment against the Jew, namely, the iniquity of reliance upon appearance and upon what passes muster in the judgment

of men.'

John 5:44 is also helpful: 'How can you believe, who receive honor from one another, and do not seek the honor that comes from the only God?' (NKJV).

Chapter 3

1. It is now believed by some researchers that babies develop an ability to listen to the language patterns and inflections native to their family during the first year. Sharon Begley, 'Your Child's Brain', *Newsweek* (February 19, 1996): pp.56-57.

2. This is the only time Chloe is mentioned in the New Testament. Though not explicitly stated, we assume that she was a Christian, perhaps even an influential Christian either in Corinth or Ephesus (the latter being the place from which Paul wrote this letter, cf. 1 Cor. 16:8). It is not clear in 1 Corinthians 1:11 whether Paul heard the message from someone in Chloe's Ephesus household who had, in turn, gotten the message from someone in Corinth, or whether someone from Chloe's Corinthian household had unearthed the division and taken the news to Paul in Corinth. It is most likely that Chloe was in Corinth. Otherwise, she would not have been known to the Corinthians. If she were so well-known from Ephesus that the Corinthians had an awareness of her, she most likely would be mentioned again – especially in conjunction with the church in Ephesus. See D. Edmond Hiebert, *Personalities around Paul*, Moody, 1973, p.225; and F. F. Bruce, *Paul: Apostle of the Heart Set Free*, Eerdmans, 1980, repr., p.258.

3. See Raymond C. Ortlund Jr., 'The Power of the Gospel in the Church Today', TrinJ, 18, 1 (Spring 1997): pp.3-13.

4. The *tois teleiois* ('those who are mature', NASB) of verse 6 probably refers to those who have been made complete, in other words, those who have been taught by the Spirit (v. 13) and who have the mind of Christ (v. 15). What Paul speaks to them is received by them as what it is, wisdom from God. How one receives the gospel depends upon one's spiritual state (cf. 1:18).

5. Jonathan Edwards, 'God Glorified in Man's Dependence', in *Jonathan Edwards on Knowing Christ*, Banner of Truth, 1990, repr., p.33: 'Those Christians to whom the apostle directs this epistle, dwelt in a part of the world where human wisdom was in great repute; as the apostle observes in [1:22] ... Corinth was not far from Athens, that had been for many ages the most famous seat of philosophy and learning in the world.'

6. Regarding *theou sophian* the sense is either 'divine wisdom' (F. W. Grosheide, *Commentary on the First Epistle to the Corinthians*, in *The New International Commentary on the New Testament*, F.F. Bruce, gen. ed., Eerdmans, 1964, repr., p.64) or 'wisdom from God'. Either one fits the context which is contrasting human versus divine wisdom or wisdom from man and wisdom from God.

7. Grosheide, *Corinthians*, p.64.

8. Andreas J. Kostenberger, 'The Mystery of Christ and the Church: Head and Body, "One Flesh"', TrinJ, 12, 1 (Spring 1991): pp.81-82, writes, 'A survey of the uses of musterion in the Pauline writings shows that it is the OT usage that is most consistent with Paul's use of the term. Paul does not teach that there is a body of religious truths that is reserved for Christian "initiates". Divine truth can be known by all Christians. It is not, as in the mystery religions, considered as communication with the intrinsically ineffable. It is therefore inaccurate to equate the meaning of the modern English term "mystery" with the Greek term ... Rather, musterion consistently denotes a divine truth which was once hidden but has now been revealed.'

9. BAGD, p.27.

10. Ibid.

11. See this same point also in 2 Thessalonians 2:13-14 and 1 Peter 5:10. Thomas R. Schreiner, *Paul, Apostle of God's Glory in Christ*, InterVarsity Press, 2001, p.453, adds, 'We have seen ... that eschatology pervades Pauline theology, particularly the tension between the already and not yet. The salvation of believers has already been inaugurated but not yet consummated. The future hope of salvation is an anchor for all of life, for it represents ultimate reality and the certain destination of all believers. The hope for future redemption runs like a thread through all of Paul's theology and it is woven into every theme in his writings ... The hope for future glorification, therefore, cannot be shunted aside to the periphery of Paul's thought, nor can we segment it so that it merely represents the last topic when organizing Paul's theology ... The hope of the future permeates every dimension of Paul's theology, reminding his readers that God's purposes will be realized.'

12. The verb, *egkakeo*, is used six times in the New Testament, five by Paul. In 2 Corinthians 4:1, 16, Paul writes that he does not become discouraged or lose heart at his tribulations. In Galatians 6:9 and 2 Thessalonians 3:13 it refers to thinking that one's well-doing or good works are not worth it. The only non-Pauline use (Luke 18:1) refers to ceasing to pray because one concludes it is not worth it.

13. Most likely Paul wrote this epistle to several churches in Asia Minor as a circular letter to be passed around – of which Ephesus was the most prominent. This is asserted because 'in Ephesus' (1:1) is lacking in some of the best and earliest manuscripts (e.g. Chester Beatty papyrus and Vaticanus uncial) and is also present in some of the best (Sinaitucus and Alexandrinus uncials). Additionally, there are the general comments Paul makes which are not in keeping with the fact that he had ministered among the Ephesians for over two years and would have known them well (e.g. 1:15; 3:2; 4:21). For this view see T. K. Abbott, *A Critical and Exegetical Commentary on the Epistles to the Ephesians and the Colossians*, in *International Critical Commentary*, T and T Clark, 1964, repr., p.vii.

14. This is also supported by 2 Timothy 2:10 where Paul writes, 'Because of this I

endure all things for the sake of the elect, in order that they also may obtain salvation which is in Christ Jesus with eternal glory.'

15. Bernard Ramm, *Them He Glorified*, Eerdmans, 1963, pp.62-63, argues that one of the ways glorification is presented in the New Testament is from the standpoint of perfection or completion.

16. See also The Westminster Shorter Catechism, No.88-99.

17. Millard Erickson, *Christian Theology*, Baker, 1994, repr., one volume ed., p.997.

18. John Murray, *Redemption Accomplished and Applied*, Eerdmans, 1984, repr., pp.174-175. Murray clarified even further (p.181): 'And glorification is resurrection.' Grudem, *Systematic Theology*, Zondervan, 1994, p.828, agrees with Murray.

19. All these are from the NKJV.

20. The Westminster Shorter Catechism, in No.38, affirms: 'The souls of believers are at their death made perfect in holiness'. The London Baptist Confession of 1689 (ch. 31) and the Westminster Confession (ch. 32) both affirm: 'The bodies of men after death return to dust, and see corruption; but their souls, which neither die nor sleep, having an immortal subsistence, immediately return to God who gave them. The souls of the righteous being then made perfect in holiness...'

21. Thomas R. Schreiner, *Romans*, in the Baker Exegetical Commentary on the New Testament, Moises Silva, ed., Baker, 1998, p.453.

22. Of course, for those still alive at the coming of Christ, the transformation of the soul and body will be simultaneous (cf. 1 Thess. 4:13-17).

CHAPTER 4

1. It is interesting that quadriplegic Joni Eareckson Tada, who has an anticipation of the physical transformation unmatched by most of us, affirms that the spiritual transformation is just as precious, if not more so, than the physical. Joni Eareckson Tada, *Heaven Your Real Home*, Zondervan, 1995, p.40.

2. Richard Baxter, *The Reformed Pastor*, in *A Treasury of Christian Books*, Hugh Martin, ed., SCM Press LTD, 1956, p.48, writes, 'The subject matter of the ministerial work is, in general, spiritual things, or matters that concern the pleasing of God, and the salvation of our people.' This is not to assert that the physical body has nothing to do with our relationship with God. On the contrary, it has very much to do with that relationship (cf. Rom. 6:12-13; 13:14). Yet, the Scriptures teach us that our relationship begins in the spiritual, in the heart. And as such, the biblical witness is that though we ought not divide the physical and spiritual as if there is no correlation, nevertheless, we can distinguish between the two (cf. 2 Cor. 4:16).

3. I am using the term transformation based upon the use of the verb metamorphoo ('transform') in 2 Corinthians 3:18 where Paul speaks of our transformation into the image of Christ – a partial metamorphosis in this age, yet,

one that will be complete in the age to come.

4. Murray J. Harris, 'Intermediate State', *New Dictionary of Theology*, Sinclair B. Ferguson, David F. Wright, eds., InterVarsity, 1988, p.399, writes that the intermediate state 'refers to the condition of mankind between death and resurrection. For unbelievers it is a state of anguish and torment in Hades (Luke 16:23-25, 28; 2 Peter 2:9) as they await resurrection – and final judgment (John 5:28-29) ... For the believer it is a period during which his bodiless soul, in conscious communion with Christ, awaits the receipt of the resurrection body.'

5. In chapter one we discussed thoroughly Exodus 33-34 which included God's revelation of himself to Moses, his assurance of his presence with Moses and Israel, the account of Moses' regularly meeting with God, and the display of God's visible glory, his radiance upon the face of Moses which must be veiled. There one of the conclusions we drew was that being in relationship with God and in his presence results in displaying his glory. Such set a foundation both for the understanding of glorification and for this particular passage. Clearly Paul is building upon that incident in the history of Israel not only to contrast the Old and New Covenants, but also to explain God's present work in the believer.

6. Simon J. Kistemaker, *Exposition of the Second Epistle to the Corinthians*, in *New Testament Commentary*, Baker, 1997, pp.128-129, argues for the translation: 'beholding the reflected glory of the Lord', and the understanding that we see and reflect the glory of the Lord.

7. Victor Paul Furnish, *II Corinthians*, in *The Anchor Bible*, William Foxwell Albright, David Noel Freedman, gen. eds, Doubleday and Co., 1984, pp.32a, 215, on ten auten eikona: 'The Greek phrase ... is loosely construed with the passive participle "being transformed" to indicate both the manner and the goal of the transformation ... The word "image" ... is used again in 4:4, where Christ is described as "the image of God". Jervell (1960: 174-5) argues that Paul has in mind Genesis 1:26-27, where the first man is said to have been created in God's image ... That passage unquestionably lies behind 1 Corinthians 15:49, which portrays Christ as "the heavenly man" by whom the life forfeited by Adam, "the man of dust", has been regained, and whose "image" believers themselves can now bear, in place of the old (cf. Col. 3:10...). Indeed, a Samaritan midrash on Deuteronomy 34:7 (M. Marqah v. 4, quoted in another connection by Meeks 1970: 363, using McDonald's tr.) shows that Moses' shining face could itself be associated with the image of God that Adam had lost...'

8. Furnish, *II Corinthians*, p.216, argues that this associates Lord and Spirit and that *apo* ('from') certainly has causal force – thus ... '"this is the work of the Lord"...'

9. Philip Edgcumbe Hughes, *Paul's Second Epistle to the Corinthians*, in *The New International Commentary on the New Testament*, F. F. Bruce, gen. ed., Eerdmans,

1962, p.119.

10. I am speaking of the popular understanding of Wesleyan teaching. Wesley actually seemed to teach that a sinner, through a second work of grace, could reach a state of perfection from voluntary, conscious sin, a state in which he/she practices mature, perfect love. However, according to Wesley, this does not mean that there would be no sin at all. Yet, on a popular level, this seems to be the take on Wesleyan teaching – and even how others have subsequently developed holiness teaching. See the article by Western Seminary professor: M. James Sawyer, 'Wesleyan and Keswick Models of Sanctification', at www.bible.org/docs/theology/pneuma/wes&kes.htm.

11. The outward man denotes, by the context, the physical and mental abilities – in other words, the main functions or aspect of one's being that has to do with this life, this age. Cf. Hughes, *2 Corinthians*, p.153.

12. Paul may have chosen this term because the Hebrew *kabod* ('glory') also connoted 'weight' and because baros was used in Classical literature to refer figuratively to the burden of suffering, thus even heightening the contrast between the light tribulation and the weighty glory.

13. BAGD, p.134, offers this translation.

14. We should not be surprised by the connection between trials and our sanctification and future glory. We have learned in our study that we are sanctified and glorified in union with Christ and, in fact, our refashioning into God-glorifiers, displaying his glory, is none other than being remade into the image of the second Adam, the perfect man, Jesus Christ himself. And, with regards to Christ we read in Hebrews 2:10: 'For it was fitting for Him, for whom are all things and by whom are all things, in bringing many sons to glory, to make the captain of their salvation perfect through sufferings' (NKJV).

15. Cited in John Calvin, *The Institutes of the Christian Religion*, vol. II, book 5, section 2.

16. 2 Timothy 2:10 makes the same point: 'Therefore I endure all things for the sake of the elect, that they also may obtain the salvation which is in Christ Jesus with eternal glory' (NKJV).

17. Regarding *katangellomen* ('we preach'), U. Becker, D. Muller, DNTT, pp.3, 44, 47, show that there is probably no technical significance to the angello word group (as distinguished from kerusso and euangelizomai). If there is any distinction, euangelizomai focuses more on the eu (good) aspect of the proclamation and kerusso on an authoritative announcement which demands compliance. The angello group has more of the aspect of an offer of information in mind. The kata prefix would emphasize or heighten the informing.

18. Cf. BAGD, p.544; F. Selter, DNTT, vol. 1, p.568; Jay Adams, *Competent to Counsel*, Presbyterian and Reformed, 1970, p.45, along with Acts 20:31, Romans 15:14, 1 Corinthians 4:13, Colossians 3:16, 1 Thessalonians 5:12, 14

and 2 Thessalonians 3:14-15.

19. Such is the sense of 'every man' in all three of its occurrences in this verse. Larry R. Helyer, 'Arius Revisited: The Firstborn Over All Creation' (Col. 1:15), JETS, 31, 1 (1988): p.62, writes, 'Ordinarily, [the] adjectival pas ("every") used with an anarthrous noun in the singular signifies "every" or "each", emphasizing the individual members of the class denoted by the noun.' Obviously, Paul is not asserting that every single person is admonished by Paul and Timothy. He must either mean 'every man they can', or 'each man with whom they can work'.

20. Bernard Ramm, *Them He Glorified*, Eerdmans, 1963, pp.62-63.

21. George Eldon Ladd, *A Theology of the New Testament*, Eerdmans, 1986, repr., pp.519-520.

22. Cf. The Westminster Shorter Catechism, No.35, along with the following texts: Ephesians 4:23-24, Romans 6:4, 6 and 8:1-4.

23. See Leon Morris, *The First and Second Epistles to the Thessalonians*, in *The New International Commentary on the New Testament*, F.F. Bruce, gen. ed., Eerdmans, 1959, p.180.

24. I agree with those commentators who argue that Paul is not expounding upon the different constitution of man, but merely revealing his desire for blameless status throughout the whole person. See Ronald A. Ward, *Commentary on 1 and 2 Thessalonians*, Word, 1980, repr., p.119; Morris, *Thessalonians*, pp.180-181. Contra Robert L. Thomas, *1 Thessalonians*, in EBC, vol. 11, p.295.

Thomas, 1 Thessalonians, p.294, helpfully calls attention to the fact that holokleron ('whole') emphasizes the quantitative aspect of the blamelessness – it is every aspect of a person such that nothing is left with sin.

25. See Arthur W. Pink, *The Attributes of God*, Bible Truth Depot, 1962, pp.47ff.

26. Morris, *Thessalonians*, p.183, comments: 'But God, besides being a Caller, is a Doer. The end of the verse fastens attention on this aspect of His being. The verbal idea is emphasized in the Greek in two ways, by the addition of "also" (God not only calls, He also acts), and by the omission of the object (there is no "it" in the Greek). There is no real doubt as to what the object is, and its omission has the effect of fastening attention on the verb "do".'

27. Morris, *Thessalonians*, p.179.

28. Some of the exhortations (e.g. 5:14) will not apply in glory since their present necessity comes from the presence of sin.

29. Richard J. Bauckham, *Jude, 2 Peter*, vol. 50 in *Word Biblical Commentary*, David A Hubbard, Glenn W. Barker, gen. eds, Word, 1983, p.124.

30. Edwin A. Blum, Jude, in *The Expositor's Bible Commentary*, Frank E. Gaebelein, gen. ed., Zondervan, 1981, vol. 12, p.396.

31. See also Bauckham, *Jude, 2 Peter*, p.119.

32. R. C. Sproul, *The Holiness of God*, Tyndale, 1998, revised, p.23.

33. '(Latin: classical source or place) is the academician's jargon for that passage

of Scripture or literature generally most frequently cited as the best illustration or explanation of a subject.' -Richard N. Solen, *Handbook of Biblical Criticism*, John Knox Press, 1981, 2nd ed., p.116. The fact that it is the locus classicus is demonstrated from the Westminster Shorter Catechism, question No.37: 'What benefits do believers receive from Christ at death?' Answer: 'The souls of believers are at their death made perfect in holiness, and do immediately pass into glory...' In virtually all editions of the catechism that have scriptural proofs, Hebrews 12:22-24 is one of the main scriptural proofs.

34. Philip Edgcumbe Hughes, *A Commentary on the Epistle to the Hebrews*, Eerdmans, 1983, repr., p.405, agrees. F. F. Bruce, *The Epistle to the Hebrews*, in *The New International Commentary on the New Testament*, F. F. Bruce, gen. ed., Eerdmans, 1985, repr., p.244, adds: 'The practical implications of the foregoing argument are now summed up in this sentence of sustained exhortation, which might well have formed the conclusion of the homily, had not our author judged it wise to expand and apply in greater detail the points made here ... In view of all that has been accomplished for us by Christ, he says, let us confidently approach God in worship, let us maintain our Christian confession and hope, let us help one another by meeting together regularly for mutual encouragement, because the day which we await will soon be here.'

35. Wayne Grudem, *Systematic Theology*, Zondervan, 1994, p.1162, agrees: '1 Corinthians 13:12 does not say that we will be omniscient or know everything (Paul could have said we will know all things, ta panta, if he had wished to do so), but, rightly translated, simply says that we will know in a fuller or more intensive way ... that is, without any error or misconceptions in our knowledge.'

36. Tada, *Heaven*, p.45.

37. Thomas Boston, 'The Kingdom of Heaven', Appendix Two in John F. MacArthur, *The Glory of Heaven*, Crossway, 1996, p.222.

38. Jonathan Edwards, 'Heaven', in 'Miscellaneous Observations', *The Works of Jonathan Edwards*, Edward Hickman, ed., Banner Of Truth, 1995, repr., vol. 2, p.618.

39. Ibid, p.626. Richard Baxter, *The Saints' Everlasting Rest*, in The Ages Digital Library, Ages Software, 1997, p.17, adds: 'Knowledge, of itself, is very desirable. As far as the rational soul exceeds the sensitive, so far the delights of a philosopher, in discovering the secrets of nature, and knowing the mystery of sciences, exceed the delights of the drunkard, the voluptuary, or the sensualist. So excellent is all truth. What, then, is their delight who know the God of truth! How noble a faculty of the soul is the understanding! It can compass the earth; it can measure the sun, moon, stars, and heaven; it can foreknow each eclipse to a minute, many years before. But this is the top of its excellency, that it can know God, who is infinite, who made all these...'

40. Edwards, 'Heaven', p.627, writes: 'But yet the glorified souls of saints in their

present state in heaven, though they cannot be said properly to see as in an enigma, is but darkly, in comparison of what they will see after the resurrection.'

41. Baxter, *Everlasting Rest*, p.14.

42. Edwards, 'Heaven', p.628.

43. Ibid, p.624. Edwards (p.623), adds, 'When the saints get to heaven, they shall not merely see Christ and have to do with him, as subjects and servants with a glorious and gracious Lord and Sovereign, but Christ will most freely and intimately converse with them as friends and brethren. This we may learn from the manner of Christ's conversing with his disciples here on earth; though he was the supreme Lord of the disciples, and did not refuse, yea, required, their supreme respect and adoration; yet he did not treat them as earthly sovereigns are wont to their subjects; he did not keep them at an awful distance, but all along conversed with them with the most friendly familiarity as with brethren, as a father amongst a company of children. So he did with the twelve, and so he did with Mary, and Martha and Lazarus; he told his disciples that he did not call them servants, but he called them friends. So neither will he call his disciples servants, but friends, in heaven.' Cf. John 15:15.

44. Baxter, *Everlasting Rest*, p.21.

45. Edward Donnelly, *Heaven and Hell*, Banner of Truth Trust, 2001, p.97. He also calls attention to Romans 7:19, 21, 24.

46. Edward Donnelly, *Heaven and Hell*, p.97.

47. Donnelly, *Heaven and Hell*, p.99.

48. Donnelly, *Heaven and Hell*, pp.99-100.

49. 'Victory', in 'To Illustrate', Leadership, 14, 3 (Summer 1993): p.61.

CHAPTER 5

1. Timothy George, 'Good Question', *Christianity Today*, 47, 2 (February 2003): p.84.

2. Murray J. Harris, *From Grave To Glory: Resurrection in The New Testament*, Academie Books, Zondervan, 1990, pp.36-43.

3. Millard Erickson, *Christian Theology*, Baker, rev., one volume ed., 1994, p.537, calls attention to the fact that man is whole only with soul and body in a view he terms 'conditional unity'. He explains: 'According to this view, the normal state of man is a materialized unitary being. In Scripture man is so addressed and regarded [cf. Gen. 2:7]. He is not to flee or escape from the body, as if it were somehow inherently evil. This ... condition can, however, be broken down, and at death it is, so that the immaterial aspect of man lives on even as the material decomposes. At the resurrection, however, there will be a return to a material or bodily condition.'

4. Harris, FROM GRAVE, p.32.

5. This wording is from the Westminster Shorter Catechism, answer No.21.

6. Joni Eareckson Tada, *Heaven Your Real Home*, Zondervan, 1995, p.41.
7. This is one of the five kinds of resurrections identified by Murray J. Harris, 'Resurrection, General', *New Dictionary of Theology*, InterVarsity, 1988, p.581. The other four are: 1. 'the past physical resurrection of certain individuals to renewed mortal life' (e.g. Luke 7:14-15; John 11:43-44; Heb. 11:35); 2. 'the past bodily resurrection of Christ to immortality' (Rom. 6:9); 3. 'the past spiritual resurrection of believers to new life in Christ' (Col. 2:12); 4. 'the future personal resurrection of unbelievers to judgement' (John 5:29; Acts 24:15).
8. Harris, *From Grave*, p.81.
9. Murray J. Harris, *Raised Immortal: Resurrection and Immortality in the New Testament*, Eerdmans, 1983, p.110.
10. George Eldon Ladd, *The Gospel of the Kingdom*, Eerdmans, 2001, repr., p.77.
11. Wayne Grudem, *Systematic Theology*, Zondervan, 1994, pp.608-609, concurs: 'Jesus' resurrection was not a merely a coming back to life. It was "a new kind of human life, a life in which his body was made perfect, no longer subject to weakness, aging, or death, but able to live eternally.'
12. That the Old Testament teaches saints will be bodily resurrected in the future has already been established in chapter one. The New Testament teaching of resurrection was assumed and alluded to in chapters two and three.
13. Other texts that demonstrate the resurrection was validation of who Christ is include: John 2:18-24, Acts 2:36 and Romans 1:4.
14. Thomas R. Schreiner, *Paul, Apostle of God's Glory in Christ*, InterVarsity Press, 2001, p.376, avers that the baptisms may very well have taken place in behalf of those who died after placing faith in Christ, yet before they could be baptized. Regardless, the Corinthians were attaching magical significance to it.
15. Some very important other mentions include (all ESV): 'Truly, truly I say to you, an hour is coming, and is now here, when the dead will hear the voice of the Son of God, and those who hear will live'. (John 5:25). 'Do not marvel at this, for an hour is coming when all who are in the tombs will hear his voice and come out, those who have done good to the resurrection of life, and those who have done evil to the resurrection of judgment' (John 5:28-29). 'And this is the will of him who sent me, that I should lose nothing of all that he has given me, but raise it up on the last day. For this is the will of my Father, that everyone who looks on the Son and believes in him should have eternal life, and I will raise him up on the last day' (John 6:39-40). 'No one can come to me unless the Father draws him. And I will raise him up on the last day' (John 6:44). 'If the Spirit of him who raised Jesus from the dead dwells in you, he who raised Christ Jesus from the dead will also give life to your mortal bodies through his Spirit who dwells in you' (Rom. 8:11). See also Matthew 22:22-33 where Jesus affirms the reality of the resurrection and Revelation 20:4-6 which most probably speaks of the believer's future bodily resurrection before the millennium and the unbeliever's resurrection

after the millennium.

16. Douglas J. Moo, *The Rapture: Pre-, Mid-, or Post-Tribulational?*, Academie, Zondervan, 1984, p.181, writes this: 'The word used by Paul to describe the "meeting" between the living saints and their Lord in the air (apantesis) occurs in references to the visit of dignitaries, and generally implies that the "delegation" accompanies the dignitary back to the delegation's point of origin. The two other occurrences of this term in the New Testament seem to bear this meaning (Matt. 15:6; Acts 28:15). This would suggest that the saints, after meeting the Lord in the air, accompany Him back to earth, instead of going with Him to heaven.' Moo goes on to guard against suggesting that this is a technical term that must mean this. He also suggests that there is nothing that says in the text how soon they return to earth. His point is simply that the use of the term favours an understanding that the saints return to earth, thus a post-tribulational scheme.

17. The Westminster Shorter Catechism, No.16, asks, 'Did all mankind fall in Adam's first Transgression?' The answer given is this: 'The covenant being made with Adam, not only for himself, but for his posterity; all mankind, descending from him by ordinary generation, sinned in him, and fell with him, in his first transgression.' The Heidelberg Catechism, Q. 7 asks, 'Whence then proceeds this depravity of human nature?' The answer given is this: 'From the fall and disobedience of our first parents, Adam and Eve, in Paradise; hence our nature is become so corrupt, that we are all conceived and born in sin.'

18. Erickson, *Christian Theology*, pp.611-615; Louis Berkhof, *Systematic Theology*, pp.258-61; Harris, *Raised Immortal*, pp.159-160.

19. Berkhof, *Systematic*, p.259.

20. Note in the preceding context that Paul writes that the Father 'will abolish all rule and all authority and power' (v. 24). Death here and elsewhere (Rev. 20:14-15) is personified as if it is ruling over one as a tyrant. Cf. George Eldon Ladd, *A Commentary on the Revelation of John*, Eerdmans, 1993, repr., pp.273-274.

21. George Eldon Ladd, *Gospel of the Kingdom*, p.129, has correctly concluded: 'Sin is an enemy of God's Kingdom. Has Christ done anything about sin, or has He merely promised a future deliverance when He brings the Kingdom in glory? We must admit that sin, like death, is abroad in the world ... Yet sin, like death and Satan, has been defeated. Christ has already appeared to put away sin by the sacrifice of Himself (Heb. 9:26).'

22. We also know this understanding is correct based upon the discussion of the crucifixion of the 'old man' in verse 6. The dying was a decisive complete event in the past. Sometime in the past every Christian has died to the realm of continual sin dominance. Just like a corpse has died to the realm of physical life and no longer exists and operates there, so also a saint is no longer the same person and no longer lives and operates in the same sin dominance

as before he was in Christ.

23. Richard N. Longenecker, *Acts*, in *The Expositor's Bible Commentary*, Frank E. Gaebelein, gen. ed., Zondervan, 1981, vol. 9, p.365.

24. Westminster Shorter Catechism, No.33.

25. For this second reason I am indebted to John Piper, *Future Grace*, Multnomah, 1995, pp.21ff.

26. Gary L. Nebeker, 'Christ as Somatic Transformer (Phil. 3:20-21): Christology in an Eschatological Perspective', TrinJ, 21, 2 (2000): p.168.

27. Nebeker, 'Somatic Transformer', p.168, helpfully comments: 'In one respect, the identification of the individuals in 3:18-19 is exegetically ancillary for understanding Paul's words in 3:20-21. However, some general conclusions may be offered based on the explicit textual clues from the context of chap. 3 and elsewhere in the letter. These persons spoken of in vv. 18 and 19: (1) are "enemies of the cross", with self-indulgent and shameful lifestyles; (2) have a limited perspective on life that is "earthly" or "this-worldly" in focus; (3) are destined for "destruction"; (4) are probably not connected with the individuals mentioned in 3:2; (5) are probably not connected to those Paul speaks of in 3:12-16; (6) are likely not connected with the opponents mentioned in 1:28; and (7) are probably not part of the Philippian community.'

28. H. Bietenhard, 'People', DNTT, vol. 2, p.804. Nebeker, 'Somatic Transformer', pp.169-170 adds, 'It may be best to render this term according to its most popular usage found in Hellenistic literature of Paul's period, namely, "commonwealth" or "state". Understood accordingly, politeuma refers to the "state as the constitutive force regulating its citizens". Moreover, [it] ... shares semantic overlap with the term basileia ... in the sense that the commonwealth parallels the idea of a kingdom's reign vis-à-vis kingdom's realm. With this suggested understanding ... Paul draws a stark contrast between the earthly-minded "enemies of the cross" and the Philippian Christians, who are ruled by a heavenly constitutive government, more specifically Christ himself.'

29. Nebeker, 'Somatic Transformer', pp.166-167: 'This passage is significant inasmuch as it is the only text in the NT where Christ himself is described as the direct agent of the believer's future bodily transformation. In other texts where Paul mentions the believer's resurrection, Christ's direct transformational agency is implicit; and, in still others, God is the agent of this future act (1 Cor. 6:14; 2 Cor. 4:14).'

30. BAGD, p.513; G. Braumann, 'Form', DNTT, vol. 1, p.709.

31. BAGD, p.805.

32. In Luke 1:48, it is found upon the lips of Mary in the Magnificat as she praises God for the announcement that she would be mother of the Messiah. In describing herself, she says, 'For He has regarded the lowly estate of His maidservant.' I. Howard Marshall, *Commentary on Luke*, in *New International*

Greek Testament Commentary, I. Howard Marshall and W. Ward Gasque, eds., Eerdmans, 1986, repr., p.82, say that it means here '"humble state" rather than "humiliation" ... It need not refer to childlessness ... but expresses the humble state of Mary in the eyes of the world ... and perhaps her humble attitude towards God...' In context, the point seems to be that compared to God and what he has done for her, she is lowly and undeserving of the blessing he has bestowed. In Acts 8:33 it is used in a quote of Isaiah 53:8 (following the LXX). It refers to the humiliation of the suffering Servant in his sacrificial death. Such is the state of being despised and rejected, not valued by the world. Finally, in James 1:10 the term refers to the state of the rich believer who has come to understand who he really is and his temporary state in this world.

33. Homer A. Kent, *Philippians*, in EBC, vol. 11, p.148.

34. Peter T. O'Brien, *Philippians*, in *New International Greek Testament Commentary*, I. Howard Marshall and W. Ward Gasque, eds., Eerdmans, 1991, cited in Nebeker, 'Somatic Transformer' p.176, affirms: 'Current physicality, affected as it is by sin, is "thus always characterized by physical decay, indignity, weakness, and finally death."'

35. Nebeker, 'Somatic Transformer' pp.178-179.

36. J. A. Schep, *The Nature of the Resurrection Body*, Eerdmans, 1964, p.166, concurs.

37. There is one other statement which deals with the subject. In 1 Corinthians 15:49 (ESV) Paul writes, 'Just as we have borne the image of the man of dust, we shall also bear the image of the man of heaven.'

38. *Future Grace*, Multnomah, 1995, p.204.

39. Harris, *From Grave to Glory*, p.102.

40. J. A. Schep, *The Nature of the Resurrection Body*, Eerdmans, 1964, p.142. The quotation from Rengstorf is taken from: K. H. Rengstorf, 'Das Evangelium nach Lukas', Das Neue Testament Deutsch, 1958. See also Grudem, *Systematic Theology*, pp.610-2, for a very helpful discussion.

It is important that we remember that the Son of God 'became man and so was and continue[s] to be God and man in two distinct natures and one person for ever' (Westminster Shorter Catechism, No.21). Even many candidates for ordination that I have had the privilege of interviewing via a denominational committee do not understand that the Scriptures teach that Jesus Christ continues to be both God and man. He did not set aside his humanity at the ascension and revert to a pre-incarnate state. The author of Hebrews who has already said that Jesus Christ is man sharing in flesh and blood (cf. 2:5-14) affirms in 7:24: 'But he holds his priesthood permanently, because he continues forever' (ESV). Then in 1 John 4:2 the apostle writes that 'Jesus Christ has come in the flesh' (the use of the perfect strongly implies that he was and continues to be in the flesh). Such is necessary if our body is to be like Christ's resurrection body (and the Scriptures teach that ours is to be a fleshly, although transformed, body). Additionally, Christ ascended in bodily form and will come again in the same manner (Acts 1:11). Such strongly implies that he presently is still the God-man. This is supported also by Paul's statement to Timothy that 'there is one mediator between God and man, the man Christ Jesus' (1 Tim. 2:5). The realization of Christ's present and continuing state has major ramifications for whether or not we believe in the future bodily resurrection of believers and the future bodily return of Christ. Likewise, it most certainly affirms the goodness of flesh and the importance that God has placed on his physical creation.

41. Certainly, as we learn of the resurrection body of saints we also learn more about Christ's body, by implication, since our body will be transformed to be like his (Phil. 3:21).

42. L. Coenen, DNTT, vol. 3, p.276; Harris, *From Grave to Glory*, p.196.

43. Grudem, Systematic, p.831, helpfully comments: 'It is appropriate to think that our resurrection bodies will have no sign of aging, but will have the characteristics of youthful but mature manhood or womanhood forever. There will be no evidence of disease or injury, for all will be made perfect.' 'The fact that the scars of Jesus' nail prints remained on his hands is a special case to remind us of the price he paid for our redemption, and it should not be taken as an indication that any of our scars from physical injuries will remain.'

44. BAGD, p.115.

45. Harris, *From Grave To Glory*, p.195.

46. Ibid. Grudem, *Systematic Theology*, p.832, writes: 'In the Pauline epistles, the word "spiritual" (Gk. *penumatikos*) never means "nonphysical" but rather "consistent with the character and activity of the Holy Spirit" (see, for example, Rom. 1:11; 7:14; 1 Cor. 2:13, 15; 3:1; 14:37; Gal. 6:1 ... Eph. 5:19).'

47. Schep, *The Nature*, pp.201-202.

48. The following three quotations are from the English Standard Version.

49. We should not be surprised that the future eternal abode would be described in language taken from Zion, Jerusalem and temple terminology. As we just saw, God's faithful presence with his people is part of his covenantal promises to them (see also Gen. 28:15; Deut. 31:6, 8; Josh. 1:5; Heb. 13:5). This was displayed to Israel through the realized presence of God among them in the tabernacle (Exod. 25:8) and later in the temple (1 Kings 8:17, 19, 20, 29; 9:3; Ezra 1:3; Hab. 2:20). From the time that David conquered Zion/Jerusalem (2 Sam. 5:7) and his bringing of the ark to this city (2 Sam. 6-7) God's presence was associated with Jerusalem. This is why the future eternal dwelling of God with man was often communicated through temple and Jerusalem imagery (cf. Ezek. 40-48; Micah 4:1-7). In fact, heaven even presently is depicted as the true tabernacle (Heb. 8-10). With all this background, we see that what John sets forth in the last two chapters of the Apocalypse is in fact the future eternal abode of God with man. As we will see in chapter 7,

this abode will be the reworked, overhauled heavens and earth.

Vos, *Biblical Theology*, p.155, adds, 'The peculiarity of the representation here is that, in dependence on Isaiah 4:5, 6, the area of the tabernacle and temple are widened so as to become equally co-extensive with the entire New Jerusalem. The necessity of a tabernacle or a temple symbolic and typical, presupposes the imperfection of the present state of the theocracy. When the theocracy will completely correspond to the divine ideal of it, then there will be no more need of symbol or type. Hence, the statement "I saw no temple therein", vs. 22. This does not, however, make it "the city without a church". Using Scriptural terminology, we should rather say that the place will be all church.'

See also George Eldon Ladd, *A Commentary on the Revelation of John*, Eerdmans, 1993, repr., pp.275-277.

50. Robert H. Mounce, *The Book of Revelation, in The New International Commentary on the New Testament*, F. F. Bruce, gen. ed., Eerdmans, 1987, repr., p.372, says that 'the first things' are part of a 'previous order which has now become history'.

51. See the parallel accounts in Matthew 22:23-33 and Mark 12:18-27.

52. Sadducees were a leading sect in Judaism which often opposed the Pharisees. Well-educated, small in number and mostly of the upper class, they affirmed that they only followed the sacred texts as opposed the traditions. They did not believe in resurrection, nor did they follow the predestinarian doctrine of the Pharisees, preferring rather to emphasize man's freedom. See F. F. Bruce, *New Testament History*, Doubleday, 1980, p.74; and J. D. Davis, *Davis Bible Dictionary*, Royal Publishers, 1973, p.703.

53. Schep, *The Nature*, p.212.

54. In the Matthean and Marcan accounts it is also made clear that Jesus affirmed that the Sadducees were 'mistaken not knowing the scriptures nor the power of God'.

55. Matthew and Mark have: 'but they are like angels' (*all eisin* [omitted in Matt.] *hos angeloi*).

56. I am indebted to Schep, *The Nature*, p.212, and I. Howard Marshall, *The Gospel of Luke*, in *The New International Greek Testament Commentary*, I. Howard Marshall, W. Ward Gasque, eds., Eerdmans, 1986, repr., p.741 for calling attention to the part of Luke 20:36 in solving this exegetical puzzle.

57. Tada, *Heaven*, pp.36-37.

58. Tada, *Heaven*, p.37.

59. The cultural mandate is found in Genesis 1:27-28: 'So God created man in His own image; in the image of God He created him; male and female He created them. Then God blessed them, and God said to them, "Be fruitful and multiply; fill the earth and subdue it; have dominion over the fish of the sea, over the birds of the air; and over every living thing that moves on the earth" (NKJV).' Part of the mandate would include helping those

in need. Isaiah includes such as part of true worship of God. Isaiah 58:6-7 (ESV): 'Is not this the fast that I choose: to loose the bonds of wickedness, to undo the straps of the yoke, to let the oppressed go free, and to break every yoke? Is it not to share your bread with the hungry and bring the homeless poor into your house; when you see the naked, to cover him, and not to hide yourself from your own flesh?'

J. I. Packer and Thomas Howard, *Christianity: the True Humanism*, Word, 1985, p.240, gives the following comments that aptly describe the cultural mandate: 'From his creation, man as male and female has been given stewardship over nature, commanded by God to develop culture and nourish human life from the productive earth.

'Labor and leisure, science and art, family and state, belong to human life as God meant it to be. Yet the meaning of life is not found in these activities but in the God who enables them.'

60. N.T. Wright, 'N.T. Wright: Resurrection is Politically Revolutionary', *Christianity Today*, 47, 5 (May 2003): p.66.

61. Adrian Dielman, in 'To Illustrate', Leadership, 15, 1 (Winter 1994): p.47.

CHAPTER 6

1. Cited in Marvin Olasky, 'The Greatest Spin Ever Sold', *World*, 17, 16 (April 27, 2002): p.14.

2. All the following quotes are from the NKJV.

3. One of the ways in which the New Testament highlights this truth is to show that the Lord rewards his people in the age to come by seating them with Christ on his throne (Eph. 2:6; Rev. 3:21) that they might participate in some way in judgement of the world (1 Cor. 6:2), which more specifically may also include the judgement of the Messiah-rejecting Israelites by the twelve (Matt. 19:28; Luke 22:30). It will be clear in the judgement what peoples will be seen as precious in the eyes of God and recipients of his grace – those who are honoured.

4. BDB, p.802.

5. Ibid.

CHAPTER 7

1. Millard Erickson, *Christian Theology*, p.1002.

2. John Murray, *Redemption Accomplished and Applied*, pp.179-180.

3. It is not absolutely clear whether we have only one vision in these two chapters or two, as George Eldon Ladd, *A Commentary on the Revelation of John*, Eerdmans, 1993, repr., p.275, suggests. Either way, we have the same effect. As virtually all commentators agree, John is being shown in these two chapters what the final state will be like. See Grant R. Osborne, *Revelation*, in the *Baker Exegetical Commentary on the New Testament*, Baker, 2002, p.726.

Concerning structure, Osborne (p.727) goes on to say, 'This section is organized like chapters 12-13, with a thesis paragraph (21:1-6, with 7-8 a parenetic challenge to the readers in light of the vision) that is then expanded in two directions, first viewing the Holy City as an eternal Holy of Holies (21:9-27) and then as a new Eden (22:1-5).'

4. Wayne Grudem, *Systematic Theology*, Zondervan, 1994, p.1158: 'When referring to this place, Christians often talk about living with God "in heaven" forever. But in fact the biblical teaching is richer than that; it tells us that there will be a new heaven and a new earth – an entirely renewed creation – and we will live with God there.'

5. See Isaiah 65:17-25, 66:22-23 for the Old Testament background to this.

6. MacArthur, *The Glory of Heaven*, Crossway, 1996, p.89 agrees: 'In other words, heaven, the realm where God dwells, will expand to encompass the entire universe of creation, which will be fashioned into a perfect and glorious domain fit for the glory of heaven.' Osborne, *Revelation*, p.728: 'It bridges the heavenly and the earthly, and the two become one.'

7. This is true of both the Hebrew *shamayim* and the Greek *ouranos*. See also Wilbur M. Smith, *The Biblical Doctrine of Heaven*, Moody, 1968, pp.27-28, and John MacArthur, *The Glory*, pp.55-56.

8. MacArthur, *The Glory*, p.56. I would add that God has accommodated himself to dwell specially in heaven in order that he might help mankind in communing with him. See Psalm 113:4-6. Grudem, Systematic, p.1159, adds: 'Heaven is the place where God most fully makes known his presence to bless.'

9. BAGD, p.84, on *aperchomai*: 'go away, depart ... pass away'. Nothing in the word itself would clear up the question of whether or not John is saying about the vision that God totally annihilated the present heaven and earth or merely transformed the present such that the former state of heaven and earth was no more.

10. Most writers do seem to favor the interpretation that the heaven and earth will be renovated. Smith, *The Biblical Doctrine*, pp.223f.; MacArthur, *The Glory*, p.89, Robert H. Mounce, *The Book of Revelation*, in *The New International Commentary on the New Testament*, F.F. Bruce, gen. ed., Eerdmans, 1987, repr., p.369, Jonathan Edwards, *Heaven*, in *The Works of Jonathan Edwards*, Edward Hickman, ed., Banner of Truth, 1995, repr., vol. 2, p.631, Anthony A. Hoekema, *The Bible and the Future*, Eerdmans, 1986, repr., p.280, Willem VanGemeren, *The Progress of Redemption*, Baker, 2000, repr., pp.451f., Grudem, *Systematic Theology* pp.1160-1161, all argue, for example, that it will be renovated, but not totally destroyed. Osborne, *Revelation*, p.730, however, favours 'a destruction of the old order and a brand "new heaven and new earth"'.

11. Ladd, *Revelation*, pp.271-272.

12. R. C. Sproul, *Surprised by Suffering*, Tyndale, 1988, p.152.

13. A.A. Hodge, *Evangelical Theology*, Banner of Truth, 1976, p.400, writes, 'Heaven as the eternal home of the divine Man and of all the redeemed members of the human race, must necessarily be thoroughly human in its structure, conditions, and activities. Its joys and its occupations must all be rational, moral, emotional, voluntary, and active. There must be the exercise of all faculties, the gratification of all tastes, the development of all talent capacities, the realization of all ideals. The reason, the intellectual curiosity, the imagination, the aesthetic instincts, the holy affections, the social affinities, the inexhaustible resources of strength and power native to the human soul, must all find in heaven exercise and satisfaction.' Cited in MacArthur, *Glory*, p.140.

14. Cf. Sproul, *Surprised*, p.153; Mounce, *Revelation*, p.370; and Ladd, *Revelation*, p.276.

15. Osborne, *Revelation*, pp.730-731.

16. The idea of a New Jerusalem unveiled at the advent of the Messiah has precedent in Jewish apocalyptic: Mounce, Revelation, p.370. See Isaiah 65:18. For an overview of the history of the concept see Osborne, Revelation, pp.731-732.

17. Ladd, *Revelation*, p.276.

18. Ibid, 276-7. Mounce, *Revelation*, p.370, adds, 'Some difference of opinion exists as to whether the New Jerusalem in John's vision should be taken as an actual city or as a symbol of the church in its perfected and eternal state.'

19. Regarding 'and they will be His people', Mounce, *Revelation*, p.372, writes, 'Apparently John modified the traditional concept (Jer. 7:23; 30:22; Hosea 2:23) and substituted a reference to the many peoples of redeemed humanity ... It is with the redeemed peoples of all races and nationalities that God will dwell in glory.'

20. Ladd, *Revelation*, p.277.

21. Geerhardus Vos, *Biblical Theology: Old and New Testaments*, Banner of Truth, 1996, repr., p.155.

22. Cf. also Psalm 84, Zechariah 2:11, 8:3, 8.

23. Osborne, *Revelation*, pp.729-730.

24. Edwards, 'Heaven', p.617.

25. Osborne, *Revelation*, p.727.

26. The term used in verse 11 for the light is phoster. Its only other use is in Philippians 2:15 where it has reference figuratively to Christians being lights in the world. It is most assuredly speaking of visible light and is describing the doxa (glory) of God.

27. Isaiah 54:11-12 forms part of the background for these verses.

Tada, *Heaven*, p.14, comments, 'Actual mountains and clouds are exalting, but even the most beautiful displays of earth's glory – towering thunderheads above a wheat field or the view of the Grand Canyon from the south rim – are only rough sketches of heaven. Earth's best is only a dim reflection, a preliminary rendering of the glory that will one day be revealed.'

28. Thomas Boston, 'The Kingdom of Heaven', in MacArthur, *The Glory*, p.221, writes, 'But the divine perfections will be an unbounded field, in which the glorified shall walk eternally, seeing more and more of God, since they can never come to the end of that which is infinite. They may bring their vessels to this ocean every moment, and fill them with new waters.'

29. Ladd, *Revelation*, p.281, concurs: 'When John tried to describe the glory of the city, he could only do what he did when he attempted to describe the presence of God himself, viz., speak of it in terms of precious stones (4:3). The word for "jasper" in antiquity was not limited to the type of stone we call jasper, but could designate any transparent precious stone. This jasper was possibly like a diamond.'

   Richard Baxter, *The Saint's Everlasting Rest*, p.198, argues that the reason the Holy Spirit describes the New Jerusalem in terms favourable to the flesh is not that we would think heaven literally made up of gold and pearl. Instead, it is 'to help us to conceive of them as we are able, and to use these borrowed phrases as a glass, in which we must see the things themselves imperfectly represented, till we come to an immediate and perfect sight'. Sproul, Surprised, p.166, however, cautions, 'These graphic images are most probably symbolic of the glory that will be present in heaven, though I shrink from being dogmatic about it. We ought not to put it past God that He may produce a city exactly as John envisioned it.'

   Tada, *Heaven*, pp.14, 20, adds, 'Heaven is best captured in art, things such as music and poetry; not straight on ... The reason that so much language about heaven in the Bible is symbolic and "clanky" is that heaven is beyond words.'

30. MacArthur, *The Glory*, p.105.

31. H. Porter, 'Gentiles', *The International Standard Bible Encyclopedia*, James Orr, gen. ed., Eerdmans, 1986, repr., vol. 2, p.1215. See also Acts 22:21-23 for an example of the animosity Jews felt toward Gentiles in the first century, A.D.

32. Ladd, *Revelation*, p.284. See also Isaiah 60:3.

33. Mounce, *Revelation*, pp.384-385.

34. Edwards, 'Heaven', pp.617-618.

35. Osborne, *Revelation*, p.727, concurs.

36. See also D. A. Carson, T*he Farewell Discourse and Final Prayer of Jesus*, Baker, 1980, pp.75-76.

37. The text does not clarify that this speaks of thickness or height. However, the height of the city (which has been given) suggests that this is thickness. Cf. Mounce, *Revelation*, p.381.

38. Mounce, *Revelation*, p.379, agrees. He adds, 'For the wall as a metaphor of security see Is. 26;1; Zech. 2:5.'

39. Richard Baxter, *The Saints' Everlasting Rest*, in The Ages Digital Library, Books

for the Ages, Ages Software, 1997, p.11, concerning the saint's rest of Hebrews 4:9, writes, 'The saints' rest is the most happy state of a Christian; or, it is the perfect endless enjoyment of God by the perfected saints, according to the measure of their capacity, to which their souls arrive at death, and both soul and body most fully after the resurrection and final judgment.'

40. In Romans 8:20 Paul writes that 'the creation was subjected unto futility'. The term translated 'futility', mataioteti, suggests that the world, due to sin, does not fulfil the purpose for which it is made, it is out of whack. Hence, presently, our occupations often bring frustration (cf. also Gen. 3:16-19). With a new heaven and earth that will all be changed. The creation 'will be set free from the slavery which results from corruption unto the freedom which results from the glory which belongs to the children of God' (Rom. 8:21).

41. Boston, 'The Kingdom', p.205.

42. Tada, *Heaven*, pp.47, 66.

43. Baxter, *Everlasting Rest*, p.38, writes, 'We shall rest from the temptations of Satan ... [and] all our temptations from the world and the flesh shall cease.' He adds (p.39), 'We shall rest from the abuses and persecutions of the world ... We shall then rest from all our sad divisions and unchristian quarrels with one another.'

44. Ladd, *Revelation*, p.286.

45. See Mounce, *Revelation*, p.386.

46. The presence of a tree of life takes the reader back to the Garden of Eden and the initial paradise (Gen. 3:24). Part of the purpose of the imagery is to show that paradise has been restored.

47. Ladd, *Revelation*, p.287.

48. Edwards, 'Heaven', pp.619, 29, 24.

49. Jonathan Edwards, 'Eschatology', in *Introduction to Puritan Theology*, Edward Hindson, ed., Baker, 1976, p.266.

50. Note that the Lamb, Jesus Christ, is on the throne. This is another reminder that the new heaven and earth is a real place. Edwards, 'Eschatology', p.262, agrees: 'It is absurd to suppose that the heaven where the body of Christ is, is not a place. To say that the body of Christ is in no place, is the same thing as to say he has no body.' 'The heaven where Christ is, is a place; for he was seen ascending, and will be seen descending again; and the heaven where the departed souls of the saints are, is the same heaven where Christ has ascended.'

51. BAGD, p.467.

52. Hoekema, *The Bible*, p.287.

A wide range of excellent books on spiritual subjects is available from Evangelical Press. Please write to us for your free catalogue or contact us by e-mail.

Evangelical Press

Faverdale North, Darlington, Co. Durham, DL3 OPH, England
email: sales@evangelicalpress.org

Evangelical Press USA

P. O. Box 825, Webster, NY 14580, USA
email: usa.sales@evangelicalpress.org

web: http://www.evangelicalpress.org